Presented to

Joanna and Daniel Rose

חג כשר ושמח

THE ENCOUNTER between the world of Torah and the realm of worldly knowledge provides a creative tension that we at Yeshiva University solemnly embrace. It challenges our minds, stirs our souls, and informs our mission.

ON THE OCCASION of this Festival of Freedom, it is my pleasure to have you explore with me this great Jewish adventure and to join with me in ensuring its continuation.

NORMAN LAMM

14 Nisan 5750—April 9, 1990

TORAH UMADDA

TORAH UMADDA

The Encounter of Religious Learning and Worldly Knowledge in the Jewish Tradition

Norman Lamm

JASON ARONSON INC.
Northvale, New Jersey
London

Library of Congress Cataloging-in-Publication Data

Lamm, Norman.
   Torah Umadda : the encounter of religious learning and worldly
knowledge in the Jewish tradition / Norman Lamm.
     p.   cm.
   Includes bibliographical references.
   ISBN 0-87668-810-5 :
   1. Judaism and science. 2. Religion and culture.   I. Title.
BM538.S3L34 1990   89-18519
296.3'875—dc20   CIP

Manufactured in the United States of America. Jason Aronson Inc. offers books and cassettes. For information and catalog write to Jason Aronson Inc., 230 Livingston Street, Northvale, New Jersey 07647.

Dedicated
to the memory of

Dr. Samuel Belkin

מורי ורבי הרה״ג רבי שמואל בלקין נ״ע

my teacher
my predecessor
my first role model of Torah Umadda

CONTENTS

vii

PREFACE

THE ISSUE

One of the distinguishing characteristics of Judaism is the value it places on the study of Torah—the sacred biblical and talmudic literatures. It regards such study as its most important precept and considers it a binding obligation on all its adherents; it does not confine it to a class of professional scholars. It explores the nature of the motivation to study Torah and is critical of any time devoted to frivolous or simply less significant activities, even cognitive ones.

Where does this leave the rest of human intellectual enterprise? What of the study of nonsacred material? Is there no place in Judaism for education in the arts and sciences, which have so profoundly influenced the nature and destiny of civilization and the self-perception of mankind?

These questions are the focus of this volume. The variety of responses tells us something about the nature of Jewish faith and the differing orientations that believing Jews bring to it, and they reflect as well on the power and scope of the Jewish commitment to Torah.

Thus, some banned any concessions to the study of worldly wisdom. Others begrudgingly permitted such study if it was limited to the vocational areas, those needed for one's sustenance. Still others were more permissive and formulated various models of accommodation between the study of Torah and the acquisition of profane knowledge. Finally, there were those who embraced both worlds in a more comprehensive vision of man's intellectual and spiritual scope, essentially denying the ultimate metaphysical validity of the bifurcation of cognitive experience into two divergent and unrelated spheres, and locating potential for the sacred in the very innards of the profane.

Before proceeding to the substance of this engaging problem, the reader is entitled to know how the author came to grapple with it and why it has proved so intriguing to him.

An Autobiographical Note

In the Fall of 1945 I came to Yeshiva University in New York as an 18-year-old freshman. As is usual with the important decisions we make in life, many elements had combined to determine this choice. I was eager to be part of a school—the only one—where I could combine my continuing talmudic studies with a good college education under one roof. I was thinking of a career in the natural sciences, but I was also considering the rabbinate, and where else could I prepare for both and thus postpone such a critical decision? I was attracted by the array of giants of talmudic learning, such as Rabbi Moshe Shatzkes and Dr. Samuel Belkin, both of blessed memory and both of whom were later to accept me as their student. And, above all, I had the ambition to sit at the feet of

that towering intellect, my master and teacher Rabbi Joseph
B. Soloveitchik, for whose health I pray. But as crucial to that
decision as all else was my fascination—from afar—with the
ideal upon which the institution was based and which it
exemplified, the "synthesis" of Torah learning and Western
culture that goes by the name of *Torah Umadda,* or the study of
sacred Jewish texts along with the secular wisdom of the
world at large.

I have experienced a lifelong romance with this ideal, a
romance that was not at all uncritical. It has inspired and
frustrated me, challenged and puzzled me, and made me feel
that, in turn, it is incapable of theoretical justification for a
believing Jew—yet so self-evident as not to require any justification. As a student I felt that, with all that Yeshiva was
providing me in the way of both sacred and profane learning,
it had failed to spell out the nature of their relationship, the
problematica, the consequences. Dr. Bernard Revel, the first
President of Yeshiva (whom, unfortunately, I did not know
personally), had spoken of "synthesis" and Torah Umadda,
but never explicated its inner meaning and its theoretical
structure. His successor, Dr. Belkin, my immediate predecessor and my first teacher of Talmud when I came to Yeshiva, was preoccupied with building the institution, although he was certainly capable of elaborating the—or *a*—
theory of Torah Umadda. His addresses and writings, when
they refer to the subject, are mostly concerned with the political aspects of the issue, namely, the confluence of Judaic
teaching and American democracy, a problem that did not
particularly concern me and my second-generation American
peers who took this for granted, perhaps uncritically. The big
void in my education was the lack of a cohesive halakhic and
philosophical theory of Torah Umadda. I soon discovered
that a number of my fellow students shared the same complaint.

Upon coming to Yeshiva as a member of its faculty in 1960, I discovered that *le plus ça change, le plus ç'est la même chose*. Most students accepted what was given to them without concerning themselves with abstract questions, no matter how consequential the answers might be; a few of the more thoughtful of my pupils were as troubled as I had been; and the intellectual leaders of the school, both administration and faculty, were too preoccupied with their truly demanding tasks to attend to questions that, their experience had convinced them, had no demonstrably ill effects if left unanswered.

That situation changed perceptibly when I became president of the institution in 1976. Student leaders were now more vocal in demanding that this ideal, Torah Umadda, be discussed as both an intellectual and halakhic problem, and there were new, bright, and capable young faculty members who encouraged such inquiry. Besides, I had myself to answer to: Could I in good conscience avoid focusing upon the single issue that had caused me such ideological distemper, both during and after my student days? Clearly, I had no excuse—other than the exigencies of a few troubled years in which the fate of Yeshiva hung in the balance—for procrastination.

With the help of Dr. Julius Cherny and Mr. Richard Herson of the Brunner Foundation, a Torah Umadda program was launched, with competent direction and faculty participation. Students were involved at every level—and their response was heartening, far better than I had expected even in my most optimistic moments. The public lectures by distinguished personalities in Jewish intellectual and academic life were attended by many hundreds of eager and inquisitive Yeshiva students as well as interested outsiders. Several books were commissioned, and the eminent scholars assigned to the tasks are expected to submit their work for publication in the near future.

Having urged the project on a sometimes reluctant and initially skeptical administration and faculty, I had no choice but to accept the invitation to address the topic myself in the form of a lecture. I now had the forced opportunity to crystallize my thinking on this subject and to try my hand at this form of apologetics—in the very best sense of the word—even though I had not yet resolved all the problems involved in what is not only a specific curricular question but, far more, a major cultural issue that has vast spiritual, halakhic, psychological, and anthropological implications.

This volume is based upon that lecture, reworked many times. Even more, it is the result of decades of an ongoing but intermittent love affair with a sublime ideal that, as the Zohar says of the Torah, is like a beautiful princess in a tower of a mighty castle, who sometimes reveals herself, sometimes conceals herself, often gives the impression that she is frostily unaware of her lover's existence—but who is always, always mysteriously attractive and unfailingly enchanting.

ACKNOWLEDGMENT

This work would never have seen the light of day without the gracious hospitality of my friends Hermann and Ursula Merkin, in whose Jerusalem home I began to prepare this volume; the month of quiet contemplation in the lovely surroundings of Yarnton Manor in England as the guest of the Oxford Hebrew Studies Centre; the competent and loyal assistance of my Academic Assistant, Professor Jeffrey S. Gurock of the University's Bernard Revel Graduate School; the needling of my dear children who, all alumni of various schools of Yeshiva University, felt that I owed this work to the students of Yeshiva; the gentle prodding of my beloved Mindella, who urged me to get on with the work and conclude it so that I might rejoin my family and become reacquainted with my grandchildren; and the challenge offered by certain opponents of Torah Umadda, especially when their criticism was unrelenting and undisguised by an excess of civility.

To all of them—my warmest thanks.

NORMAN LAMM
Sackett Lake, N.Y.
November 2, 1989
4 Heshvan, 5750

*It is best that you should take
hold of the one, and also do not
let your hand go from the other;
for one who fears God will
discharge his duty to both.*

—Ecclesiastes 7:18

*"The words of the wise are as goads,
and as nails well planted are the words of the
masters of assemblies, which are given
from one Shepherd"* (Ecclesiastes 12:11).
"The masters of assemblies"— these are the scholars
who sit in manifold assemblies and occupy themselves
with the Torah,
some pronouncing unclean and others clean, some prohibiting and others permitting,
some disqualifying and others declaring fit. Should a man
say, "How in these
circumstances shall I learn Torah?"
Therefore we read,
"All of them are given from one Shepherd"—One God
gave them, one leader [Moses]
uttered them from the mouth of the
Lord of all creation.

—Babylonian Talmud, *Hagigah* 3b

*I heard it said that God wrote a book—
the world; and He wrote a commentary
on that book—the Torah.*

—Rabbi Zadok Hakohen of Lublin
(1823–1900)

CHAPTER 1

An Introduction

to the Encounter

The secularized reader, heir to the agnosticism that characterizes most of the intellectual life of the West and skeptical of all certitudes, especially theological ones, may well be amused at this effort to formulate (or reformulate) one aspect of the encounter between an ancient faith and the basic assumptions of contemporary Western culture. An accommodation between Faith and Reason (or Religion and Science) in the last decade of the twentieth century? Hasn't that problem been solved a hundred, two hundred years ago? And is not the attempt to resurrect the issue at this late date indicative of a rather soft-headed atavism?

Such a not-unexpected reaction reveals quite another set of unspoken certitudes buttressed by its own brand of triumphalism. It ignores the persistence of man's metaphysical yearning which, though dormant for generations, wakes up at irregular intervals to stake its claim on man's intellectual curiosity as well as arousing in him a spiritual thirst and a

quest for transcendent meaning. To neglect this dimension is
to risk a warped vision of man's inner life and a cramped
understanding of culture.

Religion exists, it persists, and the questions it asks and the
answers it offers will not go away. To dismiss it as a fear
reaction to the uncertainties of this complex and scary age, or
to brand all religion as "fundamentalism" and hence unworthy of serious consideration save in self-defense, or to
view it as legitimate only as long as it identifies with one's
own social or political agenda—all of this is the kind of
simplistic reductionism that one properly ought not to expect
of a sophisticated, educated, and fair-minded person; and that,
were such sentiments in mirror image uttered by religious
folk, would rightly be condemned as parochial, narrow, and
Neanderthal.

Religiously committed individuals who participate in our
contemporary society and culture are beset by a conflict of
values and perceptions that is of the greatest personal consequence. The encounter of the two worlds within religious
individuals and communities often leaves deep scars on the
psyche of the individuals and the ethos of the community. But
it also holds the promise of fascinating creativity, of new
syntheses, of renewed efforts to grasp elusive insights.

The tension between the sacred and the secular is a perennial
one. As long as men and women keep open minds (admittedly
not a universal condition) and recognize that both these
realms embody truths that may be ignored only at the peril of
injuring one's intellectual integrity, this subject will be of deep
concern—to some as an anxious existential question, to others
as a challenging theoretical problem. It is not a contest from
which one side will emerge victorious and the other turn heel
and flee in ignominious defeat. This most vexing, complicated, and axiologically significant issue cannot be reduced to
such a simple, partisan, adversarial confrontation on the level

of a children's game. The history of the last two or three thousand years should reenforce our conviction that we are dealing with an issue so perplexing, so central to human destiny and to our understanding of our place in the world, that we must shun simplistic solutions. The two worlds—of faith and inquiry, of religion and science, of trust and reason— are destined (not doomed!) to live together, now close and now far, now attracting and now repelling, like twin stars revolving about each other in some distant corner of the galaxy.

Judaism, the world's oldest monotheistic religion, began as an act of revolt against its contemporary civilization. Abraham was the great iconoclast as well as the first Jew. He was called "Hebrew," the Sages of the Talmud declared, not only because of his ethnic origin as a descendant of Eber, but also because the term implies "side" or "over–against": Abraham was on one side and all the world on the other. Yet his opposition to the pagan Chaldean culture was one of engagement, not of indifference or seclusion. He did not ignore the heathen world, nor was he unconcerned with the idol-worshipers of his time. He was involved with them, taught them, was reprimanded by them, fought them, formed alliances with them, helped them.

This confrontation by the "knight of faith," as Kierkegaard called him, with his pagan environment, was but the first such encounter between Judaism and worldly culture. In different forms, this contest—or dialogue, depending upon the nature of the relationship and upon one's point of view—arose in Islam and Christianity as well.

In Christianity, the encounter was most often expressed as that between "Athens and Jerusalem." This term was coined by Tertullian (ca. 160–220) in referring to the struggle be- tween Hellenism, representing classical civilization, and He- braism, referring to Christianity, which considered itself the

rightful heir of Judaism. The words "Athens" and "Jerusalem" eventually became paradigms for the development of
culture in the Western world. Thus, closer to our own time,
this pair of concepts became crucially important for Matthew
Arnold in his analysis of contemporary humanism and Christianity in the nineteenth century; Arnold considered them to
have an inverse relationship with each other, and he attempted
but failed to produce a synthesis between them.[1]

Heinrich Heine too universalized this antithesis, declaring
that all men are either Jews or Greeks. The broad use of this
neat pair of categories proved attractive to many a writer.[2]
Indeed, this bifurcation into "Hebrew and Hellene" was fairly
common, especially among Jewish writers upon their en-
trance into European life at the close of the eighteenth century.
This was true of people like the early Zionist Moses Hess and
the Hebrew poet Tchernichowsky as well as Heine. Hebrews
or Jews were considered to be ascetics who questioned life,
whereas Greeks were those who loved life realistically. Jewish
covenantal assurances are opposed to Greek speculations. The
Jews represent unity, the Greeks multiplicity. The Greeks
think of life as eternal *being*, the Hebrews as eternal *becoming*.
The Greeks relate to space, the Jews to time. In the words of
Moses Hess, "The task of all cultural history is to effect a
reconciliation between these opposing principles."[3] Indeed,
one of the defining characteristics of Western civilization is
this dialectical tension between biblical religion and autonomous reason.

However, great caution must be exercised not to overstate
the value of such dichotomy and not to oversimplify the
collision between Judaism and Hellenism by elucidating from
it two universal principles. The tendency to do this is a
weakness of intellectuals, a delightful methodological toy of
academicians. Toys can be played with, and often have educational value, but should never be substituted for reality.

Tertullian himself denied the possibility of any meaningful dialogue between Athens and Jerusalem ("Jerusalem" was for him, of course, a symbol of Christian faith): "What has Athens to do with Jerusalem? What agreement is there between the Academy and the Church?" For this Latin Church Father, the gulf between them was unbridgeable. This assertion is of one piece with his famous statement *credo quia absurdum est,* that he believed *because* it is absurd. Such antirationalism never found a warm and hospitable reception among classical Jewish thinkers. They may have been, as most were, antirational*ist,* but not antirational. Skepticism of the value of reason is not the same as raising the denial of reason to the status of a virtue. Thus, the rigid separation between the two cannot be used, in Judaism, to justify a chasm between religion and the rest of the world, or, indeed, between religious knowledge and all worldly knowledge.

Judaism has, throughout its millennial history, confronted a variety of civilizations, each with its own values and perspectives. It has fought and rejected some completely, and learned from and taught others as a result of a fruitful and usually unself-conscious dialogue with them.

Often, numbers of Jews, overwhelmed by the majority culture and unwilling or unable to remain confidently independent as a cognitive and religious minority, have assimilated into the host culture; they and their descendants have been lost forever to Jewish posterity. This painful phenomenon has occurred from biblical times onward. Never, however, has that confrontation been as long, as intense, as complicated, and as fateful as the present one—Judaism as it faces Western civilization and the entire complex of modernity.

This volume addresses one aspect of that encounter, insofar as it can be isolated from the whole matrix of relationships, and that is the intellectual–educational aspect. While there are various formulations of this encounter—the contemporary

Jewish equivalent of "Athens and Jerusalem" might be "Ye-shiva and University"—the one we shall use is that of *Torah* and *Madda*: Jewish learning and the worldly wisdom of our culture. Hence, *Torah Umadda* denotes the synergistic interrelation of religious study and secular or profane knowledge. The belief implied in this locution is that the interaction between the two yields constructive results. Definitions of some key terms now follow.

TORAH

"Torah," which etymologically means "teaching" or "doctrine," usually embraces a number of related things. Often it refers to the canonical text of the Pentateuch, the Five Books of Moses. Sometimes it includes the rest of Scripture as well; that is, the books of the Prophets and the Writings. We shall be using the term primarily in its most inclusive sense, namely, the entire corpus of the Jewish religious tradition, consisting of both the Written Law (Scripture) and the Oral Law (i.e., the oral tradition) coextensive with Scripture, which was subsequently reduced to writing as the *Talmud* and its vast literature.

There are two Talmuds (or *Talmudim*), the Jerusalem (or Palestinian) and the much more voluminous and authoritative Babylonian Talmud. Each Talmud consists of the same core, the *Mishnah*—the interpretations and legislations of the teachers known as the *Tannaim*, redacted toward the end of the second century of the Common Era. The two Talmudim differ in the *Gemara*, the vast commentary and supplement to the Mishnah, as developed in the academies (or *yeshivot*) of the *Amoraim*, successors to the Tannaim. The Gemara was redacted some 300 years later. These three terms—*Talmud, Mishnah, Gemara*—are synonymous; each means "study" or "learning."

Talmud Torah, the study of Torah, has always held a place of the highest prominence in Judaism. A teaching of the Mishnah that has become part of the daily morning service, recited by praying Jews for centuries, informs us of the high esteem in which the study of Torah by all Jews is held. After enumerating those virtuous deeds "of which man enjoys the fruits in this world while the stock remains for him in the world-to-come," a list that includes honoring parents, acts of charity, prayer, hospitality, tending to the sick, and the like, the Mishnah concludes: "but the study of Torah is equal to them all [combined]."[4] The Jew who studies Torah is considered to be engaging in *imitatio Dei,* for "the Holy One, blessed be He, the King of kings of kings . . . studies Torah one quarter of the day."[5]

So deeply ingrained is the study of Torah in Jewish religious consciousness that, in happy disregard of chronological order, the tradition has Abraham observing all the *mitzvot* (commandments, plural of *mitzvah*), even those legislated by the postbiblical sages.

The effects of Torah study are vast. The Sages—the authors of the Talmud—held that the study of Torah raises the ordinary Israelite to the level of the priesthood. It elevates him to the order of freedom. It enhances brotherliness and is a source of consolation. The reward for the assiduous student of Torah will be the opportunity to continue "learning" Torah for all eternity![6]

Torah may be studied individually or in small groups of two or three. The Jewish tradition encourages study in such small groups. The teacher–student relationship is most highly prized; the title for Moses is *Rabbenu,* "our teacher." (*Rabbi* means "my master" or "my teacher.")

The *yeshiva* (plural: *yeshivot*) is the oldest institution of higher learning in Judaism. As such, it may well be the oldest form of higher education in the world; universities began to coalesce into formal schools only in the late Middle Ages. The word yeshiva means "seat," perhaps the chair from which the master, the head of the school (the *Rosh Yeshivah*), holds his lectures and directs the discussions. Another opinion derives the name from the fact that the disciples sat at the feet of their master.

The earliest yeshivot we know of flourished in both Palestine and Babylonia in the century before the Common Era. So inseparable is the idea of higher formal education from the fabric of Judaism that Jewish legend maintained that, in earliest biblical days, Abraham sent Isaac to study in the Yeshiva of Shem and Eber—thus locating the origin of the yeshiva within eleven generations of the creation of man!

It was the task of the master not only to give the lecture, which consisted of the *perush,* or explanation of the text "on the page"; but also to give *hiddushim* ("new comments")—that is, to formulate new insights and offer original explanations. Those who attended the yeshiva were called *talmidei hakhamim,* "disciples of the sages."

The yeshiva is thus an educational institution that is well over 2,000 years old. It has shown phenomenal resilience, especially in its astounding renaissance after the Holocaust both in Israel and in the Diaspora, especially in the United States.

"Torah" consists of various canons, volumes, legal collections, or literary works, and comes in a variety of genres, often intertwined in the same text. The two main genres or branches of Torah are *Halakhah,* Jewish law, and *Agadah,* all the nonlegal material in the sacred literature, from legends to ethics to didactic parables to biblical exegesis to theology and mysticism. Halakhah is normative and, because of its broad influence on all forms of practical behavior, has always been accorded the position of preeminence. Agadah is the poetry to Halakhah's prose; it captures the heart and fires the imagination of the student, and holds up for him the highest and most sacred ideals, often unattainable by average mortals. But it is the Halakhah that governs his daily activities in all areas of life, from the most critical to the most minute, and indirectly encapsulates the sublime insights and principles of the Agadah.[7]

HALAKHAH

The Hebrew root *H-L-KH,* "go" or "walk," is both etymologically and substantively the source of *Halakhah,* the Jewish "way" or, as it is usually translated, "Jewish law." The discipline of Halakhah is rooted in the effort to "walk before" the Almighty, as in the divine command to Abraham, "Go [or: walk] before Me and be whole" (Genesis 17:1), to live a life sanctified by carrying out the divine will. By its commitment to Halakhah, Israel achieves its mission of becoming a "holy people" (Exodus 19:6), and individual Jews thus live in consonance with the divinely revealed Law. And the highest activity in the halakhic life is learning—*Talmud Torah,* the study of Torah (especially Halakhah) itself. The primacy of Talmud Torah, as mentioned, is a most salient characteristic of the Halakhah. Its emphasis, especially on the study of Halakhah, is evident throughout the Talmud and its literature.

However, an exclusive emphasis on Halakhah risks ignoring an important principle: that *Halakhah is minimal Judaism,* and not its totality; it does not exhaust the content of Torah. Halakhah is the necessary but not sufficient condition of Torah existence. It points beyond itself to higher achievements and greater challenges: to extending one's self beyond the Law; to supererogatory piety (*lifnim mi-shurat ha-din*), which implies social-communal and ethical as well as ritual punctiliousness;[8] to the refinement of one's character both socially and spiritually; to the universal transformation of

mankind at the Messianic End of Days; to the flight of the soul
in the ethereal realms of Agadah and the stringent demands
the latter makes upon us spiritually, morally, and psychologically, demands no less heroic than the practical and intellectual demands made upon us by the Halakhah. (The great poet
of the nineteenth-century East European Jewish Enlightenment, Hayyim Nachman Bialik, missed this point in a famous
introduction to his work on the Agadah. He considered Halakhah harsh and demanding in its discipline, and Agadah
compassionate and forgiving; Halakhah had an angry visage,
Agadah a smiling mien. But this is an error. As Rabbi Joseph
B. Soloveitchik pointed out in a lecture many years ago, it is
Halakhah that, in setting the minimal criteria for conduct,
avoids superhuman demands on Jews, whereas Agadah often
ignores the all-too-human limitations of the majority and
challenges the Jew to transcend his conventional social and
psychological constraints and moral limitedness.)

Thus, Halakhah retains, as it must, its axiological primacy.
Halakhah must take the lead, and its judgments must always
be sought and respected and obeyed. But primacy is not
exclusivity. Beyond the Halakhah lies all the rest of God's
creation, and that too must be considered in the religious
perspective of the believing Jew. Judaism is capacious enough
to include all the world in its comprehensive purview, including religiously neutral knowledge and learning.

MADDA

We refer in these pages to such worldly wisdom as *Madda*,
which in its plain sense means knowledge, and the effort to
integrate it with Torah as *Torah Umadda*. In the last century, in
Germany, the preferred term was *Derekh Eretz* (literally, the
way of the world). There is justification for use of the term
Madda in the sources; Maimonides, the illustrious twelfth-

century talmudist, philosopher, and physician, named the first of the fourteen volumes that constitute the immortal *Mishneh Torah,* his halakhic code, the *Sefer ha-Madda,* the "Book of Madda." Perhaps most accurate would be *hokhmah,* Wisdom, the term often employed in the sources. For instance, in the introduction to the Midrash on Lamentations we are told that whereas the non-Jews do not possess Torah, they do possess hokhmah, Wisdom—indicating the universality of such learning. The Talmud legislated a special blessing upon encountering a gentile scholar: "Blessed art Thou O Lord . . . who has given of His wisdom to flesh and blood." And Maimonides is fairly consistent, in his *Mishneh Torah,* in referring to such learning as hokhmah. The expression "Torah and Wisdom" may therefore be used as an alternative to "Torah Umadda."[9]

Nevertheless, the term *Madda* does have warrant in Maimonides, as mentioned, and it has gained wide currency. It is engraved as the motto of Yeshiva University, "Torah Umadda," and was introduced at Yeshiva by its first president, Dr. Bernard Revel. The term "Torah Umadda" was used by the eminent Rabbi David Zvi Hoffmann, successor to Rabbi Azriel Hildesheimer as head of the Rabbinical Seminary in Berlin, as the title of an article he published in *Jeschurun* in 1920. In Lithuania, the Yavneh group, which is discussed in Chapter 2, founded a school in 1928 that it named "The Universal School of Torah Umadda." Dr. Revel preceded them both, however. In a collection called *The Alperstein Letters,* recently acquired by the Yeshiva University Archives, we find a letter by Dr. Revel to Rabbi A. Alperstein. His salutation refers to his correspondent as a man "rich in both Torah and Madda" and describes some of his hopes and plans and anxieties as he takes on the responsibility of heading the yeshiva. He sees his role as *mashgiah al limmudei ha-torah ve'ha-madda,* "supervisor of Torah and Madda studies." The letter was written in the summer of 1915. Madda, therefore, understood as "wisdom" in the sense noted above, is the name we shall be using, both by itself and in conjunction with the study of sacred literature, as Torah Umadda.

Torah Umadda is thus an effort, not at all unprecedented in the history of normative Judaism, to expand the area of religious interest to include all of creation, and to bring all of humanity's cultural creativity and cognitive achievements within the perimeters of Torah. The intersections of Torah and Madda are not always clear; indeed, they are more often than not elusive and indeterminate.

The culture or specific Madda that the overwhelming majority of Jews in the contemporary world face today—indeed, in which so many of them participate not only as consumers but also as producers—is that of modernity.

The salient elements of modernity, which has so profoundly shaped the scientific–technological megalopolis in which most Jews of the world live today, include the following things: the substitution of experience for tradition as the touchstone of its world view; a rejection of authority—at the very least a skepticism toward it, at worst a revolution against it; a radical individualism that draws upon the sources of both the Protestant faith and, in its more extreme manifestations, the French Revolution (specifically, the notion that people can and ought to recreate their society by destroying it first), and thus a preoccupation with the self; a repudiation of the past and an orientation to the future, and thus a fascination with the new (what Jacques Maritain has felicitously called "chronolatry"); and secularism, not as a denial of religion as much as an insistence upon its privatization, drawing largely upon the Kantian distinction between private and public morality, with moral issues relegated to the private realm and unenforceable in the public arena; and a rejection of particularisms of all sorts and an affirmation of universalism, the dream of the Enlightenment.

Of course this does not exhaust the list, and—equally self-evident—not all of the elements have to be present to qualify a point of view as modern. Indeed, some of these elements can be extrapolated to lead fairly rapidly to mutual inconsistency. Besides, there are currents and countercurrents, some of which we are experiencing at the time of this writing.

Thus, for instance, the decade of the '70s was highly hedonistic, with its much touted sexual revolution, experimentalism with dress and morality (especially its legitimization of homosexuality as an acceptable "alternative life-style"), general permissiveness, easygoing attitude toward drugs and pornography, open life-style, apotheosis of the self (evidenced by the emphasis on self-gratification, self-expression, and self-realization), youth culture, feminism (in its more extreme manifestations), and so on.

Yet the '80s have seen a reaction set in against some of the excesses of the modernism of the '70s, leading a prominent sociologist to dub it "the revolt against modernity."[10] Hence there has developed a new social conservatism, with its attack on permissiveness and cultural modernism, its attempt to restore traditional values (however one defines them), Pope John Paul II's conservatism within the Catholic Church, the Moral Majority and the "New Right," the social-political agenda of the Reagan and Bush administrations, the counter-attack by political philosophers against the assertion that rights are anterior to the good, and so on.

Yet, despite these forays on the fringes of modernity, the basic characteristics of modernity have survived, all premature reports as to its demise and succession by "postmodernity" notwithstanding.

This, then, is the culture of modernity, in its broadest

outlines, with which believing Jews must contend. That it presents a problem of overwhelming proportions cannot be denied. But the social, communal, and general cultural challenge of modernity is not our central concern here. Rather, we shall focus on the intellectual and educational dimensions of the encounter. This is the Madda aspect with which Torah Umadda must deal. Hence, the question of the *study* of the literature and sources of the modern experience, rather than the experience itself, is what occupies us; and, in this sense, the Torah Umadda problem of our period in history is a continuation of the problem first formulated in Alexandria (see, on this, the beginning of the next chapter) and perhaps even earlier.

However, before leaving the topic of modernism, the reader deserves to know the general approach of the writer to the fundamental cultural questions which, as stated, we do not entertain here in any great detail. This point of view is informed by a number of premises, among them the following two, which are most relevant to the more restricted question of Torah Umadda.

First, religion is not just one of a large number of social phenomena or interpretations of existence and, particularly, human experience. It addresses the most fundamental issues in a most fundamental way and demands the most fundamental and unconditional response or responses. In this sense, it denies the secularist thesis that religion is simply one more phenomenon that has no special claim on modern man's attention. Religion deals with truth—"the Lord your God is Truth"; "the Torah of truth was in his mouth"; "Moses is true and his Torah is true"—even if, in this post-Kantian period, one insists that this truth of religion has no cognitive value in the realm of the natural order.

Second, this response, and the comprehensive commitment that flows from it, does not imply that all the rest of existence is of no or only peripheral interest to the faithful Jew. His belief in the binding nature of Halakhah and the priority given to the study of Torah in his intellectual life does not exclude concern with all else. It is a failure of intelligence to confuse priority with exclusivity. To ignore all the rest of existence because of the commitment to Torah as the channel to the Holy One is to insult the Holy One and deny His infinity—as if He too has no interest in the rest of His creation. (Theologically, this can result in an eccentric dualism—a God who is theistic in relation to Israel and deistic in relation to all else!) Even in the most radical interpretation of the mystical origin of Torah, to which we attend in a later chapter, it is Torah that is an aspect of God, not the other way around. Ignoring the world is an insult to Torah as well: the Midrash (the literature of both agadic and halakhic interpretation of biblical verses) maintains, using agadic language, that God employed the Torah as a blueprint in creating the world, and that hence it is sacrilegious to remove the world from the purview of the interest of the Jew committed to Torah.

Purpose and Plan of the Book

This book is primarily, but not exclusively, intended for readers who are as troubled as is the writer by the vexing problems thrown up by the confrontation of Judaism and the Jewish tradition on one side, and, on the other, modernity and the secular civilization in which we live; specifically, by the teachings of Torah, the eternal resource of divine wisdom and guidance, as it collides with the ever-changing wisdom of the secular culture of our scientific, technological, cosmopolitan society. This dilemma is the contemporary version of the predicament experienced by the Judean exiles who, by the shores of Babylon, hung up their harps and lamented, "How shall we sing the Lord's song in a foreign land?" (Psalm 137:4).

I hope that those who are fully committed to Torah and yet unabashedly participate in contemporary culture on its highest levels, and who gladly accept the tensions engendered by the encounter between Torah and Wisdom, will find here—if not solutions—at least challenges for further thought, and maybe even a hint or two as to directions in "singing the Lord's song" in a cultural landscape that appears foreign to the faith of Israel.

Those who stand outside the Jewish tradition, either because of the accident of birth or because they do not accept the theistic basis of Torah or the binding authority of Judaism as expressed in the Halakhah, may at least benefit from observing the difficult but happy struggles of those committed to both Torah and Madda; observing these struggles can be, for them, an exercise in cultural and religious anthropology. Such readers are welcome as interested spectators of this internal debate—or, better, search. An attempt has been made to clarify and define terms for the uninitiated reader so as to facilitate following the argument.

Those who locate themselves within the Jewish tradition but experience no dilemma because they ascribe no value to secular wisdom as such, who affirm "Torah Only"—it is with them whom, in a special chapter, the writer conducts this dialogue, as brothers in the halakhic fraternity who differ on their orientation to Madda. If he fails in this attempt at convincing them, or even in drawing them into genuine dialogue, perhaps at the very least they will learn to appreciate the religious authenticity and spiritual earnestness of those who are seized by this metaphysical tension and who seek, in one way or another, to integrate Madda into their vision of Torah.

We begin with a brief recapitulation of past efforts at developing an open attitude toward the encounter of Torah and the environing culture. This short impressionistic historical survey is then interrupted in order to present the views of those opposed to Torah Umadda, emphasizing especially the ideas of the "Torah Only" school of thought, and to respond to their criticisms. We then turn to the Torah Umadda concepts of Moses Maimonides, Samson Raphael Hirsch, and Abraham Isaac Hakohen Kook, and essay a critical evaluation of their contributions—which we term the rationalist, cultural, and mystical models of Torah Umadda, respectively. Following that, we posit some basic premises and sketch in the ideational background of Jewish religious thought in the Eastern Europe of the late eighteenth and early nineteenth centuries, with some assistance from more contemporary figures, in order to extrapolate to three newly formulated varieties of Torah Umadda. These yield for us the instrumentalist, inclusionary, and hasidic models. We then adumbrate the consequences of these new formulations, follow this with some observations on the Torah Umadda impact on the personal aspiration for religious growth and spiritual wholeness, and conclude by addressing the ideological–political question of the coexistence of divergent conceptions of the role of Madda in the framework of Torah Judaism—the view of Judaism that continues undiminished the centrality of the commitment to Halakhah.

A final note: Although we offer historical material as background, presenting a number of illustrations drawn from Jewish history, we have made no attempt to be comprehensive. This is not a book on cultural or intellectual history. Our approach is more phenomenological than historical; indeed, this work is primarily one of advocacy of a definite point of view, and the analytic, historic, and philosophic materials are used mainly to support the thesis so advocated.

NOTES

1. See, for instance, David J. DeLaura, *Hebrew and Hellene in Victorian England: Newman, Arnold, and Pater* (Austin & London: University of Texas Press, 1969).

2. Lionel Trilling, *Matthew Arnold* (New York: Columbia University Press, 1949), p. 256.

3. Hans Kohn, "The Teachings of Moses Hess," in the *Menorah Journal,* 18:5, May 1930, p. 403.

4. *Pe'ah* 1:1, and see note 6.

5. *Avodah Zarah* 3b.

6. For references and further elaboration, see my *Torah Lishmah: Torah for Torah's Sake in the Works of Rabbi Hayyim of Volozhin and His Contemporaries* (New York: Yeshiva University Press, 1989), Chapter 3. Hereinafter, *Torah Lishmah* refers to this work and not to its Hebrew precursor of the same name, published in 1972 by Mosad Harav Kook in Jerusalem.

7. The relation of Halakhah and Agadah to each other is as complicated as it is significant. For further treatment of the theme here alluded to—the underlying identity of Halakhah and Agadah—see the Introduction to my *Halakhot ve'Halikhot* (Jerusalem: Yeshiva University Press and Mosad Harav Kook, 1990).

8. Compare Nahmanides' famous dictum about *naval bi'reshut ha-torah,* "a scoundrel within the boundaries of Torah," in his commentary to the Torah, Leviticus 19:2.

9. The logo of Yeshiva University prior to the present one, which bears the words *Torah Umadda,* cited the verse from Isaiah 33:6—"And the stability of thy times shall be a hoard of salvation—wisdom (*hokhmah*) and knowledge, and the fear of the Lord which is His treasure."

10. This is the title of an article by Daniel Bell in *The Public Interest,* 54:81 (Fall 1985), pp. 42–63.

CHAPTER 2

HISTORICAL PRECURSORS

EARLY PRECEDENTS

The Hellenistic period is the most obvious choice for a beginning point in locating precedent for the Torah Umadda approach. This encounter of two vital cultures was stormy indeed, but it also resulted in a cross-fertilization, and it had enormous consequences for world history, let alone Jewish history.

The high point in the sympathetic encounter between Judaism and Hellenism was reached in Alexandria, Egypt, at the beginning of the Common Era when Philo Judaeus, who embodied the culmination of the fusion of the two cultures, wrote his seminal works that were to exercise an enormous influence over the religious philosophy of all monotheistic faiths for centuries to come.

In his educational program, Philo reserved a special place for the liberal arts and sciences, the *enkyklios paideia* or encyc-

19

lical studies.[1] He held that one who has studied the arts and sciences must arrive at a belief in God; indeed, only by studying the Creation can one arrive at a knowledge of the Creator. The atheist errs by drawing the wrong conclusions from his encyclical studies, especially astronomy.[2] Of course, Jewish education is presumed; Philo's own knowledge of Jewish sources testifies to a working system of Jewish education in Alexandria during that period (although there is no evidence that it even began to rival the educational system in Palestine, about which more follows).

Scholars are divided over the venue of the secular education of Jews in Philo's time. The consensus is that that young Jews received training in the encyclical studies in the Greek gymnasium, although others hold that it took place in schools under Jewish control.[3]

Philo held that it is God who is the ultimate source of encyclical knowledge, not because He is the Author of the world, but specifically because He is the One who makes it possible for men to know;[4] this theme was to be picked up and developed a thousand years later by Maimonides. Nevertheless, he believed, without proper caution such encyclical studies can lead one to heresy by implying that the human mind rather than God exercises "leadership and sovereignty in human affairs," failing to realize that it is God who is the ultimate guarantor of the truth of such studies.[5] Philo was concerned—and here he sounds contemporary—that Jewish youths appeared to be acquiring Greek culture merely to further their social and political ambitions, instead of utilizing the encyclia in the striving for divine knowledge. Despite the danger of the seductive charms of secular learning, he held that the benefits were such that they were worth the risk. Philo was criticized both by the radical Hellenists and by those traditionalist Jews who felt the risk was unwarranted.[6]

Philo of Alexandria is thus a distinguished precursor of the varied attempts since then to address the problem of Torah and Wisdom. Yet Philo and his Alexandrian peers somehow remained tangential and never really entered the mainstream of Jewish history.

One significant and salient fact that emerges from a study of this era of utmost importance to the contemporary problem of Torah Umadda, is that an authentic and viable Torah Umadda approach requires the Torah part to be genuine, to be studied with enormous seriousness, and never to be considered a mere adjunct of Madda.[7]

The key as to why the Jews of the Land of Israel, unlike those in the Diaspora, were, on the whole, successful in resisting assimilation, lies in a passage in the works of the ancient historian Josephus in which he declares that the Jews place a premium not on the mastering of languages but on knowledge of the Torah and its interpretation. The Jews of the Land of Israel—alone—instituted, as early as the first century, a system of universal education for males; established a chain of yeshivot, institutions of higher Torah education; and studied and eventually codified the Oral Law. In Alexandria, however, despite the numbers and wealth of the community—as evidenced, for example, in the tremendous loans that Philo's family was able to give to Agrippa I and in the huge synagogue (so reminiscent in size and lavishness of our own postwar synagogues and centers) in Alexandria—we hear of no comparable system of education and no yeshivot.

The works of Philo and of other Hellenistic Jews were not mentioned by the rabbis, and, indeed, were not even translated into Hebrew until the sixteenth century. Yet the attempted syntheses of Jewish and secular studies in medieval Babylonia and Spain did become part of the mainstream of Jewish literature, though admittedly, in many cases, only after a struggle. Why so?

The answer would seem to be that Hellenized Jews such as

Philo examined the Torah through the prism of the Greek language and culture, whereas Maimonides viewed the Greek philosophers through the prism of the Torah and the Talmud. The cultured Jews of Alexandria derived their knowledge of Plato by reading Plato in the original, but their understanding of the Torah came second-hand, through a translation, whereas the educated Jews of medieval Spain derived their understanding of Aristotle through translation and their knowledge of Torah first-hand.

That lesson must not be lost on us as we attempt to fashion an approach for Torah Umadda for our times, one that will resonate with the fundamental structures of Judaism and issue out of Torah itself. The primacy of Torah must be a given in any viable Torah Umadda approach. This precludes any version of Torah Umadda that treats Torah as a form of human culture only, as a literary-religious adjunct of the ethnic or national polity of Israel that remains supreme and absolute.

While we shall be giving major attention to the medieval period, some mention must be made of the positive views of the encounter of Judaism with other branches of learning during the Mishnaic, Talmudic, and Geonic periods (first to eleventh centuries). Thus, for the early Mishnaic era, the Talmud relates in the name of R. Simeon b. Gamaliel that his father had a thousand youngsters studying in his school, five hundred learning Torah and an equal number engaging in "Greek Wisdom."[8] In the Geonic period, according to the eleventh-century R. Joseph Ibn Aknin (in his commentary to the Song of Songs), R. Hai Gaon (939–1038), "the last and greatest of the Geonim," did not hesitate to use Arabic sources, including Arabic love songs, to prove a talmudic point; in addition, he quotes the Koran and the Hadith (the sayings and doings of Mohammed). The same source tells of the famed talmudist R. Samuel Hanagid quoting Christian exegetes. Moreover, he quotes R. Masliah, a well-known *dayyan* (halakhic judge) in Sicily who, in a letter to R. Samuel Hanagid, tells of a personal experience with R. Hai Gaon. The latter had encountered difficulty in understanding a verse in Psalms, and directed R. Masliah, much to his consternation, to approach "the Catholic of the Christians and ask him what he knows about the interpretation of this verse." Noticing R. Masliah's discomfort, R. Hai rebuked him, saying, "Our early fathers and righteous men never hesitated to inquire from people of different religions, even from shepherds, concerning obscure words in Scripture."[9] The late-eleventh-century sage R. Yehudah Barceloni reports in the name of the same R. Hai Gaon that it is permissible to teach schoolchildren Arabic and arithmetic. Interestingly, and quite to the contrary of a number of nineteenth-century as well as contemporary Ashkenazi (Franco-German) authorities, he insisted that these be taught *only* alongside their Torah studies, not separately.[10] The tenth-century talmudist and philosopher R. Saadia Gaon is so well known for his openness to nontalmudic studies that it is unnecessary to document his views. It is sufficient to point to his Introduction to his *Emunot ve'Deiot,* where he mocks those who reject scientific and speculative studies lest they lead to heresy. They are no better, he says, than those ignoramuses who believe that an alligator swallowed the moon; "like so many others, they are laughable."

Interestingly, the Sephardi (Spanish) experience, especially during the Italian Renaissance and in Southern France as well, included a very natural, relaxed, and unapologetic acceptance of what we now call Torah Umadda, without even bothering much to explain and defend it as an ideology. On January 17, 1466, over five hundred years ago, four centuries before the founding of a small yeshiva on New York's Lower East Side that was destined to blossom into Yeshiva University, King John of Sicily granted authorization to his Jewish subjects to establish a Jewish university. Unfortunately, the project was never realized. In the sixteenth century, R. Abraham Provencal tried to found a Jewish university in Italy, and that too failed. These efforts, though they came to grief, reveal an orientation to Torah Umadda half a millennium ago.

In other Sephardi centers, the integration of sacred and secular studies was less common, but when it occurred it did not usually encounter great resistance. One thinks, in this connection, of the fifteenth-century sage R. Elijah Mizrachi, the leading Turkish rabbi of his time and the great commentator on Rashi (the illustrious eleventh-century French commentator on the Bible and the Talmud); he not only knew but taught his students mathematics and other subjects alongside Talmud.[11]

No survey of medieval thought on the relationship of sacred to profane knowledge can possibly be complete without reference to the immortal Maimonides. Because of his enormous achievements, however, he is treated separately in a later chapter.

The Ashkenazi experience was, for a variety of historical reasons, much more tense, anxious, and withdrawn than the Sephardi. Of course, this is meant as a general rule only, for there were notable exceptions. Thus, in the sixteenth century, R. Moses Isserles (RaMA), the renowned commentator on the *Shulhan Arukh* (the standard code of Jewish Law composed in the sixteenth century), in an exchange of letters with the illustrious R. Solomon Luria (MaHaRSHaL), defends the study of other branches of Wisdom on religious grounds, much to the discomfort of his interlocutor. Other Ashkenazi giants who were favorably disposed to non-Torah learning alongside Torah studies include, in the seventeenth century, R. Loewe (known as MaHaRaL of Prague, ca. 1525–1609); R. Mordecai Yaffe (author of *Levush,* 1530–1612), disciple of both Isserles and Luria; in the eighteenth century, R. Jacob Emden (1697–1776), who was an autodidact in secular studies and whose ambivalence toward them was expressed, on the one hand, in confining the time and place where they may be pursued, and, on the other hand, in declaring them a necessity for the development of proper social relationships in a changing society; also his antagonist, R. Jonathan Eybeschuetz (1690/95–1764); R. Mosheh Margalit (1710/20–1781), author of *Penei Mosheh* on the Jerusalem Talmud; the Gaon of Vilna (1720–1797); two disciples of the Gaon, R. Baruch of Shklov (1740–1812) and R. Menashe of Ilya (1767–1831); and others.[12] Overall, however, East European authorities were generally averse to permitting non-Torah studies to enter the curriculum.

MODERN PRECEDENTS

The nineteenth and twentieth centuries saw renewed attempts at introducing Torah Umadda, both conceptually and institutionally, into Ashkenazi Jewish life in both Central and Eastern Europe. Because the efforts of Rabbi Samson Raphael Hirsch were so extensive and consequential, we accord them separate treatment in following chapters, and instead proceed here with a brief sketch of such ventures in Russia and Lithuania.

Russia

The Russian version of Torah Umadda is represented by the efforts of Rabbi Yitzhak Yaakov Reines.[13] Reines, a Mizrachi (religious Zionist) leader in Russia, had always dreamt of building a yeshiva in Lida. He began his project in 1896, but for a variety of reasons it was aborted. Some seven years later, he returned to the task and assumed the role of publicist on behalf of his dreams. In one public letter, he offered sharp criticism of the yeshivot of his day, maintaining that they failed to achieve their mission and did not educate students to be "people filled with Judaism and humanity alike." Their training in the yeshivot, he averred, did not leave the students prepared to deal with the revolutionary atmosphere then prevalent in Russia. Many of them remained in the yeshivot because of the lack of alternatives—surely not a tribute to the yeshivot or their students. He therefore proposed a new kind of yeshiva.

The yeshiva planned by Reines was to be founded on the following principles:

1. Thorough knowledge of Talmud and its commentaries and Codes.
2. Knowledge of other vital Jewish studies, such as Bible, Hebrew, grammar, history, and literature.
3. Secular studies at least on a par with those offered in the city schools.

In 1905 the school, formally named "Torah Va-Daat" (Torah and Knowledge), opened its doors to its first class. Before long it boasted over three hundred students in five grades, and even one class of a postgraduate talmudic institute, today known as a "kollel."

A short time after the school was founded, Reines invited Rabbi Shlomoh Poliachek, the famed Illui of Metchit, educated in Brisk and a student of Rabbi Chaim Ozer Grodzensky of Vilna, to be the teacher of Talmud. Despite the best efforts of a number of distinguished rabbis, including Rabbi Hayyim Soloveitchik of Brisk, to prevail upon Rabbi Poliachek to reject the offer, Poliachek went to Lida and left an indelible impression upon it during the years of its existence. (Rabbi Poliachek later taught at the Rabbi Isaac Elchanan Theological Seminary, now an affiliate of Yeshiva University.)

The purpose of the yeshiva of Lida, as Reines wrote in his *Shenei Me'Orot,* was to educate rabbis—whether the "authentic" kind accepted by the masses of religious people or the "official" rabbinate established by the government—as well as pedagogues who would teach Talmud, Hebrew, and general studies; also, for future laymen, there would be a course of general studies specifically for those who intended to go into the nonclerical fields, such as business. Hence, the school had a spectrum of goals and missions. In 1907, Reines made it clear that he believed the time had come to emphasize the training not of rabbis but of ordinary laymen, and to elevate their standards of learning.

The Zionist orientation of the yeshiva, as well as its broad curriculum—the very thing that attracted parents who were more modern and progressive in their educational views—aroused the opposition of the less modernist groups at the very beginning of the yeshiva's history. Representatives of other yeshivot lost no opportunity to defame Rabbi Reines's yeshiva, spreading rumors that "the school has no direction, students sit bareheaded, they are taught to sing and dance," and so on. It did not take long before these rumors were proven false and the school became so popular that Reines had to turn away hundreds of students for lack of space.

The school continued to exist until the beginning of the First World War. In the second year of the war, with the advance of the German army to Lida, people fled the city and the yeshiva was forced to leave as well. Unfortunately, Rabbi Reines died just as the Germans were about to come into the city, and after a short period of moving elsewhere, the yeshiva—as a result of the terrible pogroms that broke out in Southern Russia after the war—finally came to an end.

The very name of the school, "Torah Va-Daat" (Torah and Knowledge), indicates the goals of Rabbi Reines—a Russian version of Torah Umadda.

Nevertheless, although practical work was done in establishing a curriculum reflecting a willingness to confront the encounter between Torah and Wisdom—even as this was being done in Germany, the United States, and Lithuania—Rabbi Reines did not elaborate a fundamental philosophy upon which to base his practical labors. It is a pity that this singularly impressive and heroic individual did not have the opportunity to complete his life's work, in both its theory and practice, because of the exigencies of war and exile and, ultimately, death.

Lithuania

The Lithuanian version of Torah Umadda goes back to the First World War.[14] That war brought about major changes in the educational complexion of Lithuanian Jewry.

The various yeshivot, *Talmudei Torah,* and *hadarim* (elementary schools) were originally meant only for boys, and included no significant secular study. However, during the German conquest of Lithuania, the Germans legislated compulsory schooling for various sections of Lithuania and set aside special schools for Jewish children in which the language of instruction would be German instead of Yiddish and the main studies would be secular. After the war, these schools began teaching in Hebrew or Yiddish, and three educational streams developed: a Hebrew-speaking secular group, a Yiddish-speaking secular group, and Yavneh, a religious group that was taught in Hebrew.

Yavneh thus became heir to the older religious education system in prewar Lithuania. The two innovations added during the postwar period were the use of Hebrew as a language of instruction in all courses, and the introduction of secular or general studies, including the Lithuanian language. Even the most extreme antimodernists in Lithuania did not oppose Hebrew as a language of instruction and conversation among students, and neither was there any opposition by these circles to the introduction of secular studies in religious schools.

In 1928, Yavneh opened a high school—"The Universal School for Torah Umadda"—which included ten grades, building on the first four years of elementary school (equivalent to grades five through high school and the first two years of college). All subjects were taught from the point of view of traditional Judaism, which created a sense of harmony.

The Yavneh schools were founded by a group called "Tze'irei Yisrael." This group was the successor to a previous organization called "Bet Yisrael" and was founded after the Bolshevik Revolution, in the year 1919, under the aegis of Rabbi Chaim Ozer Grodzensky of Vilna.

With the establishment of the Yavneh schools, the following three items were declared as the principles of the school:

1. Wide and deep knowledge of Torah (including Bible, Talmud, Codes, Jewish Philosophy, Kabbalah, etc.).
2. Broad knowledge of Jewish history and adequate knowledge of general history.
3. Proper study of general education. (This was already presaged in the term "Torah Umadda" included in the name of the school.)

A year later, in 1920, a meeting was called in Kovno to formally establish the school. Chairman of the occasion was the distinguished scholar Rabbi Abraham Duber Kahana Shapira, Chief Rabbi of Kovno. The committee included representatives of both the Mizrachi group and their opponents within Orthodox Judaism, the anti-Zionist Agudath Israel (which, in the 1930s, effectively took over the Tze'irei Yisrael group).

The first year alone saw the opening in Lithuania of forty Yavneh schools, and a year later there were requests to open branches in eighty other locations. Over a third of all Jewish schools in Lithuania belonged to the Yavneh stream, which received the backing of the leading rabbis of Lithuania.

In 1921, a Yavneh Teachers Seminary was opened in Kovno. In order to ensure that a religious spirit would prevail in the seminary, it was decided to place it under the guardian-ship of Rabbi Joseph Leb Bloch, the rabbi and rosh yeshiva of Telshe. It was effectively the only seminary in Lithuania for the preparation of Jewish teachers, because the other educa-tional streams did not have any real teacher education. Most of the students in the seminary were former yeshiva students. The first three years were devoted primarily to Talmud stud-ies; these were taught in the first part of the day, with the afternoons devoted to other Judaic studies, general studies, and professional studies, such as pedagogy, psychology, his-tory of education, and methodology.

The diploma from the seminary gave graduates the right to enter the university. Yavneh lasted in Telshe until the Soviet conquest some ten years later.

In 1923, a Teachers Seminary for Women was opened, headed by Dr. Y. R. Holzberg. The latter speaks in tones of reverent admiration of the work of Rabbi Joseph Leb Bloch. One of the great and more stringent rabbinic figures of Li-thuania, Rabbi Bloch was the first one to understand the need for modern Hebrew religious education for both boys and girls. As early as 1915, he proposed establishing a modern religious school that would fulfill all government require-ments and yet be conducted in the spirit of Torah and piety. He did not hesitate to include secular studies in the curriculum of the preparatory school for the Telshe Yeshiva; and when the Lithuanian government agreed not to draft yeshiva students into the army on condition that they would receive a secular education equivalent to the four grades of high school, he consented to such a program in his preparatory school.

Despite the difficulty, at the beginning, in finding religious teachers with a higher education, Yavneh soon found itself well supplied with faculty as a result of its own earlier initiatives. It had succeeded in raising a generation of young Lithuanian–Jewish academics who were committed to Torah. In the only Lithuanian university in Kovno, a group named "Moriah" was founded, comprised of religious students and academicians. This group called a convention of religious academicians from all the Baltic countries in 1932, meeting in Riga where the organization had been formed. This was a direct result of the educational efforts of Yavneh.

Hence, Lithuania, like Russia, reflecting also what was happening in the United States, empirically implemented the concept of Torah Umadda. However, it did so considerably later than Germany—the first Jewish community to undergo modernization—and without developing a coherent philosophy such as had been under discussion in Germany.

Latvia

Mention should be made of another such experiment in nineteenth-century Eastern Europe in integrating secular studies into the Torah curriculum, one of more modest success but earlier than the two that have been discussed. This was a high school established by the well-known musarite, Rabbi Simcha Zissel Ziv Broide (1823–1897) of Kelm, the most distinguished disciple of the founder of the movement, R. Israel Salanter. In both the Talmud Torah he founded in Kelm and the one he later started in Garubin in Latvia, not far from the Baltic Sea, he introduced non-Torah studies into the curriculum for three hours a day. He wrote the following:

General knowledge helped men to understand nature, God's own handiwork. It is an act of *kiddush ha-Shem* (sanctification of the divine Name) to demonstrate in this age of Enlightenment that a Jew may be modern in manners, dress, speech, and general education, and yet be a scholar of Torah with a high ethical and pious disposition.[15]

R. Simcha Zissel set forth four major pedagogical principles that were to guide his schools. Third of the four was:

> Acquisition of polite manners (*derekh eretz*) in keeping with the spirit of the times, to be able to get along with people in conversation and action. All these studies are based upon deep piety, skillfully woven into the subject matter. The reading and writing of the Russian language, arithmetic, and geography are taught in this house under our supervision.[16]

The school lasted about twenty years and produced such luminaries as Rabbi Nathan Zvi Finkel (the "Old Man" of Slobodka), Rabbi Moshe Mordecai Epstein, Rabbi Naftali Tropp, and others.[17]

The United States

The most profound and pervasive expression of the Torah Umadda philosophy, both conceptually and institutionally, would ultimately be found within the confines of the Yeshiva Rabbi Isaac Elchanan (Theological Seminary), today an affiliate of Yeshiva University. But this now self-evident fact was not initially true of this venerable institution. When founded in 1897 by transplanted Lithuanian rabbis—Moses Meyer Matlin, Yehudah David Bernstein, and Isaac Bernstein—as an extension of the elementary *heder* Etz Chaim (founded in 1886), its mission was to provide immigrant rabbis and their American-born scions with a home where Torah would be studied exactly as it was in Eastern Europe. The intellectual world of Torah Umadda was foreign to their consciousness.

Even the instrumentalist value of secular studies, which was to provide rabbis with the general philosophy and sociological training necessary to address the needs and proclivities of their own emerging American Jewish community, was unknown to them.

They went as far as frowning on their students studying the English language, and they were dismayed when some of their best charges ultimately sought to expand their intellectual horizons at American colleges and universities. For the yeshiva's founders, if their school was to have a practical goal, it would be the production of scholars who would write talmudic treatises, thereby raising the prestige of the Torah among those in America who were still interested and who wished to garner respect for their American Torah enclave in the estimate of the world religious community.[18]

The yeshiva's slow, often tortuous move away from this stance was first precipitated by its own rabbinical students, who complained that their training—their proficiency in Talmud, Rabbinics, and Codes notwithstanding—was not equipping them to communicate effectively to the next generation of American Jews. They demanded an integrated curriculum, retaining Talmud as the bedrock but exposing them also to the widest streams of Jewish culture and texts and, of course, facilitating their addressing their American constituency by instruction in English public speaking.[19]

Initially, the yeshiva's rabbinic and lay officialdom rejected their demands, causing some students to leave the school either to pursue alternate professional callings or to enroll at the Jewish Theological Seminary. Others stayed and fought their teachers and leaders. With the help of newspaper support, in 1906, they initiated a strike at their school. Clearly at an impasse, the yeshiva's directors first sought to mollify the protest by electing Rabbi Philip Hillel Klein as president. Significantly, the Hungarian-born Klein, holder of a Ph.D.

from the University of Jena, had earned his ordination from
Rabbi Azriel Hildesheimer's Berlin-based Rabbiner Seminar.
But the directors did not follow through in their modernization efforts beyond the presidential appointment, and they
failed to bring into the school that type of multifaceted Torah
Umadda curriculum to which Klein himself had been exposed
in Western Europe. Eventually renewed protests ensued, new
promises were made, and two new esteemed rabbinic personalities, East European in training but clearly attuned to at least
the instrumentalist aspects of Torah Umadda, were installed
as presidents. Rabbi Moses Zebulun Margolies (RaMaZ) was
elected in 1908, with Rabbi Klein serving as honorary president. In 1910, both men stepped aside in favor of Rabbi
Bernard Levinthal, who was equally sympathetic to the students. Still, truly substantive changes in philosophy and curriculum at the Yeshiva Rabbi Isaac Elchanan had to await the
arrival in 1915 of American Orthodoxy's earliest and most
committed champion of Torah Umadda, Dr. Bernard
Revel.[20]

A talmudic prodigy, ordained a rabbi at the age of 16 at the
Telshe Yeshiva, a voracious autodidact of various secular
disciplines and later to attain advanced degrees in Semitics and
Law, Revel personified the educational possibilities implicit in
the philosophy he would name Torah Umadda. (Revel was
equally comfortable with the term Torah ve'hokhmah, discussed earlier.) Despite opposition from various quarters,
Revel was determined—and indeed successful—in making his
yeshiva not only a bastion of traditional Torah learning, far
beyond what Rabbis Matlin and Bernstein had foreseen, but
also a home for the serious study of Judische Wissenschaft (academic Judaic studies) as well as a professional school for the
training of English-speaking American rabbis.[21]

From the late 1920s until his death in 1940, and through his
organization of Yeshiva College, Revel limned the institu-

tional integration of Torah study with the wide universes of secular knowledge as exemplified by American institutions of higher education. As Revel developed it, the student of Torah would be exposed on a daily basis and within the same precincts ("the beauty of Japheth in the tents of Shem") to both intensive Torah study and a university curriculum. The general structure of the day for an undergraduate student as formulated by Revel—and so it remains essentially to this day—called for the first half of the day, usually from 9:00 A.M. to about 3:00 P.M., to be spent in Torah, and the rest of the day in Madda. It would be left to the thinking individual himself, with the assistance of the examples of appropriate rabbis and teachers, to perform within his mind and personality the essential synthesis of the teachings that made up Torah Umadda—articulated first in the United States at the core institutions that would evolve into Yeshiva University.[22]

It is of some interest to record, in this connection, an event that never occurred.[23]

On July 18, 1946, a provisional charter to found the American Hebrew Theological University was granted by the Regents of the University of the State of New York to two prominent Brooklyn institutions not particularly distinguished by a favorable attitude toward Torah Umadda. This was in response to a request by the heads of these institutions, the late Rabbis Shraga Feivel Mendlowitz of Mesivta Torah Vodaath and Yitzchok Hutner of Mesivta Rabbi Chaim Berlin, who were slated to lead the Board of Trustees of the new institution. The charter application declared that the school would offer a basic liberal arts program on the level of a junior college, and three graduate schools that would require a baccalaureate degree for admission: a school of theology (leading to the D.Th. and Ph.D. degrees), a school of social studies (leading to the M.A. degree), and a school of administration (offering an M.S. degree).

When Rabbi Harold Leiman, the principal of the Chaim
Berlin High School and originator of the idea to found a
college, was asked how this effort could be reconciled in the
face of the declared opinion by such rabbinic eminences as
Rabbi Elchanan Wasserman and Rabbi Baruch Ber Leibowitz
forbidding university studies, his answer was, "It was done
because we faced a serious problem and we approved it
because of the circumstances of the day."[24]

Less than a year later, on June 20, 1947, the application was
withdrawn. In later years, there was some question as to why
the project was stillborn; in a long conversation with Rabbi
Mendlowitz,[25] Rabbi Leiman attributed this to the strong
opposition by the late Rabbi Aaron Kotler, head of the Lake-
wood Yeshiva and a powerful and pivotal personality in
yeshiva circles.

What this nonevent seems to prove is that even outside
Yeshiva University circles, the opposition to Torah Umadda
was not as solid and unanimous as is sometimes imagined.
There were moderate Orthodox rabbinic leaders who were
beginning to appreciate the need for a Torah Umadda education on a higher level, but countervailing forces were developing at the same time, and the latter proved too powerful for
the former. Had Rabbis Mendlowitz and Hutner succeeded, it
is quite possible that the complexion of Orthodox Jewry,
especially with regard to the question of Torah Umadda,
would be considerably different today.

Notes

1. See Alan Mendelson, *Secular Education in Philo of Alexandria* (Cin-
cinnati: Hebrew Union College, 1982), p. 3 et passim.
2. Ibid., pp. 23, 81.
3. Ibid., p. 29f.
4. Ibid., p. 39.
5. Ibid., p. 43.
6. Ibid., p. 82.

7. The comments that follow are based on Professor Louis H. Feldman's article, "Torah and Secular Culture: Challenge and Response in the Hellenistic Period," in *Tradition* 3:26–40.

8. *Sotah* 49b. See, on this, Saul Lieberman, *Hellenism in Jewish Palestine* (New York: Jewish Theological Seminary, 1962), p. 104f.

9. See *Hitgalut ha-Sodot ve'Hofaat ha-Meorot,* ed. Abraham S. Halkin (Jerusalem: Mekitzei Nirdamim, 1964), pp. 493–495. The story is cited as well in the autobiography of Rabbi Baruch Halevi Epstein, *Mekor Barukh* (New York: Grossman Publishing Co., 1954), vol. 1, p. 80f. In a later work (*Sefer ha-Iyyunim ve'ha-Diyyunim,* Jerusalem: Mekitsei Nirdamim, 1975, p. 227), Halkin cites a passage by the famous R. Moses ibn Ezra, grammarian and poet, that is worth translating:

> I have quoted from the Arabic Koran and paid no attention to the widespread enmity adopted by contemporary halakhic thinkers, because I noticed that the greatest of those involved in [both] Halakhah and philosophy, including R. Saadia Gaon and R. Hai Gaon, and others, availed themselves [of the Koran] when they sought help in understanding obscure passages in the Prophets, even of Christian commentaries despite the [latter's] imperfect knowledge.

10. R. Hai Gaon, *Sefer ha-Ittim* (Krakow, 1903), p. 256.

11. Responsa R. Elijah Mizrahi, no. 56 (Constantinople, 1559).

12. See Yehezkel Cohen, in his *Ha-Yahas le'Limmudei Hol be'Yahadut* (Tel Aviv: Hakibbutz Hadati, 1983), and Yehudah Halevi, "Hokhmat ha-Torah u-She'ar he-Hokhmot," in *Yad Re'em* (Jerusalem: Defus Daf-Hen, 1974), pp. 189–212. On Emden, see especially Jacob J. Schacter, *Rabbi Jacob Emden: Life and Major Works* (unpublished doctoral dissertation, Cambridge, MA: Harvard University, 1988), Chapter 6. Emden, a highly idiosyncratic individual, was favorably inclined to the study of the natural sciences and even to what is today called humanistic studies, but bitterly opposed to philosophy—and most especially to Maimonides' *Guide of the Perplexed*—though he had read widely in the field. On R. Israel of Zamoscz, R. Baruch of Shklov, and R. Menashe of Ilya, see Emanuel Etkes, "Immanent Factors and External Influences in the Development of the Haskalah Movement in Russia," in *Toward Modernity,* ed. Jacob Katz (New Brunswick: Transaction Books, 1987), pp. 20–24. This list is not intended, of course, to be complete.

13. The material on Reines was culled from the recent biography by Geulah Bat-Yehuda, *Ish ha-Me'orot: Rabbi Yitzhak Yaakov Reines* (Jerusalem: Mosad Harav Kook, 1985), Chapter 43.

14. The information on Yavneh is derived from an article by Dr.

Yitzchak Raphael Etzion (Holzberg), "The Yavneh Educational Movement of Lithuania" (Heb.), in *Yahadut Lita,* ed. Natan Goren and A. Yary (Tel Aviv: Iggud Yotz'ei Lita be'Yisrael, 1972), vol. 2, pp. 160–165.

15. Eliezer Ebner, "Simha Zissel Broida (Ziff)," in *Guardians of Our Heritage,* ed. Leo Jung (New York: Bloch, 1958), p. 334.

16. Dov Katz, *Tenuat ha-Musar* (Tel Aviv: A. Zioni, 1954), vol. 2, pp. 193–194.

17. William Z. Low, "Some Remarks on a Letter of Rabbi E. E. Dessler," in *Encounter: Essays on Torah and Modern Life,* ed. H. Chaim Schimmel and Aryeh Carmell (Jerusalem/New York: Feldheim, 1989), p. 210.

18. For biographical sketches of the Lithuanian rabbinic founders of the American yeshiva, see Hayim Dov Baer Gulevsky, *Sefer Du Yovlin* (Brooklyn: Edison Lithographers, 1988), pp. 23–27. On the early history of the yeshiva, see Jeffrey S. Gurock, *The Men and Women of Yeshiva: Higher Education, Orthodoxy and American Judaism* (New York: Columbia University Press, 1988), pp. 18–19. See also Gilbert Klaperman, *The Story of Yeshiva University: The First Jewish University in America* (New York: Macmillan, 1969), pp. 50, 56–57, 63, 64.

19. Gurock, pp. 24–25.

20. For biographical sketches of Rabbis Klein, Margolies, and Levinthal, see Jeffrey S. Gurock, "Resisters and Accommodators: Varieties of Orthodox Rabbis in America, 1883–1983," in *The American Rabbinate: A Century of Continuity and Change, 1883–1983,* ed. Jacob Rader Marcus and Abraham J. Peck (Hoboken NJ: Ktav, 1985), pp. 31, 32, 36, 37. On the careers of this rabbinic triumvirate at Yeshiva, see Gurock, *The Men . . . ,* pp. 30–36.

21. For a full-length biography of Dr. Bernard Revel, see Aaron Rothkoff, *Bernard Revel: Builder of American Jewish Orthodoxy* (Philadelphia: Jewish Publication Society, 1972).

22. On the founding and educational structure of Yeshiva College, see Gurock, *The Men . . . ,* pp. 80–95 et passim.

23. See, on this aborted effort, William Helmreich, *The World of the Yeshiva* (New York: Free Press, 1984), pp. 47–50.

24. In response to a question by Professor Helmreich, ibid.

25. Helmreich, p. 50. Hillel Goldberg, in a biographical article on Rabbi Hutner for *Tradition* (22:34), tells of Rabbi Hutner submitting to the will of Rabbi Kotler and abandoning the project.

CHAPTER 3

OPPOSITION

TO TORAH UMADDA

IN RECENT HISTORY

Before the major models and exemplars of Torah and Wisdom are presented in greater detail, it is instructive to consider the views of the adversaries of any form of positive engagement between sacred and secular studies. This is in keeping with the teaching of the House of Hillel that one must always give the courtesy to one's intellectual opponent of presenting his views before expounding one's own ideas.

The opposition to Torah Umadda is as old as Torah Umadda itself. Indeed, the more powerful and creative the ideological, educational, and institutional achievements of Torah Umadda advocates, the more persistent the antagonism to it. Perhaps the best illustration of this phenomenon is the bitter anti-Maimunist campaign that began toward the end of the life of Maimonides and reached a crescendo after his death but has continued, indeed, to this very day. Because even the lightest treatment of this controversy tends to take one far afield—there is a whole literature on it, more than can be quickly summarized here—we shall confine ourselves to a brief historical survey of the opposition to Torah Umadda in relatively recent times, before proceeding to a more systematic presentation of the views of the "Torah only" advocates, a rebuttal of their arguments, and an examination of the major Torah Umadda models.

Despite a number of glowing exceptions, Ashkenazi Jewry had little to do with secular learning. The curriculum of the schools and the research of the scholars was overwhelmingly confined to Talmud and Codes; even biblical studies and Hebrew language studies received precious little attention. Secular wisdom usually did not come into consideration at all, and if it did, it was spurned.

When, in the nineteenth century, Rabbi Samson Raphael Hirsch—under the influence of Rabbi Jacob Etlinger and Hakham Isaac Barnais—developed his *Torah im Derekh Eretz* movement (see Chapter 5), East European rabbinical figures turned a cold shoulder to Hirsch's ideas, even though they respected and welcomed him personally. The Talmudists of the Lithuanian yeshivot were especially negative. Such an eminent figure as Rabbi Hayyim Soloveitchik of Brisk had a totally rejectionist attitude toward general education, including even the study of the language of the land in which he lived and the reading of newspapers or books of any kind.[1] Perhaps the most dramatic proof of the seriousness with which the Lithuanian yeshivot viewed the incursion of secular learning as a threat to their whole way of life is the decision by the Netziv (Rabbi Naftali Zevi Yehudah Berlin) to close the Yeshiva of Volozhin rather than accept the demand by the Russian Minister of Education, in 1881, to introduce even the most elementary general studies into the curriculum of the yeshiva. The yeshiva, indeed, remained closed for a number of years.

Nevertheless, this may indicate not a radical stance concerning secular learning as such, but rather a curricular policy that would not permit the commingling of sacred and secular studies (taking the reverse position of R. Hai Gaon, discussed earlier). Thus, the Netziv's son, Rabbi Meir Bar-Ilan (Berlin), writes:

> Once, my father, of blessed memory, came into my room, just when I was studying Russian from a teacher who was a yeshiva student from Minsk. My father inquired from the teacher about my progress in my studies and, as usual, the teacher complained that I did not prepare my lessons properly. My father said to me, "Study, my son. I wish that I had known Russian, because then things would have appeared quite differently to me." . . . What in those days was called "Haskalah" [higher secular education] and in certain, indeed most, Haredi circles was despised, appeared quite differently to my father. Neither in Volozhin or in his later years did my father ever speak slightingly of "Haskalah" as such.[2]

Of all the places in which the linking of secular to Torah studies was abjured, the most aggressive and absolute was that of the Old Yishuv in Jerusalem. A short digression into recent history may prove illuminating: When Ludwig August Frankel, an Austrian Jewish poet, came to Jerusalem in 1856 in order to set up a school in which secular studies too would be taught, and which received the approval of the Sephardi Chief Rabbi, Rabbi Haim Nissim Abulafia, the Ashkenazi Jerusalem community was aroused and a ban pronounced upon the school. This ban on the linking of sacred and secular wisdom was declared absolute and eternal and, indeed, was observed by the vast majority of the Haredim—the most stringent and most antimodernist religious Jews. (Haredim is the plural of

Haredi and derives from the Hebrew expression denoting those who fear the Lord.)

The same community, under the strong pressure of its Hungarian Haredim, also frustrated the attempts of Rabbi Azriel Hildesheimer, the eminent co-developer of the *Torah im Derekh Eretz* school with Rabbi Samson Raphael Hirsch, to set up an orphanage in Jerusalem in which some small part of the day was to be devoted to secular studies and the learning of a trade. Hildesheimer's goal was to prevent these orphans from being preyed upon by Christian missionaries, who were very active in Jerusalem at that time. In the vigorous reaction to Hildesheimer's effort by such Hungarian rabbinic dignitaries as Rabbi Akiva Joseph Schlesinger and Rabbi Hillel Lichtenstein (one of the leading students of the famed Rabbi R. Moses Sofer, the *Hatam Sofer*), Hildesheimer was accused of wreaking havoc with Jewish children and handing them over "to the foreign harlot" and, ironically, of facilitating the work of the Christian missions in converting the orphans!

Nevertheless, the non-Hungarian Haredim were far more pluralistic in their approach. Thus, Agudath Israel—a worldwide organization founded in 1912 in Kattowitz as a reaction against secular Zionism, Reform, and the socialist Bund, and which serves as the political arm of Haredi Jewry—consisted of Polish and Rumanian Hasidim (adherents of the pietistic movement founded in the last half of the eighteenth century), Lithuanian Mitnagdim (opponents of Hasidism), Hungarian Haredim, and "neo-Orthodox" German Jews of the *Torah im Derekh Eretz* school, who affirmed the value of a secular education and culture but shared the anti-Zionism and communal segregation policy of the others. At its first convention, the "Kenesiyah Gedolah" in 1923, the Gerer Rebbe declared that whereas the organization and convention were designed to establish unity among all Orthodox groups, nevertheless each country or constituent community was to continue its

own traditions and customs undisturbed by others. The principle was established that what is right for one community
may not be acceptable to another, and no coercion should be
exercised.

Nevertheless, inner tensions developed. In the 1930s there
took place a confrontation between the Hungarian Haredim
in Jerusalem and German immigrants, both groups belonging
to Agudath Israel. The latter wanted to educate their sons and
daughters according to the pattern set by Hirsch in Frankfort
rather than in the educational institutions of the Old Yishuv in
Jerusalem. The Agudah leaders felt that there was no way of
overcoming the resistance of the Jerusalem Hungarian
group—the precursors of the Neturei Karta, the extremist
fringe group that broke away from Agudath Israel, considering it too moderate, and which to this day is uncompromis-
ingly anti-Zionist and does not recognize the legitimacy of the
State of Israel.[3] This group "created scandals," a situation that
had caused Hildesheimer, earlier, to complain bitterly in his
correspondence of "religious terrorists" and of otherwise
good people who were petrified of them and were intimidated
by them into signing all kinds of bans. In this case, however,
the German Haredim decided to go ahead with their project.
In January 1934 they opened the Horev School for their own
children, offering not only Torah studies but a broad general
studies program as well. Moreover, the lower grades were
coeducational, and in the upper grades, although boys and
girls were kept in separate classes, they studied in one building
and shared one sports field.

The reaction was not long in coming. Posters decrying the
terrible desecration of Jerusalem described in gory detail the
sins of the German modernists: Boys and girls studying in
mixed classes; men and women teachers working together;
other signs of corruption such as the use of blackboards,
school bells, and maps. . . .[4]

Closer to our own time, some forty or fifty years ago, a number of Torah giants in Eastern Europe responded to a query from America about the study of secular wisdom, especially in universities; these responses were recently published by Yehuda (Leo) Levi.[5] The responses of Rabbi Elchanan Wasserman and Rabbi Baruch Ber Lebowitz were completely negative. The reaction of Rabbi Abraham Isaac Bloch of Telshe is discussed later in this chapter.

Of special interest is the responsum of the famous Rabbi Joseph Rosen, "the Rogotchover." Most of his reply seeks to demonstrate that knowledge of natural sciences has halakhic significance and standing, and is not simply tolerated. Beyond that, pointing to a Maimonidean halakhic text, Rabbi Rosen expresses the opinion that, according to talmudic law, the wisdom that a father is required to impart to his son includes not only such things as astronomy, medicine, and surveying, which result in a more accurate knowledge of Halakhah, but also other kinds of secular study whose goal is the enhancement of the state (*yishuv medinah*) and of society.

However, on the negative side he holds that the stricture of the *Sifra* (an early Tannaitic halakhic midrash on Leviticus) against worldly learning refers to the *intermingling* of secular and religious studies; but if they are studied separately, such study is permissible. This ruling contradicts a much earlier opinion by R. Hai Gaon[6] permitting non-Torah learning *only* when it is taught together with Torah. Additionally, Rabbi Rosen holds that the permission to teach secular wisdom is limited to allowing the father to teach his sons, as individuals, but does not include the entire community. Formal schools, in other words, are ruled out. Levi shows that others too have restricted the teaching of secular subjects to private lessons and have forbidden it in public; hence the decision of Netziv to close down the Yeshiva of Volozhin rather than submit to the Russian authorities, who insisted on having secular studies taught at the Yeshiva. But Rabbi Rosen seems to indicate halakhic warrant for his ruling, whereas others came to this decision as a matter of policy. Professor Levi is hard-pressed to find the sources for Rabbi Rosen's decision. Moreover, it is an old Jewish tradition that in the elementary Jewish schools children were taught arithmetic and spelling. This goes back, as mentioned, at least to the days of R. Hai Gaon. So does Rabbi Akiva Eger write:

> "Torah is beautiful with *Derekh Eretz*"; thus we should teach the children for an hour or two every day writing and arithmetic, as indeed has been our custom.[7]

TORAH ONLY

At this point it is worth considering, in more systematic fashion, some of the major objections to the whole philosophy of cultural symbiosis implied by Torah Umadda.

"Torah and . . ."

Some critics of Torah Umadda aver that they believe in "Torah *only*" and deride any kind of "Torah and . . .," such as Torah and Madda. Such a purism has an appealing ring to it, but it is mistaken; it ignores the facts. This facile dismissal has to explain a host of talmudic terms, such as the famous triad, *Torah, avodah, u-gemillat hasadim* (the study of Torah, worship, and doing deeds of loving-kindness),[8] implying preoccupation with social philanthropy as well as with Torah study. Or, more to the point:

> Rabban Gamaliel the son of R. Judah the Prince said: Beautiful is the study of Torah combined with some worldly occupation. . . . All study of Torah without work must in the end prove futile and become the cause of sin.[9]

Surely this express mishnaic requirement that one combine Torah study with work or worldly occupation (*derekh eretz*— some form of economic, social, or culturally useful activity) cannot be ignored. The exaltation of Torah does not require contempt for all other forms of wisdom or experience. Indeed, the Talmud taught that whoever maintains that he possesses only Torah, possesses not even Torah.[10]

The same critics argue that Torah Umadda is premised on a flawed appreciation of Torah; namely, that it fails to subscribe to the wholeness and self-sufficiency of Torah. Torah Umadda, they aver, implies that Torah is not complete, that it is lacking; else, why the need for Madda?

This critique is usually based upon the Mishnah in *Avot* (5:26) that says, "turn it [i.e., Torah] over and turn it over, for all is in it"; in other words, delve into Torah intensively and you will discover that it contains everything. Hence, the Tannaim believed that Torah is the repository of all wisdom, and therefore independent study of other systems of thought and culture is a denial of this authoritative comprehensiveness of Torah.

While this is indeed the interpretation of this mishnah by the Gaon of Vilna in his commentary, that fact does not close the issue. First, as we later expound at greater length, the Gaon himself holds an instrumentalist view of Torah and Wisdom, believing that the secular disciplines are necessary to unlock the vault of Torah in order to reveal the wisdom stored in it. A casual interpretation of a single passage in an agadic mishnah is less expressive of the Gaon's overall view than are his explicit approval of certain kinds of secular knowledge and his instructions to his disciples to arrange for the translation into Hebrew of certain classics of mathematics and other sciences.

Furthermore, the Gaon's is not the only authoritative exegesis of this mishnaic dictum. R. Menahem ha-Meiri sees this passage as teaching that any problem within Torah itself is solvable without having recourse to sources outside of Torah.[11] Thus, Torah is self-sufficient as sacred teaching; it makes no claim to be the sole repository of *all* wisdom, human as well as divine.

This much more modest interpretation is certainly more palatable for those living, as we do, in an age that has witnessed the explosion of information and knowledge and the incredible advances of science and technology. The view some ascribe to the Gaon, that there is no autonomous wisdom outside of Torah, because all is contained in Torah, would leave committed contemporary Jews profoundly perplexed. No amount of intellectual legerdemain or midrashic pyrotechnics—or even sophisticated but capricious computer analyses of sacred texts—can convince us that the Torah somehow possesses within itself the secrets of quantum mechanics, the synthesis of DNA, and the like. No such problems arise if we adopt the interpretation of ha-Meiri. And the latter is perfectly compatible with the outlook of Torah Umadda, whose advocates do not agree that ignorance—any ignorance—should be raised to the level of a transcendental good and a source of ideological pride.

Yet this "Torah only" school must not by any means be dismissed cavalierly. Its ideology not only nourished the opposition to Maimonides in the great Maimunist controversies that erupted after his death, but it has prevailed in the majority of the great yeshivot, and its renaissance in the contemporary Western world is astonishing. Our greatest objection to "Torah only" is that it considers itself as the *only* legitimate expression of Torah Judaism; it is not, even though it has distinguished precedent and represents *a* legitimate interpretation of the Torah tradition.

The "Torah only" school is based on a number of propositions, all of which militate against Torah Umadda and all of which deserve sober, respectful, and critical analysis. We shall here discuss three of them in detail.

First is the fear that exposure to Madda is potentially dangerous to religious people, especially the young and those who are Jewishly underdeveloped and spiritually immature (an elastic category that can be expanded to include almost everyone). Second is the talmudic statement, enshrined in a centuries-old tradition extending from the talmudic period to our own day, that Halakhah is the only subject that is religiously valid and spiritually meaningful, and that other areas of intellectual endeavor are not to be countenanced for a Jew committed to Torah. Third is the concern that any time available for intellectual advancement not devoted to Torah constitutes a violation of the important injunction against *bittul Torah,* wasting time that should be better spent in Torah study.

The Danger of Heretical Notions

The first premise of the "Torah only" school is the fear that the open attitude of Torah Umadda to the secular disciplines carries with it the danger of infecting the student with the virus of heresy. Thus, the late Rabbi Elchanan Wasserman prohibited all secular learning because it required the study of heretical texts. When faced with the question of why the great Maimonides engaged in such studies, Wasserman's response is characteristic of the Haredi treatment of Maimonides, who represents an embarrassing anomaly for the Haredi world generally: The great Maimonides was permitted to do such things precisely because of his greatness; the usual rules do not apply to him, but we spiritual Lilliputians cannot afford to take such risks.[12] Hence, whatever might be gained in cultural breadth and increased knowledge is paid for in the coin of religious defection and spiritual devastation. And the price is too high. The flame of faith cannot survive the buffeting winds of atheism and agnosticism, abetted by the torrential downpour of a paganized hedonism and scientifically sanctioned materialism, unless it is protected by a powerful and secure container—namely, "Torah only," which alone can ensure its survival.

There is much merit to this argument. Madda certainly does confront the student with an array of ideas, many of which are thoroughly incompatible with traditional Jewish beliefs, and many more of which pose indirect challenges to the premises of religious faith. Moreover, the life-styles of modernity, enshrined in literature—much of which is sheer pornography disguised as art—and often justified by the social sciences, are inimical to sacred Jewish values of modesty, sexual temperance, family cohesiveness, respect for parents and elders, and the like. (We have more to say about literature and the rest of the humanities in Chapter 12.) Believing Jews are a tiny cognitive minority in a vast sea of *kefirah* (apostasy), and "Torah only" beckons as a haven, as perhaps the only viable solution. Hence, the opposition to Torah Umadda and the inclination to "Torah only."

In a sense, however, all this is beside the point. Dogmatic assertion, theological persuasion, and religious apprehensiveness cannot change the reality that the problem of Torah Umadda is part of the cultural and intellectual landscape and will not go away. We may ignore it for a while, but it will not therefore sneak away like a thief in the night.

The infiltration of modernity into Jewish life is inexorable. The permanent return to the shtetl, whether one considers it desirable or not, is impossible. The current revival of what might be called "shtetlism" is admittedly an astonishing phenomenon, but its success should not be seen as an irreversible process. The very forces that eroded the shtetl in the first place are bound to reassert themselves one way or another. "You can't go home again" is completely true in this case.

Technology, which insinuates itself into every nook and cranny of civilization, is not only a means, a technique, but also a harbinger of other things to come; and indeed, in its own right it introduces major cultural transformations. As it penetrates even ghettoized life, it becomes a battering ram of modernity. The argument that the ubiquitousness of technology does not necessarily lead to a meaningful encounter with the scientific culture that produced it, as can be demonstrated by the Ayatollah Khomeini's revolution in Iran in the 1980s, in which he used the telephone, tape recorder, and television from his exile in Paris and, subsequently, his headquarters in Qum, suffers from two defects. First, not enough time has elapsed for the revolutionary zeal to have spent itself in order to test whether indeed, in more normal times, Shiite fundamentalism can coexist for a long period with a technological culture. Second, if the answer to this question is in the affirmative, it would clearly reduce Iran to permanent technological sterility and condemn it to remain forever a consumer and never a producer of technology. Is this the kind of scientific aridity and impotence that we wish upon Jews and upon the State of Israel?

Hence, the problem that gives rise to Torah Umadda in the first place—and was responsible for the emergence of *Torah im Derekh Eretz* a century ago—is unavoidable, and that means that Torah Umadda, in one form or another, will always be with us. The confrontation between Torah and the contemporary culture of modernity can be held off for a while, but not forever. As successful as "Torah only" may be for a period of time, it is not a permanently impenetrable and invulnerable cocoon.

Even if all faithful Jews should agree to adopt such a policy, it must ultimately fail—and not only because modernity, in a world transformed into a village by the miracles of telecommunications and all the other marvels of technology, will inevitably break through the protective cordons of such ideological and communal isolation.

It must fail lest it succeed—and thereby change the very nature of the Jewish people in relation to the mission that it received at Sinai. To turn our backs on the accumulated knowledge of the Western world, even for the meritorious reason of protecting the tender flower of Jewish faith, means to abandon our role as a *people* and to opt for the safer role of a *sect*. Such a decision, of course, would constitute a revolutionary break with Jewish history. It is unthinkable that the "holy nation and kingdom of priests" (Exodus 19:6) should be transformed into a "sacred sect and denomination of priests" and that a nation founded with the promise of becoming a blessing for "all the families of the earth" (Genesis 12:3) should abandon its destiny for the security of the Jewish equivalent of an Indian reservation. Our religious purity and ideological safety would thereby be purchased at the cost of our historic claims, our pretensions both nationalistic and universalistic, and our ancient vision of a redemptive destiny that encompasses *all* Israel and *all* humanity. And that price is too high.

Lest the reader suspect that this distinction between sect and people (a distinction already used by perceptive sociologists), and this fear of sectarianism, are a rhetorical exaggeration, the author has before him some writings that confirm these fears. They come from the more (or most) strident of the Haredi community and are presented here not as polemical arguments—for surely they are not representative of the majority of moderate Haredim—but as a glimpse into what the future portends if the Orthodox community allows this "shtetlism" and its implied closedmindedness to new ideas, experiences, people, and any change whatever, no matter how innocent, to continue unchecked.

The January 13, 1989, edition of the organ of the Satmar Hasidim, *Der Yid* (which announces itself as the "Voice of American Orthodox Jewry") carries an article on page 45 by a Rabbi Landsman, one of a series on "The Trials of the New Generation." The column offers us some rather piquant information about this group's formulation of the trials and temptations of being a Jew in the modern world. Addressing itself to the relatively large number of published works on Halakhah by people of suspect ideological purity, it tells us that the late Satmarer Rebbe, Rabbi Joel Teitelbaum, taught that no volume of pure Halakhah, even if it contains no discussion of ideology, may be used if the author is not one of the "in group," that is, not one of those who identify with their brand of Orthodoxy. Previous articles in the series by the same author offer similar cautionary notes to the unsuspecting pious student.

Such insistence on mental straitjackets and paranoid witch-hunting is not confined to the pages of a weekly newspaper. Thus we read in the responsa *Be'er Mosheh* by a prominent Haredi scholar, Rabbi Moses Stern, the Debrocziner Rav, that the author was asked if it is permitted to buy holy books written by earlier acknowledged authorities and printed in our time by various institutions and movements whose names are synonymous with heresy. His answer was that it is the duty of all rabbis and leaders of the generation to proclaim both verbally and in writing that it is forbidden to purchase works from such publishers because, somehow, they will cause the innocent reader to be attracted to their false ideas. The following are some choice comments by this contemporary doyen of Hungarian Haredism:

> One may rightly fear that [the reader] will learn from [the author's deeds], since he will detect in the book the latter's greatness in Torah,

and therefore erroneously conclude that the author, with his great ability, determined that it is permissible to be a Zionist or a heretic[13] and others of the sort. Or, for instance, if one studies from a book the author of which is a *rosh yeshiva* in some (*sic!*) Yeshiva University, and he will notice his great knowledgeability in Torah, he will certainly, Heaven forbid, say that it is permissible to teach in Yeshiva University, and it is permissible to study there, since a rabbi as great in Torah [as the author] stands at the head of it, whereas in truth he is blasphemous and abominable, as is well known.[14]

Should the Haredi community continue on its path of accelerated radicalization, the many moderate and rational Haredim will be outnumbered, outmaneuvered, and delegitimized. The disqualification of Torah Umadda will then be only the first step in the successful transformation of religious Jewry into a ghettoized sect that will be a caricature of Judaism.

Moreover, such a posture means to step out of history itself—just in the very epoch, beginning in 1948, when the Jewish people decided to enter the arena of history after a millennial hibernation in which we were passive objects instead of assertive subjects, spectators instead of actors. If all the brainpower of the religiously observant Jewish community is to be reserved for "Torah only"—a logical extension of its whole philosophy—then no observant Jew endowed with intellectual capacity of any significance may enter the professions or government. "Torah only" Jews aspire to a State of Israel (that is, those who do not reject it even *de facto*) that will abide by all the rules and regulations of the Halakhah. But how is this to be done without Orthodox physicians and psychologists, Torah-educated writers and economists and sociologists, Halakhah-committed lawyers and poets and professors? The theory of "Torah only" is certainly a precious one, one that attracts our admiration for its courage in refusing to conform to the rest of society and our gratitude for fostering talmudic learning on a scale unknown in generations past. But in a time when a Jewish state has been founded on the ashes of the greatest cataclysm ever to have struck our people, and an independent Jewish polity established for the first time in two millennia, such a theory is self-destructive. And one need not subscribe to the Zionist credo to appreciate the dangers of such anti-intellectualism and provincialism to the welfare of "the nation that dwells in Zion." One thinks of the remark of Jefferson Davis, President of the Confederacy during the Civil War, who was frustrated by the South's doctrinaire devotion to its States' Rights principle and the strict construction of its Constitution, even if this ideological consistency meant certain defeat in that bloody war. Davis said that if the South succumbed, its epitaph should read, "Died of a Theory."[15]

Such a policy is tantamount to conceding the future of the State of Israel to the nonreligious. And this is precisely a sectarian rather than a national vision of Torah, and one that articulates nicely with a secularist view as well. Advocates of Torah Umadda are not prepared for this negotiation, one that requires the attainment of absolute religious security—a myth at best, for nothing in life is absolute—at the cost of abandoning the whole Jewish vision of Israel's role in the comity of nations. We were not meant, as Eliezer Berkovits once put it, to become the Neturei Karta of the nations.

Torah Umadda does not, of course, imply the acceptance of all that goes by the name of modernity. Who, after all, is willing to swallow whole the bait of a triumphant modernism that reeks of the burnt corpses of millions of victims of Nazi gas chambers? Torah Umadda holds that modernity is neither to be uncritically embraced nor utterly shunned nor relentlessly fought, but is to be critically engaged from a mature and responsible Torah vantage. It does not assume that all that is new is good—or bad. It holds that the potential spiritual havoc wrought by confronting the insights and values of contemporary Western culture is far less pernicious to the truth of Torah than that caused by ignoring the whole of man's cultural heritage and thus not knowing how to deal with it at all. Problems may become exceedingly painful when met frontally, but at least there is the possibility of a successful accommodation, even of a solution. A theology of fear solves nothing but the need to rationalize fear itself.

Blinding oneself to a problem may be psychologically more comfortable, less taxing, and produce less tension, but it is a sure formula for defeat and failure. For the studied neglect of Madda means not only that we fail to benefit, intellectually and otherwise, from the undoubted historic triumphs of this culture, but equally that we do not know and understand its demonic aspects and thus find ourselves defenseless before them. Such vulnerability is surely no virtue.

A Nightmare:

I am driving in a comfortable automobile while the weather outside is decidedly inclement—the lights wavy and confusing as they are reflected from the wet pavement, and traffic heavy in both directions. The windows are tightly closed, shutting out the nerve-wracking sounds of blaring horns, screeching brakes, and grinding gears. The car's "climate control" creates an artificial environment of exquisite peace and comfort as the cassette softly plays my favorite musical piece in four-way stereo, and the ceaseless metronome of the windshield-wipers taps out its own dull rhythm. For a moment—and more—I am utterly distracted from the tumultuous world beyond the car. The glare and the disorder and the irritating noise evaporate from my consciousness as I luxuriate in irenic repose within my automobile, my gaze averted from the windshield and wafting gently over the soft lights twinkling their reassuring digital numbers from the automated dashboard like so many beckoning stars. I smile inwardly as my autohypnosis successfully wards off the pandemonium and perils of the

*outside world, the churning chaos of the approaching highway or
urban intersection with roaring behemoths of the road careening
toward me; I imagine the interior of the car as a World unto itself, my
own self-contained Universe, following its own rules and reaching for
its own destiny, going off in any direction it wishes, an autonomous
sovereign. The hint of euphoria leads my eyelids to close. Suddenly, a
jarring crash . . .*

The Sages of the Mishnah did not unanimously opt for this
closed attitude toward dangerous ideas. Ideas certainly can be
dangerous; were they not so, they would be of no value in the
first place. But the Sages held that such ideas must be confronted and fought, not ignored and dismissed. "Be diligent in
your study of Torah," they cautioned, "and know what to
answer the heretic (*apikores*)."[16] MaHaRaL (R. Loewe of Prague) commented on this mishnah:

> [This means] one should study Torah in order to know how to respond
> to the heretic, for just as it is a *mitzvah* for a man to study and acquire
> Torah which is the "Torah of truth," so is it important to banish false
> opinions from the world in order that truth be magnified in it. For if one
> regularly ignores falsehood, it can ultimately, Heaven forbid, destroy
> the truth and annihilate it while falsehood gains strength in the world.
> Therefore [the Mishnah] warns us to deny that which is false by
> knowing what to answer to a heretic.[17]

In another magnificent passage, the same MaHaRaL went
even further, offered a decisive rebuttal to all forms of pietistic
obscurantism, and emphasized the need for forceful yet respectful dialogue with those with whose ideas and opinions
we differ. The power of his plea for open-mindedness and
intellectual courage loses none of its cogency and reasonable-
ness despite the passage of some 400 years since the lines were
first penned, and they are relevant both to our specific theme
and to the larger issues that concern Jews and Judaism in our

times. The following is a translation of some of his words, after he quotes the Aristotelian commentator Averroes, who advised citing the opinions of one's adversaries before recording one's own views, because such opposition lends strength to one's arguments and because the latter become more acceptable to those who seek the truth if they know that the ideas of others were properly considered before they were rejected:

> [Averroes'] words hold true for religion as well. . . . It is not proper that we despise the words [of our adversaries], but rather we must draw them close as we can. [Averroes] wrote there that if one does not do so, and he refuses to accept the words of his opponents with love but rejects them [out of hand], this certainly points to the weakness of his own arguments. . . .

> Therefore it is proper, out of love of reason and knowledge, that you not [summarily] reject anything that opposes your own ideas, especially so if [your adversary] does not intend merely to provoke you, but rather to declare his beliefs. And even if such [beliefs] are opposed to your own faith and religion, do not say [to your opponent], "Speak not, close your mouth." If that happens, there will take place no purification of religion. On the contrary, you should, at such times, say, "Speak up as much as you want, say whatever you wish, and do not say later that had you been able to speak you would have replied further." For one who causes his opponent to hold his peace and refrain from speaking, demonstrates [thereby] the weakness of his own religious faith, as we said. This is therefore the opposite of what some people think, namely, that when you prevent someone from speaking against religion, that strengthens religion. That is not so, because curbing the words of an opponent in religious matters is naught but the the curbing and enfeebling of religion [itself]. . . .

> When our Rishonim found something written against their faith, they did not reject it [out of hand], for it stands to reason that [such opposition] ought not be a cause for rejecting it and for silencing a man when it comes to religious matters; for religion is given to all. This is

especially so with regard to the written word. . . . Should there not have been a reaction against the books of the philosophers who, following their own investigations, repudiated [traditional religious teachings] and asserted the Eternity of the Universe and thus denied the creation altogether? Nevertheless, [the Rishonim] read their books and did not dismiss them. For the proper way in order to attain the truth is to hear [others'] arguments which they sincerely hold, not out of a desire to provoke you. Thus, it is wrong simply to reject an opponent's ideas; instead, draw him close to you and delve deeply into his words. . . .

When a powerful man seeks out an opponent in order to demonstrate his [own] strength, he very much wants his opponent to exercise as much power as he can, so that if he defeats him his own victory will be more pronounced. What strength is manifested when the opponent is not permitted to fight? . . . Hence, one should not silence those who speak against religion . . . for to do so is an admission of weakness.[18]

These words of MaHaRaL are not a concession to coercive external pressures. They are a heroic assertion of self-confidence in his faith as a believing Jew, one ready to meet all challenges on his way to attain the ideal of "wholeness."[19] They are a clarion call to religious courage in the face of all the pressure for doctrinal homogeneity. Truly faithful Jews have nothing to fear from the truth, and they should therefore welcome all genuine learning, as long as it is not motivated by spiteful polemics. The opposition must be given a sympathetic hearing and not be silenced by either contempt or fear.

It is true that not everyone is as capable as MaHaRaL of confronting heretical views in confidence and equanimity. But if one's intentions are genuinely to attain or ascertain truth; if one knows that, as MaHaRaL writes, the adversary is not merely being polemical or provocative but that he too is engaged in searching for truth; if one's commitments are grounded in knowledge; and if one's education has included the basic elements of discourse in which the dialogue is to be conducted, then MaHaRaL's encouragement remains an inspiration to this day—and is worthy of emulation.

If MaHaRaL wrote so about philosophic writings, he most certainly would have held the same views with regard to Madda, which encompasses far more than the medieval or Renaissance philosophers dreamed of. Speculating about how a historic figure would have reacted if placed in a different age is always a risky business, but the breadth of MaHaRaL's vision and the scope of his tolerance and intellectual self-confidence defy the restraints of historical particularities and speak to us with the same persuasiveness as when they were first written.

The Four Ells of the Halakhah

We now direct our attention to a source that, the "Torah only" school asserts, conclusively delegitimates any form of intellectual activity other than the study of Torah. That source is the talmudic teaching in the name of Ulla that, after the destruction of the Temple in Jerusalem, "the Holy One has nothing (left) in His world but the four ells of the Halakhah."[20]

At first blush, this passage effectively decides the question: only the study of Halakhah can be religiously justified.

Our response is twofold. First, those who use this passage to justify the disqualification of any other pursuits neglect the beginning of the passage: Ulla said that *from the day the Holy Temple was destroyed* the Holy One ... The Talmud is not celebrating this restriction on the Divine; on the contrary, it is bemoaning such narrow focus as the result of the Destruction and, apparently, an exilic phenomenon to be overcome in the fullness of time with the coming of Redemption.

Second, and more important, no such facile conclusions are evident from the way Maimonides treats this talmudic dictum. Because the lengthy exegesis by Maimonides is rather obscure, we shall sacrifice brevity for the sake of enlightenment in endeavoring to understand the interpretation by Maimonides.

After praising the Sages and declaring that they spoke the truth, and that those who are intoxicated by sensuality cannot hope to understand them, Maimonides writes as follows:

> So it is in truth, and [the Sages] said, "the Holy One has nothing (left) in His world but the four ells of the Halakhah." Think upon these words, for if you take them at face value they will appear very far from the truth, as if the four ells of the Halakhah are the purpose and [we are bidden] to reject all other sciences and branches of Wisdom. . . . But if you delve into these words with profound understanding, you will discover in them marvelous wisdom, and you will find in them much intelligence. I will therefore explain them to you so that they will be an example of how to digest all [similar passages] which you chance upon. Therefore, understand it well.[21]

In order to clarify this talmudic passage, which would seem to contradict his whole *Weltanschauung* by denying legitimacy to secular studies, Maimonides then proceeds to a lengthy explanation that seemingly is completely beside the point.

He begins by invoking the accepted truth that every created thing has a purpose, and then concluding that in this sublunar realm, all was created for man, the *telos* and crown of this planet. But then the question is, What is the purpose of man himself? To this Maimonides answers, as is to be expected: the perception of truth, especially the knowledge of God and His unity, a knowledge and a cognitive enterprise to which all other studies and disciplines are subordinate and propaedeutic. However, in order to attain this highest intellectual perfection, it is necessary as well to achieve moral perfection, for one who has surrendered to sensuality and the natural appetites can never hope to gain the greatest of all ideas; the satisfaction of the body and that of the soul are in reciprocal relation to each other.

The question then arises: What of all those humans who neither aspire to nor achieve this sublime goal of the intellectual knowledge of God? Maimonides, combining teleology and elitism, offers two answers: First, that such people are created to serve those who do devote their lives to divine contemplation ("because if everyone would be a philosophizing scholar, the world would be destroyed and man could not survive"); and second, that they provide companionship for the God-seekers. Thus, even those who are not at all aware of their divine mission still fulfill their *telos* or *takhlit* indirectly, at one remove.

The next and final paragraph on this theme is the most puzzling of all, both because Maimonides here comes to a conclusion that seems a total non sequitur and because the paragraph is tightly condensed, compared to his literary luxuriation in all the preceding paragraphs. This is what Maimonides writes:

> Thus, from all that we have said, it is now clear that the purpose of all that exists in this world of change and deterioration is the perfect man, [which term] includes both wisdom and conduct, as we explained. And since we learn from [the Sages] two things, namely, wisdom and conduct, as we explained and to which we alluded, [the Sages] correctly stated that, "the Holy One has nothing (left) in His world but the four ells of the Halakhah."

Maimonides here refers to a point that he says he had made elsewhere (I do not know the source; he does elaborate on this in his *Guide,* written much later than this work) that the study of the Oral Law, or Halakhah, leads to perfection in two realms, that of theory (wisdom, *hakhmah*) and of practice (*ma'aseh*). Hence we understand, concludes Maimonides, the statement that God is restricted to the four ells of Halakhah.

How does the conclusion follow from the premises?[22] Maimonides is consistent in his view that the ultimate goal of man is the correct philosophical apprehension of divine unity, and that the way to such fulfillment of the purpose of human existence is through the study of the requisite sciences. For instance, Maimonides says, concerning the branches of learning that the Talmud calls *Pardes* (Paradise, or orchard):[23]

> Even though [the rabbis] were great men of Israel and great sages, not all possessed the ability to know and grasp all these [metaphysical] matters thoroughly. I say that one may not stroll in the *Pardes* except if he has first filled his belly with bread and meat—and this "bread and meat" are the knowledge of what is forbidden and what is permitted and the like concerning the *mitzvot*. . . . Even though the Sages called [this halakhic knowledge] "a small matter"—for the Sages said that "a great matter" is the [study of Ezekiel's] Divine Chariot [for Maimonides this is metaphysics] and a "small matter" is the colloquia of Abaye and Rava [the halakhic discourses in the Talmud]—nevertheless, it is proper that they take precedence, for they primarily compose the mind. Moreover, they are the great boon which the Holy One bequeathed for the promotion of social well-being in this world so that we may deserve to inherit eternal life; for [halakhic studies] are accessible to knowledge by all—young and old, men and women, both those of broad and those of shallow understanding.[24]

Clearly, Maimonides is of the opinion that the philosophically correct understanding of divinity is a "great matter," whereas Halakhah remains a "small matter."[25] Nevertheless, although Halakhah is propaedeutic, it remains an absolute prerequisite to such speculation, and the reason is that practice precedes theory in the philosophic enterprise of the knowledge of God. "For they settle a man's mind" is not meant to describe Halakhah as an educational experience, providing mental gymnastics for the budding philosopher, but to say rather that Halakhah provides for two practical goals without which the speculative mission cannot be undertaken.

These goals are *tikkun ha-middot,* the personal perfection of the moral character of individuals, especially the potential student of philosophy; and *tikkun ha-hevrah,* the perfection of society that will make such dedication to study safe, secure, and possible. The latter, societal perfection, assures us that the masses of human beings who have no direct contact with or interest in such undertakings will serve their function of providing for the elite their elemental needs and fulfilling their need for companionship. The former, moral perfection, is necessary for the scholar himself, to liberate him from subjugation by the senses. This is the function, direct or indirect, of the Halakhah—"settling the mind of a man"—thus making it possible for the elite scholar to proceed with the study of those branches of wisdom that will enable him to continue with his quest for knowing God. Halakhah having tended to the practical and behavioral preparations, the choicest of men can now proceed to achieve the purpose of all humankind: the knowledge of God.

We now understand the conclusion to which Maimonides comes. The entire mission for which man was brought into being cannot begin in a corrupt society and cannot be advanced by people who are morally inferior. Thus, Halakhah is the indispensable beginning. Only if it comes first can we hope to achieve the ultimate goal—that of the divine Chariot, which is the "great matter." If not for Halakhah, there is no entree for man to the divine Presence. Thus, indeed, "the Holy One has nothing (left) in His world but the four ells of the Halakhah." The Holy One is restricted to the four ells of Halakhah. *However,* this restriction is for the purpose of leading man to those studies for which Halakhah is preparatory—the sciences, which will lead to true speculation.

Hence, far from denying the legitimacy of and the need for secular wisdom, the statement by the Sages that "the Holy One has nothing (left) in His world but the four ells of the Halakhah" reaffirms the high role of such wisdom in the fulfillment of man's purpose on earth.

For Maimonides, then, our talmudic passage cannot and may not be used as a facile put-down of secular studies. Quite the contrary emerges from Maimonides' sage and authoritative commentary.

Bittul Torah—*A Halakhic Digression*

This third premise of the ''Torah only'' school is that the study of any discipline other than Torah constitutes a violation of a particularly significant prohibition, that of *bittul Torah*,[26] the nullification or neglect of Torah—that is, the wasting of the time that ought to be reserved for the study of Torah.[27]

The most often quoted source for the study of Torah as an ongoing mitzvah is the verse in Joshua 1:8, ''This book of the law [Torah] shall not depart out of thy mouth; but thou shalt meditate therein day and night. . . .'' Hence, the study of Torah is required of us *constantly,* ''day and night.'' The question then arises: How can the performance of this mitzvah be reconciled with the realities of everyday life: sleeping, eating, attending to one's natural functions, and, especially, earning a livelihood? This problem is treated in two different passages in the Babylonian Talmud, and they seem diametrically opposed to each other.

In *Berakhot* 35b, R. Ishmael asserts the halakhic right to work for one's sustenance, and hence its legitimacy as an exception to the commandment to devote all one's time to the study of Torah. R. Simeon bar Yohai disagrees: One's ''work'' can well expand to fill all available time, and hence what will become of Torah? He therefore rules that even time spent on earning one's daily bread is a violation of the commandment to study Torah; one should have faith, and Heaven will provide. The Talmud then records the views of two later scholars, the famous Amoraim Abaye and Rava. Abaye said that many followed the ruling of R. Ishmael and they succeeded, whereas those who tried the way of R. Simeon bar Yohai did not succeed. Of Rava it is told that he instructed his students to absent themselves from his lectures during the two harvest months, so that they might earn enough of a living to be able to afford to study for the rest of the year without distraction.

A major problem arises, however, when we compare these views to the talmudic discussion in *Menahot* 99b. Here we are told by R. Yohanan in the name of the same R. Simeon bar Yohai that the mitzvah to study Torah "day and night" is fulfilled by the minimum of studying one chapter (of Torah text) by day and one by night. R. Yohanan adds that this ruling should not be shared with the ignorant (who, presumably, will accept the minimal standard and make no attempt at increasing the time spent studying Torah). Rava disagrees and holds that there is nothing wrong with publishing this ruling even among the unlettered. We are then told that R. Ishmael was asked by his nephew if, in light of the fact that he had studied all of Torah, he was permitted to study "Greek wisdom." The uncle's answer was to refer to our verse in Joshua and hence, humorously, to advise his nephew to seek out an hour that is neither day nor night, and to study his Greek wisdom then. This ruling, however, is opposed by R. Jonathan, who interprets the verse neither as an obligation nor as a mitzvah but as a blessing: If you will not allow the Torah to "depart from your mouth" and will study it constantly, then—as the rest of the verse has it—"that thou mayest observe to do according to all that is written therein, for then thou shalt make thy way prosperous, and then thou shalt have good success." As a "blessing"—and the exact halakhic meaning of this word is more than a perfunctory promise or expression of good wishes—the verse implies no obligation concerning the mitzvah to study Torah constantly.

Now, the contradictions between these passages of the two

leading Tannaim, R. Simeon bar Yohai and R. Ishmael, are glaringly obvious. "Much ink has been spilled and many quills have been broken," as the talmudic expression goes, in essaying a solution to this problem.

Perhaps the key to the solution lies in a famous story recorded in *Shabbat* 33b concerning the threatened arrest by the Romans of R. Simeon bar Yohai and his son, R. Elazar. Father and son were forced to stay in a cave for twelve years, during which time they studied Torah and survived by the fruit of a carob tree. When they emerged, they were scandalized by the "normal" behavior of their fellow Jews, who engaged in worldly pursuits and neglected the transcendental demands of Judaism; whereupon a Heavenly Voice ordered them back to their cave. Their level of sanctity was too great and constituted a threat to Jewish society. Twelve months later they were again permitted to leave their cave, and this time the father became reconciled to the world, declaring that the two of them alone would suffice for the rest of Israel (in completely fulfilling the high demands of constancy in the study of Torah). Eventually, the son too joined the father in a new-found appreciation of "ordinary" Jews and their far less intense way of showing their love of the mitzvot.

This story hints at a basic change in attitude by R. Simeon bar Yohai. It is reasonable to assume that his view of *hoi polloi,* highly elitist from the start, was powerfully enhanced and reenforced during his isolation in the cave, and that this view was radically altered by his experience upon emerging.

With the above in mind, we may summarize the views of the different Tannaim and Amoraim so as to eliminate the obvious contradictions mentioned. (The reader is reminded once again that the discussion and analysis is not being repeated here; only the conclusions are presented, and of them only those relevant to our theme.)

R. Ishmael holds that the commandment to study Torah

must be pursued at all times, "by day and by night," save for those times that must be devoted to "normal" living, by which he intends primarily the earning of a livelihood. Hence, the study of "Greek wisdom" is prohibited, since it does not fall within the parameters he set. Such study is therefore to be shunned as *bittul Torah*.

R. Simeon bar Yohai is consistent in his view that biblically, *mi-de'oraita,* the mitzvah to engage in the study of Torah is fulfilled by the minimum of studying one chapter in the morning and one at night.[28] Beyond that, however, he originally held that as a matter of policy this would ultimately lead to the wholesale neglect of Torah, and he therefore insisted on legislating a *seyag* or special regulation requiring the study of Torah constantly, and not even agreeing to a dispensation for pursuing a livelihood. But after his experience upon leaving the cave and hearing the reproach of the Divine Voice, R. Simeon bar Yohai changed his mind and abandoned the *seyag* he had earlier proposed. He now held that the original biblical law on the study of Torah was adequate even from the point of view of public policy and rabbinic legislation. (The passage in *Berakhot* would then be dated before his sojourn in the cave, and the one in *Menahot* after he left it.) R. Yohanan, who reports this postfugitive opinion of R. Simeon bar Yohai, determines, however, that given the situation in his own day it is best not to impart such information to the masses who might misuse it, whereas Rava is clearly satisfied to accept the (new) view of R. Simeon bar Yohai publicly and without any dissembling. Abaye, commenting on the *Berakhot* passage, clearly sides with R. Ishmael in rejecting the radical *seyag* of R. Simeon bar Yohai, holding that it is impractical as public policy for the masses.

The third opinion is that of R. Jonathan, who denies that the verse intended any obligation to study Torah all the time; it is a blessing, not a commandment. Apparently, he will agree

with the view of R. Simeon bar Yohai after the cave experience; that is, that a chapter by day and a chapter by night
suffices to qualify for the general biblical mitzvah of Torah
study (and this law is not related to the verse in Joshua). Rava,
therefore, may be said to side with either R. Simeon bar Yohai
in his postcave period, or with R. Jonathan, there being no
practical difference between them. Accordingly, there is no
obligation to study constantly (that is, one must study constantly, but "constantly" is now redefined as meaning *every*
day and *every* night, not *all* day and *all* night); and there is
therefore no banning of Greek wisdom, which prohibition
was predicated upon the obligation to study Torah all the
time.

With this in mind, we may summarize the talmudic opinions adumbrated in this chapter and draw the relevant conclusions.

For R. Ishmael, any activity not involving the study of
Torah, other than the basic necessities for human existence
and the pursuit of a livelihood, was considered *bittul Torah,* for
such time must be devoted to the study of Torah. Because *all*
one's time must be devoted to the study of Torah, there is no
relevance to the concept of *keviat ittim le'torah,* setting aside
regular times for study. Greek wisdom is therefore unacceptable (because of *bittul Torah,* not because of heresy).[29] This
view was apparently espoused by Abaye. Thus, working for a
living is acceptable; the study of Madda is not.

For R. Simeon bar Yohai, *bittul Torah* as a biblical law
applies only to one who fails to fulfill the minimum requirement of one chapter by day and one by night. His precave
view was that *any* activity, including working for the basic
necessities of life, involves the rabbinic transgression of *bittul
Torah.* Hence, not only the worldly intellectual pursuits but
also ordinary working for a living is prohibited as an act of
bittul Torah. His later view reverts to the biblical law that

establishes the minimum of two chapters, as mentioned. This view considers both working to support oneself and the intellectual pursuit of Madda as acceptable, provided there is some form of ongoing daily study of Torah.

For R. Jonathan, one must establish a daily regimen of Torah study (*keviat ittim le'torah*); should he violate that routine (which minimally should be one chapter by day and one by night), he is guilty of *bittul Torah*. (This accords with the later view of R. Simeon bar Yohai.) Rava agrees, as mentioned, both with this point of view and with the later view of R. Simeon bar Yohai, there being no difference between them. R. Yohanan agrees with Rava, differing only on policy regarding the publicizing of this ruling among nonscholars. Madda is therefore acceptable, as is engaging in work in order to sustain oneself.

Now, the "Torah only" school opts either for the opinion of R. Simeon bar Yohai (which we have interpreted as limited to his experience before emerging from the cave, and reflected in *Berakhot*), thus prohibiting not only secular studies but any form of working for a livelihood; or for the ruling of R. Ishmael, thus banning Madda but permitting the earning of a livelihood.

The first of these two alternatives, what might be termed "educational perfectionism," is advocated by Rabbi Baruch Ber Leibowitz.[30] Rabbi Leibowitz is thus more stringent than Rabbi Wasserman, whose responsum was mentioned above and who is permissive with regard to earning a living. One wonders how the former envisions an entire people studying Torah without paying attention to earning their daily bread in these pre-Messianic times. To leave young Torah scholars unprepared for the rigors of life by denying to them the rudiments of gainful occupation ("takhlis," according to this view, is a reprehensible concession to necessity unworthy of a Torah scholar) is to create—for those not blessed with rich fathers or fathers-in-law—an underclass of the impoverished and embittered who, instead of eliciting well-deserved admiration for their self-sacrifice for principle, will earn derision for their otherworldly naiveté and readiness to live on the dole. Maimonides' long and passionate disquisition (based on unassailable talmudic sources) on the need to combine study with a respectable way of earning a living, and his opposition to the notion that Torah scholars should become permanent wards of the community, should be required reading for all who are responsible for the fate of young scholars. These are the harsh words of Maimonides in his halakhic code:

> One, however, who makes up his mind to study Torah and not work, but lives on charity, profanes the Name of God; brings the Torah into contempt; extinguishes the light of religion; brings evil upon himself; and deprives himself of life hereafter. For it is forbidden to derive any temporal advantage from the words of the Torah. The Sages said, "Whoever derives a profit for himself from the words of the Torah is helping in his own destruction."[31] They further charged us, "Make not of them a crown wherewith to aggrandize thyself, nor a spade wherewith to dig."[32] They likewise exhorted us, "Love work, hate lordship."[33] "The study of the Torah, not cojoined with work, must, in the end, be futile, and become a cause of sin."[34] The end of such a person will be that he will [resort to] stealing from his fellow creatures.[35]

Were the responsum of Rabbi Leibowitz limited to a cadre of promising scholars who would be designated the future spiritual–halakhic leaders, they and they alone being required to focus exclusively on *Talmud Torah,* that would be unexceptionable and, indeed, thoroughly acceptable and commendable. The problem arises with the universalization of the ban against any non-Torah activity, even working to feed one's self and one's family.

The second opinion, that of "educational pragmatism," permitting the pursuit of a livelihood, is held by a number of

authorities of the "Torah only" school. Perhaps most characteristic, and certainly well known and articulate, is Rabbi
Eliyahu Dessler.[36] His dispensation, however, is begrudging.
He limits it to those of inferior intellectual or spiritual capac-
ities and confines the right to work to such activities as those
of a shopkeeper and the like, clearly banning the professions
and most especially the academic professions. In the light of
the Leibowitz and Dessler opinions, contemporary "Torah
only" proponents would have difficulty explaining the permission granted by some heads of yeshivot to certain students, ostensibly of intellectual ability equal to their peers, to
enter the learned professions, such as accountancy or the law,
especially academic law.

Those who wish to do so are entitled to accept for themselves a more stringent attitude. What is impermissible is to
delegitimize those who follow the majority opinions of the
giants of the Talmud: R. Jonathan; R. Simeon bar Yohai in his
later stage (according to the interpretation presented in this
chapter); and Rava and R. Yohanan, the Amoraim whose
opinions always prevail.

It is these latter who afford a broad range of legitimacy for
the study of Madda without running afoul of the prohibition
of *bittul Torah*. The accepted rule is that Rava prevails over
Abaye in all cases save six; and R. Yohanan was the preeminent authority in the first generation of Palestinian Amoraim.
Moreover, if Madda is accepted in the form of the instrumentalist, inclusionary, or hasidic models described later in this
book, the problem of *bittul Torah* is solved for advocates of
Torah Umadda.

In reacting to the charge that Torah Umadda violates the
prohibition of *bittul Torah* by its indulgence of the study of
Madda, we have been operating wholly in the halakhic
sphere. Yet it is questionable whether, indeed, this is necessary
or advisable, for basically the question as a whole is not by its

nature susceptible to a halakhic decision, for it is meta-ha-
lakhic and refers to one's total *Weltanschauung*.

We are, in this, in complete agreement with the late Rabbi
Avraham Yitzhak Bloch, the rabbi of Telshe and its Rosh
Yeshiva, who, in response to a query from a New York rabbi,
began his *teshuvah* (responsum) with the following words:

> In these matters, it is exceedingly difficult to offer a clear halakhic
> response, because the issues are largely based upon ideological stances
> and opinions which are linked with the Agadic sections of the Talmud
> and which operate under the specific rules of Agadah which has its own
> definitions of the positive and negative commandments. It is, therefore,
> difficult to offer clear principles and unequivocal halakhic decisions, as
> is normally done in the halakhic areas of the Oral Law. As a result, the
> law will vary and will be contingent upon the nature of the individual as
> well as the conditions that are peculiar to that place and time.[37]

Rabbi Joseph B. Soloveitchik is obviously of the same
opinion. In an address that was later published, he states (in
another context, but with clear relevance and applicability to
our question):

> When it comes to Halakhah, the Holy One gave the Sages of Israel the
> authority to decide questions of law . . . ; but with regard to historical
> questions, those that apply not only to the mundane specifics or ev-
> eryday life, but to the very destiny of the eternal people, the Holy One
> *Himself* decides the Halakhah! No one has the right to reject the halakhic
> decision of the Holy One. . . .[38]

NOTES

1. See Rabbi Meir Bar-Ilan (Berlin), *Mi'Volozhin ad Yerushalayim* (Tel
Aviv: Yalkut, 1939–1940), vol. 1, pp. 238–259. However, other leading
figures disagreed and held that the study of the Russian language was not
only permissible but mandatory; see next note for references.

2. Ibid., vol. 1, pp. 139, 97–101. See too Moshe Tzenovitz, *Etz
Hayyim: Toledot Yeshivat Volozhin* (Tel Aviv: Mor, 1972), pp. 319–344.
While Netziv firmly opposed formal secular studies (especially the curric-

ulum that the radical Maskilim sought to impose on the yeshiva by reporting them to the Russian governmental authorities, and which would have effectively spelled the demise of the yeshiva as a serious school of rabbinic learning), he was not antagonistic to private self-education. His fear was that submission to the demands of the government and their Haskalah puppets would occasion massive *bittul Torah* and cause the study of Torah to be perceived as secondary to Haskalah studies. Also see on this Shaul Stampfer, *Three Lithuanian Yeshivot in the Nineteenth Century* (unpublished dissertation, Jerusalem: Hebrew University, 1981), pp. 79–80, especially note 194, and pp. 120–121, especially note 107.

3. On the views of Neturei Karta, see my "The Ideology of Neturei Karta—According to the Satmarer Version," *Tradition,* Fall 1971, pp. 38–54.

4. On the above, see Yehezkel Cohen, *Ha-Yahas le'Limmudei Hol be' Yahadut* (Tel Aviv: Hakibbutz Hadati, 1983), pp. 29–43.

5. Yehuda Levi, "Two Responsa on Secular Studies" (Hebrew), *Ha-Ma'ayan* 16:3, pp. 1–16.

6. Cited in Chapter 2, note 9.

7. *Teshuvot Rabbi Akiva Eger* (New York: Daat, 1948), no. 67. The opening citation is from *Avot* 2:2.

8. *Avot* 1:2.

9. *Avot* 2:2.

10. *Yevamot* 109b.

11. R. Menahem ha-Meiri, *Bet ha-Behirah,* ad loc.

12. The responsum first appeared in *Ha-Pardes* 13:9, pp. 5–22, and was reprinted by Yehuda Levi in *Yad Re'em,* p. 208. See the end of the next chapter for a fuller discussion of the assertion that Maimonides was too great, and we too inadequate, for us to learn from him.

We have not cited here a text that, for many, has become the *locus classicus* of the halakhic disqualification of secular studies on the grounds that they constitute heresy. That text (in *Menahot* 99b) reads:

Ben Dama, the son of the sister of R. Ishmael, asked R. Ishmael, "Is one like myself who has mastered all of Torah permitted to study Greek Wisdom?" R. Ishmael applied to him the verse in Joshua (1:8), "Thou shalt meditate in [Torah] day and night," [and said to him], "Go and find a time which is neither day nor night and study Greek Wisdom."

It is assumed that R. Ishmael's circumlocution (. . . "neither day nor night") is a homiletically inspired derision of "Greek wisdom" which, presumably, includes all non-Torah studies. The reason we have omitted mention of this passage in this context is that the interpretation is fallacious. It should be obvious that in quoting the verse from Joshua, R. Ishmael is formulating his objection to Greek wisdom on the grounds of *bittul Torah,* the neglect of the study of Torah, rather than on the principle of heresy. A later ban on the study of Greek language was similarly understood as issuing from extraneous reasons rather than a *per se* disqualification as heresy; see the Jerusalem Talmud, end of *Sotah* (and *Pe'ah* 1:1), which attributes the prohibition to the fear that it will encourage informing to the Roman authorities. See Saul Lieberman, *Hellenism in Jewish Palestine* (New York: Jewish Theological Seminary, 1962), pp. 100–114, who concludes that this latter prohibition was intended to restrict the teaching of Greek to children, not to bar its self-study by adults; and ibid. on the content of the term "Greek wisdom." We take up the question of *bittul Torah* on the basis of this text later in this book.

13. The term used is *misrahim,* a play of words on *mizrahim,* the name of the religious Zionists; the former is a harsh, odious word that literally means people who emit a foul odor.

14. Rabbi Moses Stern, *Be'er Mosheh* (Brooklyn: Defus Balshon, 1970–1971), Chapter 3.

15. Quoted in Eli Evans, *Judah P. Benjamin: The Jewish Confederate* (New York: Free Press, 1988), p. 212.

16. *Avot* 2:14.

17. R. Loewe of Prague (MaHaRaL), *Derekh Hayyim* (Warsaw; 1833), commentary on *Avot* 2:14.

18. *Be'er ha-Golah,* end.

19. See, on this, Chapter 13 below.

20. *Berakhot* 8a.

21. Introduction to *Perush ha-Mishnayot,* Kapah edition (Jerusalem: Mosad Harav Kook, 1963–1968), pp. 39–45.

22. I am indebted to Rabbi Joseph Kapah for suggesting this interpretation of the Maimonidean passage.

23. See my Hebrew essay on "The Sage and the Saint in the Writings of Maimonides," in Moshe Carmilly and Hayim Leaf, eds., *The Samuel Belkin Memorial Volume* (New York: Erna Michael College, Yeshiva University, 1981), pp. 11–28, and my *Torah Lishmah* (New York: Yeshiva University Press, 1989), pp. 174–176 and note 33.

24. *Hilkhot Yesodei ha-Torah* 4:13.

25. As a consequence, Maimonides in his *Guide* (3:52) regards the talmudists as inferior in rank to those who competently engage in philosophy or theology.

26. A detailed discussion in English of the nature of *bittul Torah* as a halakhic construct is too ponderous for this volume. The reader is therefore referred to Chapter 5 in my forthcoming *Halakhot ve'Halikhot* (Jerusalem: Yeshiva University Press, 1990), where I deal with the question more comprehensively. What follows in this text is a summary of my major findings there.

27. See, for instance, the responsum that appears in the commentary on *Kiddushin* by Rabbi Baruch Ber Leibowitz, one of the leading disciples of Rabbi Hayyim Soloveitchik of Brisk.

28. For the sake of accuracy, it should be mentioned that there are a number of different definitions of the minimum required to fulfill the obligation to engage in the study of Torah "day and night." In addition to a chapter each day and each night, we find the following: an hour each by day and by night; the recitation of the Shema by day and by night; two halakhot each by day and by night; and, according to some, even a single word by day and by night.

29. See end of note 12.

30. See note 27. Rabbi Leibowitz insists, surprisingly, that Maimonides shared this view.

31. *Avot* 4:17.

32. Ibid., 4:7.

33. Ibid., 1:10.

34. Ibid., 2:2.

35. *Hil. Talmud Torah* 3:10.

36. See, for instance, Rabbi Eliyahu Dessler, *Mikhtav Me'Eliyahu,* ed. Aryeh Carmel and Chaim Friedlander (B'nai B'rak, Israel: 1963), vol. 3, p. 357.

37. This *teshuvah* was first published in the Israeli journal *Ha-Ma'ayan* (Nisan 5736), pp. 11–16. See note 5.

38. Rabbi Joseph Dov Soloveitchik, *Hamesh Derashot* (Jerusalem: Machon Tal Orot, 1973), pp. 22–23.

CHAPTER 4

THE RATIONALIST MODEL:

MOSES MAIMONIDES AND PARADISE

We shall begin our analysis of the major expositors of Torah and Wisdom with a recapitulation of the views of the most distinguished exemplar of Torah and secular learning in the Spanish Golden Age, Moses Maimonides.

MADDA AS AN OBLIGATION

Of all the views on the integration of Torah and other studies, the most assertive and comprehensive is that of Maimonides. His educational policy issues from the background of his larger philosophical vision, and it results not in a declaration of the *permissibility* of secular studies, but of the *obligation* to pursue them as an act of mitzvah. We shall sketch briefly the Maimonidean view, mentioning some relevant passages from his *Guide of the Perplexed,* and then his halakhic decisions in his *Mishneh Torah.* (The reversal of the chronological order is of no consequence; Maimonides was remarkably consistent throughout his life, especially on this issue.)[1]

The study of metaphysics is, for Maimonides, the pinnacle of wisdom, for it leads to a true apperception of God insofar as it is given to man to understand Him. But there are many prerequisites to such study. In the *Guide*[2] he tells us that we can obtain a knowledge of Him only through His deeds (rather than His essence) because they provide the evidence for His existence and inform us about Him both affirmatively and negatively; that is, what He is and what He is not. "It is thus necessary to examine all things according to their essence, to infer from each species" those truths that can assist us in solving metaphysical problems. Thus we must study the nature of numbers and geometry. Astronomy and physics help in comprehending the "relation between the world and Providence—as it is in reality, and not according to imagination." Other disciplines, although not preparing the way for metaphysics directly, train us in the proper use of reason and thus minimize confusion. Hence, the study of logic and various branches of mathematics is obligatory. In Chapter 5 of his Introduction to *Avot* (the "Eight Chapters"), Maimonides adds the biological sciences and medicine to his list, and elsewhere he includes grammar and etymology.[3] Not only does metaphysics require such learning; even the proper performance of the *mitzvot maasiyot,* the practical commandments, necessitates such intellectual preparation in the secular branches. In the Introduction to the *Guide,* he addresses his student, R. Joseph Ibn Aknin, concerning these practical commandments:

> The Almighty, desiring to lead us to perfection and to improve the state of our society, revealed to us *His* laws which are to regulate our actions. These laws . . . presuppose an advanced state of intellectual culture. We must first . . . have a knowledge of metaphysics. But this discipline can only be approached after the study of physics. . . . Therefore, the Almighty commenced Scripture with the description of Creation, that is, with physical science.

The word "His" is here italicized in order to emphasize a point made by Rabbi Kapah: it would seem simple enough to perform mitzvot such as taking the *lulav* and *etrog* or laying the *tefillin* without such an extensive education. Why, then, the imposing list of prerequisites? The explanation is that with the proper perspective and understanding provided by a higher education, these halakhic acts are not merely *man's* practical commandments, but *His,* God's. Informed by the knowledge of His cosmos, the halakhic performance leads to the knowledge of God, and thus becomes *His* practical mitzvot. For "there is no way to know Him save through His works."[4]

The Torah, Maimonides tells us,[5] teaches only the final results to which our cognitive labors should lead us—such as the existence, unity, omnipotence, and will of God. "But these cannot be understood fully and accurately except after the acquisition of many kinds of knowledge." We are commanded to love God (Deuteronomy 6:5), a mitzvah repeated time and again, and this love "is only possible when we comprehend the real nature of things and understand the divine wisdom displayed therein."[6] Madda enhances the life of Torah.

In the concluding chapter of his philosophical *magnum opus, The Guide of the Perplexed,*[7] Maimonides tells us that in the Prophets and the Talmud we find two categories of knowledge: that of Torah and that of *Hokhmah,* Wisdom. The latter is called upon to provide the intellectual, scientific, and speculative infrastructure for the former. Thus, Moses is praised as being a master (or "father") of both Torah and Wisdom. The Sages teach us that a man is required to give an account of himself first for his study of Torah and then for his study of Wisdom. Chronologically, one must first engage in the former, but it is the latter that helps us attain spiritual perfection and bestows immortality upon us, and, indeed, fulfills us as human beings.

We have enough evidence to justify the view of Rabbi
Kapah, who states that "if one studies all these disciplines and
sciences which for some reason are called 'secular,' in order
thereby to attain greater understanding and knowledge of
God—which is the foundation of all wisdom and without
which, according to Maimonides, it is impossible to reach
such a state of knowledge—such studies are the holy of
holies."[8] It is with this firm conceptual underpinning that one
can appreciate Maimonides' halakhic decisions concerning the
study of Torah and of ("secular") Wisdom.

In *Hilkhot Teshuvah* (10:6), Maimonides states that the love
of God is contingent upon one's knowledge of God. Hence,
one must take care to study and ponder all branches of
wisdom that lead us to understand Him. Such study, as he
later reiterates in his *Guide,* as quoted earlier, is thus a fulfillment of the mitzvah to love God.

IN PARADISE

But Maimonides goes beyond that. In the first four chapters
of his halakhic code, *Mishneh Torah,* he outlines the basic
premises or beliefs incumbent upon every Jew in order to
serve the Lord properly. In *Hilkhot Yesodei ha-Torah,* he writes:

> The subject of these four chapters, which constitute five [separate]
> mitzvot, is what our early Sages called *Pardes* [Paradise; literally: or-
> chard], as when they said, "four entered the *Pardes.*" And even though
> they were giants in Israel, not all of them were able to know and
> understand all these matters properly.[9]

The subject matter of *Pardes* is conventionally assumed to be
an esoteric probing into the mysteries of the Creation nar-
rative at the beginning of Genesis (*maaseh bereshit*), and the
obscure vision by the prophet Ezekiel of the "Divine Chariot" (*maaseh merkavah*). For Maimonides, however, these are

not mystical or kabbalistic passages. Rather, they represent, respectively, physics and metaphysics. Natural science and philosophy are thus the contents of *Pardes.*

Now, in the same *Mishneh Torah,*[10] Maimonides recommends dividing one's study time into three: one third for the Written Law, or Scripture; one third for the Oral Law; and one third for the study of Gemara (or Talmud). In this last category he includes *Pardes.* Thus, for Maimonides, Madda (what he more accurately calls Wisdom) is incorporated in *Talmud Torah;* in other words, it has value as the study of Torah. (Indeed, he often couples Torah and Wisdom with regard to a number of halakhot where others speak only of Torah. The term *Hokhmah,* Wisdom, for Maimonides specifically refers to secular wisdom, as indicated in the *Guide* passages cited earlier.)

Thus, Maimonides holds the proper study of worldly wisdom to be, halakhically, the fulfillment of the commandment to study Torah.

It is strange, indeed, that such a remarkable ruling, *in his halakhic code,* by the greatest halakhic authority of the entire posttalmudic period—an authority whose every paragraph, indeed every nuance, has been analyzed in enormous depth and the halakhic implications of which have been spelled out and relied upon for the past eight or nine centuries—is usually glossed over in silence by most rabbinic commentators in the vast literature of exegesis of the *Mishneh Torah.* Later we shall return to probe the halakhic consequences of Maimonides' decision and attempt to attain the same goal by a different route.

We have here, then, a fully developed presentation of Torah Umadda, buttressed both philosophically (in the rationalist idiom) and halakhically. Madda is not alien to Torah but, if studied in the manner and for the purposes described by Maimonides, becomes part of Torah itself.

THE RESPONSUM TO R. JONATHAN

This point should be emphasized and certainly not over-looked. But we are faced with a problem presented by an oft-quoted passage from one of Maimonides' famous responsa. Maimonides was widely admired by the scholars of Provence, who sent him a list of their halakhic queries—some of them echoing the critical glosses of his older contemporary R. Abraham Ibn Daud of Posquieres (the RaAVaD)—and asked that he send them a copy of his *Guide of the Perplexed,* about which they had heard but which they had not yet seen. Maimonides' delayed response (which he attributes to his failing health and his heavy schedule of communal responsibilities) is devoted to the halakhic inquiries, but it also contains an interesting introduction, written in a rather florid style. In this introduction of the responsum to R. Jonathan of Lunel and his fellow scholars, Maimonides writes:

> I, Moses, hereby inform the eminences R. Jonathan ha-Kohen and all his sage colleagues who read my letter, that—although ere I was born the Torah knew me in [my mother's] innards, and ere I left the womb it dedicated me to its study and appointed me to spread its wellsprings abroad, for it is my lovely hind [doe], the wife of my youth whom I have loved since my childhood—I married many strange women: Moabites, Amonites, Edomites, Sidonites, Hittites. [But] the Lord knows that I took them from the very beginning [only] to be perfumers and cooks and bakers for [the Torah] so as to display her beauty to all nations and princes, for she is very attractive. Nevertheless, I have not paid adequate attention to her for I have divided my heart into many parts, attending to many branches of wisdom. I toiled for ten years without end, day and night, in composing this work [the *Mishneh Torah*]. . . .[11]

The implication is that the study of Torah is preeminent for Maimonides, and that all other studies are merely instruments for the better comprehension of Torah—the academic equivalents of "perfumers and cooks and bakers" (a paraphrase of I Samuel 8:13). Does this not vitiate our argument that Maimonides reserved a place of importance per se for non-Torah studies in his *Weltanschauung?*

The question is a good one, but not a decisive one. First, Maimonidean scholars are divided as to the authenticity of the entire responsum, including both the introduction and the twenty-odd halakhic replies.[12] If the responsum is indeed pseudepigraphic, as Kapah maintains, the question disappears.

Second, one can hardly dismiss the clear opinion of Maimonides in the many works in which he focuses directly on the relation of Torah studies to the study of Wisdom, on the basis of his wistful remarks in the introduction to a long halakhic responsum in which he apologizes for procrastinating in his reply to criticisms of his *Mishneh Torah* and protests his loyalty to halakhic study as his first love. Indeed, talmudic studies *were* his "lovely hind," and indeed he regretted that the limitations of time made it impossible for him to devote adequate attention to his study of both Torah and Wisdom, but he does not offer any substantive change in his larger view. He is merely uttering a perfectly human complaint and expressing an admirable and unexceptional preference for the study of Halakhah. Most students of Maimonides would be shocked were that not the case. The same has been true of students who have followed his tradition in their own education: the emotional and spiritual hold of Torah is incomparable and unassailable—and that is as it should be. Yet that does not gainsay the autonomous role that Wisdom plays in Maimonidean thought. Both Torah and Wisdom are, philosophically, ultimately instruments through which one may attain the highest good of Judaism, that of *daat ha-Shem,* the knowledge of God. In one sense, they are each autonomous; in another, they are interdependent in that both are necessary for the attainment of this knowledge of God, each with its role to play, as each enlightens the other. But neither can be reduced to the role of a "mere" instrument for the other, otherwise devoid of innate value.

IMPACT OF MAIMONIDES' MODEL

In assessing the impact of the views of Maimonides on our theme, let us make two observations, one grateful and another rather ungrateful.

The ungrateful but necessary remark is that while his precedent is, in and of itself, adequate for a contemporary reaffirmation of the central thesis that is our concern, the reconciliation essayed by Maimonides and other medieval Sephardi philosophers is—with full respect and infinite admiration for their brilliance, virtuosity, and moral seriousness—of limited value. That is so because they restricted their intellectual efforts to the particular philosophies of their day—Aristotelianism, the Kalam, Neo-Platonism—which have long since become obsolete.[13]

Now, that in itself would not be critical. Maimonides dealt with *his* contemporary Madda, and it is ludicrous for modern observers, endowed with infallible hindsight, to fault him for not considering the Kantian critique of metaphysics and the whole modern epistemological framework according to which the knowledge of Nature is irrelevant to religion in that it does not add philosophically to our knowledge of God. Rather, the problem with Maimonides' *Guide,* and perhaps even his failure from our perspective, was that he tackled the *specific* issues of the Torah Umadda problematica with which he was confronted. Hence, once the Aristotelianism he confronted evaporated from the cultural scene, his solutions largely lost not only their cogency but also their relevancy. His contribution for the ages would have been much greater had he bequeathed to us an approach to the larger, more *general* aspects of the encounter between Torah and his then contemporary Wisdom.

Nevertheless, while he failed to provide a generic or structural solution, we can extrapolate as to methods and patterns, ignoring what the history of thought and culture has proved ephemeral, and salvaging central guidelines that have enduring value for our present and future Madda encounters. Such an attempt is made later in this work.

The grateful observation with regard to Maimonides' views is the indebtedness of all Jewish history to this towering intellect who taught us—although we, his pupils, are often obstreperously reluctant to be taught—that a believing, thinking Jew needs a large and embracing vision, a more capacious theoretical framework into which he can integrate his most precious Jewish ideals, a vision that will be uplifting to his soul and luminous to his mind, and that will endow with renewed vigor his most fundamental commitments. It is, alas, a teaching more observed in the breach these days when the fear of contamination by the hedonistic, assimilationist environment often extends to any serious thinking in a large and comprehensive manner.

As long as halakhic Jews persist in isolating Halakhah from integration into *Hashkafah* (a larger theoretical outlook or *Anschauung*), it runs the risk of becoming a form of religious behaviorism with inadequate relevance to the perennial problems of the human spirit. (Conversely, the formulation of *Hashkafah* without a solid foundation in Halakhah tends to deteriorate into a form of sacred semantics, a *façon de parler* instead of a *façon de vivre*.)

Whether this larger conceptual framework is the Maimonidean brand of Aristotelianism, or any other view, is not as important as the fact that such a more comprehensive structure is necessary if Halakhah is to address our hearts and minds and souls as well as it speaks to our wills and directs our external functioning in the world.

What Maimonides taught in the twelfth century, Rav Kook reiterated in the twentieth, and they both must be listened and responded to very carefully and thoughtfully. In the words of Kook:

> The Torah and the religion of Israel must be presented in the light of the most profound religious thought. Talmudic scholarship must be supplemented by careful study of the great Jewish thinkers, whether of the philosophical, ethical, or mystical traditions. Only thus can a point of departure be attained for a needed rejuvenation of religious thinking. Even the more recondite aspects of religious thought must be popularized, since naive theological conceptions are unacceptable even to the uneducated. . . . Religion without sophistication is no longer viable.[14]

Without such a larger vision, it is easy enough to dismiss all worldly wisdom as insubstantial, irrelevant, or dangerous. With it, the encounter between Torah and Wisdom simply cannot be ignored. For it not only *can* and *may* take place, but indeed *must*. Torah Umadda thus may change its style and flavor, in keeping with the changing content of Madda as it evolves and grows throughout the ages, but its essential dynamism and its claim on our religious and intellectual attention remains unchanged. Paraphrasing the Zohar, it "divests itself of one form and garbs itself in another form."

THE DEGENERATION OF THE GENERATIONS

Reference was made in the last chapter to the argument by "Torah only" advocates that expressions of support for secular studies by the likes of Maimonides cannot be used to legitimize such study by us in the contemporary world because of *yeridat ha-dorot,* an irreversible degeneration of the generations in their qualities of intellect and spirit. We are—as we often read in rabbinic literature—*yatmei de'yatmei,* "orphans among orphans": too inadequate, too weak, too vulnerable, to take risks permitted to the ancients.[15] This argument effectively undercuts any effort by proponents of Torah Umadda to justify their point of view; either they have no sources to support their thesis, or, if they do find precedent, it is disqualified because *nitkatnu ha-dorot,* the generations have become diminished, and therefore such precedents do not apply to us.

This criticism deserves to be treated seriously. The degenerative model of time—which is really a mirror image of the modernist fallacy that all that is new is better than all that is old—has respectable sources in the Jewish tradition. Indeed, it is a major theme in most of rabbinic literature. It is based on reverence for earlier authorities because of their proximity to the time of Revelation; hence the superiority of their traditions. Thus, the Halakhah generally does not permit the Amoraim (Sages of the Talmud) to overrule the Tannaim (Sages of the Mishnah); and once the Talmud has decided an issue, it is impermissible for later authorities to diverge from that decision. In general, earlier authority prevails over later authority.

The Talmud gave expression to this principle in a number of direct statements:

> The later generations are unlike the early generations: the early generations regarded their study of Torah as fixed, and their (worldly) labors as provisional, and they succeeded in both. The later generations regarded their labor as fixed and their study of Torah as provisional, and they failed in both.[16]

Furthermore, "The heart of the early masters was as broad as the gates of a chamber, and that of the later ones—like the eye of a needle."[17] "Previous generations plowed and sowed—and we do not even have a mouth wherewith to eat."[18] "If the early ones were angels, we are humans; and if they were

humans, we are like donkeys—and not (special) donkeys, such
as those of R. Hanina b. Dosa and R. Pinhas b. Yair, but like
ordinary donkeys."[19] "Better the fingernail of the early masters than the waist of the later ones."[20] Moses, whom the
Torah describes as the most humble man on the face of the
earth, was the most humble only in his generation; in earlier
generations there were those who exceeded Moses in their
meekness.[21] The law of levirate marriage required a man to
marry his deceased brother's wife if the brother died childless.
If, however, the brother refuses to perform this marriage
(*yibbum*), he must undergo a humiliating procedure called
halitzah.

> In the beginning, when people could be trusted [to perform *yibbum*],
> intending the act for the sake of the mitzvah [rather than out of lust, the
> Sages] said that *yibbum* takes precedence over *halitzah;* now, however,
> that people do not intend [their acts] for the sake of the mitzvah, *halitzah*
> takes precedence over *yibbum*. Said Rabba bar bar Hama in the name of
> R. Isaac, [the Sages] later reconsidered and said that *yibbum* takes
> precedence over *halitzah*. R. Nahman b. Isaac said to him: Did, then, the
> generations become more perfect?[22]

The answer is that, of course, they did not; and the reason for
the changed ruling was not an observable improvement in the
moral quality of the later generations, but a purely halakhic
decision to favor one authority over the other.

This theme continues, as is to be expected, in the rabbinic
tradition of the Middle Ages. Thus, in his commentary on the
verse, "Say not, 'why were the former days better than these?'
for you do not inquire wisely concerning this" (Ecclesiastes
7:10), the eleventh-century Rashi says: "The earlier generations were better and more righteous than the later ones,
therefore the former times were better than ours; for it is
impossible that the later [generations] were the equal of the
early ones."[23] The degeneration of the generations is thus
taken as self-evident.

It would seem, therefore, that the issue is closed: the degeneration of the generations is total and invariable. And if, indeed, that is so, then we are forced to a number of inevitable conclusions. First, no Torah Umadda precedent, such as that of Maimonides or the many like him, is relevant, for they are inimitable by virtue of their chronological priority to us; and, hence, our inferiority does not permit us to risk the involvement in non-Torah disciplines that was permissible to them.

Second, it follows that all significant questions in life have been answered, and there is no place in Judaism for *hiddush* or creativity—either philosophically or halakhically; for how can we, of an epoch so lowly, so humble, so mediocre, presume to contribute anything of value and thus imply that it was overlooked by predecessors so vastly superior to us? There are, indeed, indications that such a grotesque view is beginning to make itself felt in contemporary Jewish life. Whereas nothing of this nature has yet appeared in print explicitly—and it certainly is not now taken as standard doctrine by any group—murmurings of such nature ought not to be dismissed. Such an attitude is nourished by a failure to distinguish between authority and authoritarianism, and by suspicion that *hiddush be'halakhah* (innovation or creativity in halakhic exposition) can lead to *hiddush be'deiot* (changes or reform in religious practice and doctrine).

Third, we are left with a decidedly pessimistic view of the future: the inexorable decline in the quality of our successor generations indefinitely into the future.

However, the matter does not end here, and there is not sufficient warrant for the technique of "kicking upstairs" all earlier authority, whose differing and more permissive views we seek to circumvent by ascribing to them powers far exceeding our own. Nor is it conceivable that Judaism would subscribe to such a narrow, constricting, suffocating view of human creativity and such a bleak and dismal view of the future development of our people and their qualities. We have six points to make in this regard.

For one thing, the talmudic sources we cited nowhere articulate a clear, unambiguous conception of the degeneration thesis; even the very terms *yeridat ha-dorot* (the degeneration of the generations) and *nitkatnu ha-dorot* (the generations have become diminished) are not mentioned explicitly. The idea is a mood, not a doctrine. Indeed, there are talmudic sources that are at least ambivalent and implicitly or explicitly question the thesis of the total superiority of the past over the present. Thus, in implied disagreement with the Rashi interpretation just mentioned, Tosafot adds this gloss: " 'The former days were better than these, and therefore we must hearken to the earlier ones more than to the later ones'—say not thus, for it is incumbent upon you to obey only the judge in your own times."[24] Tosafot is here apparently taking exception to the assumption of the necessary superiority of the past over the present.[25]

Furthermore, the Talmud does not take the leap of faith from the assumption of the superiority of the *rishonim* (earlier authorities) over the *aharonim* (later ones), to the dogma of the infallibility of the former; on the contrary, the Talmud regards the imperfections of the ancients as an act of divine grace, providing for their descendants a place in the sun of scholarly innovation and a sense of intellectual fulfillment. Thus, it is related[26] that "Rabbi" (R. Judah the Prince) heard reliable testimony that the illustrious R. Meir, a generation earlier, had eaten vegetables in Bet She'an without tithing them first. This flew in the face of the accepted practice of requiring vegetable produce to be tithed in that locale. On the basis of this report, presumably informed by the view that Bet She'an was not halakhically considered as within the borders of the Holy Land, Rabbi permitted all such produce of that town to be consumed without offering the tithe. Rabbi's family was outraged by the decision. "How can you permit that which your fathers and their fathers before them prohibited?" His response was to demonstrate, by biblical references, that no generation, no matter how far back in time, is perfect, and that each one leaves to its successors to repair that in which it failed. *Makom hinihu lo avotav le'hitgader bo*—"His ancestors left him space to grow." The Talmud adds: From this the Sages concluded that one must not rebuke a scholar who offers a novel halakhic interpretation of his own.[27]

This is a far cry from the reactionary tendency to stifle all *hiddush* and regard halakhic creativity with suspicion, referring to R. Moses Sofer's famous homiletic interpretation of the halakhic ruling that *hadash asur min ha-torah*—all innovation is biblically proscribed. And it is a definitive rebuttal to the attitude that all questions have been answered and that it is for us of the wretched present only to remember and repeat and apply what our forbears bequeathed to us.

Hence, even while agreeing with the doctrine of the moral and spiritual superiority of the *rishonim* and the subsequent degeneration of the generations, and the reverence owed by the *aharonim* to the *rishonim,* this by no means precludes the gift of and necessity for creativity by the hapless later generations, and certainly offers no solace or support for the assertion that the right (and even obligation) to engage in Madda is restricted to the likes of Maimonides and other such mental and spiritual giants but is forbidden to us of the benighted present.

Indirect evidence that the degeneration hypothesis was not accepted categorically comes to us from yet other talmudic sources. Thus, R. Eliezer was asked if the later generations are better than the earlier ones, and he replied with verses indicating that the sinners whose malfeasance caused the destruction of the First Temple were less heinous than their equivalents in the Second Temple.[28] The comparison of these two generations is given as an example of the deterioration of the generations, but it is a *historical* fact, not an inexorable law of the nature of moral retrogression; else the question was out of place.

Moreover, we find instances where the Talmud compares the later generations favorably with the earlier ones when it comes to being learned in the Law: "The earlier generations were not expert in (preparing a divorce) *lishmah* (with the proper intention of executing it for this specific man and woman); but the later generations are expert in *lishmah*."[29]

Another example: according to biblical law, the sabbatical year releases all debtors from their debts. The result was that the economy came to a halt: the rich stopped lending and the poor were unable to borrow. Thus, the Torah's injunction to the well-to-do to lend to the needy, and not to begrudge them, was being subverted. Hillel therefore ordained the *prozbul,* a document declaring that the creditor's debts are transferred to the courts (which are exempt from the sabbatical decree regarding the release of debts).[30] The Talmud asks whether Hillel's *takanah* was meant to obligate his own generation or all subsequent ones.[31] The difference is this: If it only obligates his own, then any properly constituted court can later revoke it if social and economic conditions warrant such a change; if the obligation is incurred for all generations, only a court greater than Hillel's "in wisdom and numbers" can revoke the ordinance. Now, what conditions can one foresee that would justify cancelling the *prozbul?* Rashi[32] comments: (*ee ikshar dara*), "if a (new) generation is (more) worthy"; that is, if there will arise a generation of greater moral fortitude that will be amenable to lending to the poor in adequate amounts despite the imminent cancellation of debts on the sabbatical year and without the protective benefit of the *prozbul*—then the *prozbul* may be cancelled. Again, a later generation can be superior to an earlier one; the theme of the degeneration of the generations cannot be taken as an indisputable dogma.[33]

It is clear that the degeneration theme in talmudic literature refers to sociological facts and historical data of specific kinds, not to some general metaphysical truth or absolute moral norm. The rabbis observed a deterioration in piety, morality, and devotion to study, and they drew therefrom certain legal consequences. When their observations proved otherwise—as in the case of writing a bill of divorce (*lishmah*)—they drew the opposite conclusions. They did not extrapolate from sociology to ontology. Hence, the tendency of our own "later generations" to create an ideology out of *nitkatnu ha-dorot* (a term not mentioned in the talmudic literature), so that examples from the past of intellectual breadth and openness are inapplicable to us, is misplaced.

Second is a halakhic point: not always may we assume the uncontested superiority in wisdom of the earlier over the later generations. Indeed, a well-known passage in the Mishnah itself teaches that a court may not overrule the decision of another court unless it is greater than the previous one both in numbers (of judges) and in wisdom,[34] thus implying that a later court may in fact exceed an earlier one in wisdom. This contradicts the assumption of the necessary degeneration of the generations.

Indeed, the impermissibility of an Amora to disagree with a Tanna's decision should not by any means be taken as unconditional. Nahmanides[35] lists a number of cases where Amoraim successfully overruled Tannaim, and the halakhah was decided in their favor. R. Joseph Karo maintained that Amoraim do have the right to challenge Tannaim but by general agreement decided that they would refrain from such challenges and generally accept the authority of the Tannaim; similarly, the authority of the Amoraim was accepted by later generations, after the publication of the Gemara.[36] Hence, the right in principle for an Amora to challenge a Tanna, or for a post-Amoraic authority to challenge an Amora, clearly contradicts the idea that the decline of the generations implies a diminution of inherent value. The consensus, in practice, not to exercise this right to overrule earlier authority undoubtedly indicates a desire to establish an official corpus or canon of law to avoid juridical chaos, as, indeed, precedent is given weight in any functioning legal system; it says nothing of innate worth or worthlessness.

Moreover, in a conflict between earlier and later decisors, the Halakhah decides with the later authorities: *halakhah ke-'batrai.* This is given as one reason for the higher rank universally granted to the Babylonian over the Jerusalem (or Palestinian) Talmud: The former talmudists came later in time, obviously knew the latter, and found them wanting.[37]

Justice Menahem Alon, in his monumental work on Jewish law,[38] makes the trenchant point that this legal maxim—*halakhah ke'batrai*—establishing the halakhah in favor of the later authorities (a rule formulated in the posttalmudic Geonic period) seems to run counter to the general tendency to defer to the superiority of the earlier sages. Professor Yisrael Ta-Shma takes exception to Alon's broad use of the principle and prefers to see it in rather narrower terms: One legal rule among many, this one is meant to decide between conflicting decisions in the Talmud itself and is not intended to enhance the autonomy of later and therefore contemporary courts and judges. It is only the Ashkenazi authorities, beginning with the fifteenth-century scholar R. Joseph Kolon (MaHaRIK), and including such distinguished halakhists as R. Israel Isserlin, R. Jacob Pollak, R. Shalom Shachna, and R. Moses Isserles (RaMA), who applied the maxim to posttalmudic authorities "until the end of all generations." The Sephardi world did not go along with this extension of the Geonic innovation and its extrapolation to posttalmudic times.[39] The authority of the *aharonim,* that is, the contemporary courts of each generation, derives not from *halakhah ke'batrai* but from the principle that "Jephtha in his generation was like Samuel in his generation." Granted the inferiority of *aharonim* to *rishonim,* the courts or decisors of each generation are empowered to decide the halakhah for its own time. According to Ta-Shma, the tradition of judicial and intellectual autonomy does indeed have a long and honorable history, one that is spelled out most explicitly by R. Isaiah the Elder of Trani. (The views of R. Isaiah are offered presently, but they are unrelated to *halakhah ke'batrai.*)

Whatever the outcome of the debate between Alon and Ta-Shma, this much is certain: Over the last 500 years Ashkenazi authorities did broaden the applicability of the Geonic legal maxim, deciding even in the posttalmudic era with the later over the earlier authorities (provided the former were aware of the latter). This does, indeed, represent a countercurrent, in the halakhic tradition itself, to the conventional assumption of the progressive devolution of the generations. Moreover, beyond the question of the exact interpretation of the significance of *halakhah ke'batrai,* there certainly existed a profound commitment, if not always articulated, to the authenticity of halakhic creativity and innovation. There is no more convincing proof than the most eminent of all Sephardi greats—Maimonides himself.

Third, it stands to reason that the ascription of superiority to the ancients derives primarily from their proximity to the source of the tradition, that is, to Revelation, as mentioned earlier; and therefore their reports are more reliable because they were less likely to have been distorted by the passage of time and the transmission through so many more generations. The authority of the teacher and hence his superior position are thus linked to his role as an indispensable agent in the transmission of Revelation to succeeding generations. This would account too for the preference for Mishnah over Talmud, because the Sinaitic tradition (or Oral Law) was indeed transmitted orally. Once the Oral Law was committed to writing, however, and especially with the advent of printing in the fifteenth century, this explanation no longer served to assume automatically the inferiority of the present to the past.[40] The text now stands as the authority, not the chronological position of the person. In this manner, creativity is salvaged, for otherwise all later generations are reduced to exegesis and, eventually, to repetition alone.

Fourth, whereas we consider the ancients *as individuals* to be our superiors, collectively we may assume the reverse, for we have the advantage of having learned from them. This theme has been expressed in aphoristic fashion by Isaac Newton: "If I have seen farther, it is by standing on the shoulders of giants." (Actually, this statement by Newton, in 1676, goes back to the early twelfth-century French savant, Bernard of Chartres, and has been repeated in writing some eighteen times until the beginning of the twentieth century.)[41] The first mention of the aphorism by talmudic authorities, and hence a counterargument to the degeneration theme, is by the aforementioned twelfth-century sage R. Isaiah de Trani[42] and has been repeated often since. Thus, we may indeed be dwarfs compared to our predecessors, but we are the fortunate beneficiaries of the cumulative wisdom of the ages—bequeathed to us by them—and therefore have the capacity to see farther than they did.

Fifth, one must distinguish between different kinds of knowledge. There were centuries in the history of Western civilization when religious devotion was normal and expected, and subsequent ages when religion went out of fashion for Western man and appeared alien to his very mentality. Similarly, in Jewish life the sensitivity to *kedushah* (sanctity) and the quality of religious experience were far more prominent in the past when life was perhaps less complex, less distracting, less fragmented, and thus more hospitable to the dimension of spirituality. Yet, granted that earlier generations were superior to us in the moral and spiritual realms, that does not exhaust the areas of human endeavor. The progress in science and technology is massive and demonstrable and needs no elaboration here. That the fruits of such scientific and technological development can be and indeed have been used to destroy and threaten the existence of whole peoples and all of mankind is no reason to deny all the good that has been wrought by scientific progress. Modern no less than primitive technological achievements are but tools. The caveman could use fire either to warm his primitive abode or to incinerate that of his rival; we have similar options with regard to the enormous power that modern technology has made available to us. Such progress, especially as it relates to the successful extension of longevity and the increase in health, quality, and dignity of life, is not to be derogated even from a spiritual point of view. On the contrary, it is a historic achievement that must be applauded and fostered.[43]

Finally, there is the simple but critical element of intellectual integrity. Authority, whether of the past or any other kind, is unquestionably a major element in tradition and in law, especially in Judaism generally and in Halakhah specifically, and must be respected. But truth has a prior and stronger claim upon us as a matter of religious principle.

R. Isaiah de Trani (the Elder), mentioned a few paragraphs earlier, is quite forthright in refusing to yield to prior authority simply because of differences in chronology, and refusing, therefore, to stifle his own halakhic creativity and his perception of the truth. Thus:

What I can prove from the text is what I write. . . . I recognize full well that "the fingernail of the early masters is better than the waist of the later ones," but this I hold true, that if because of the way I read a text I do not agree with a certain view [of an earlier authority], "even if Joshua the son of Nun were to tell it to me, I would not obey him,"[44] and I would not refrain from writing what I think is right. For this is the way of the Talmud: the last of the Amoraim did not refrain from criticizing the earlier [Amoraim] or even the Tannaim, and they fully contradicted Mishnayot, and often decided against the majority [of earlier authorities] and sided with the minority. . . .[45]

In a similar vein, the twelfth-century sage R. Abraham Ibn Ezra writes:

The spirit of God made us all and from matter were the early ones formed as were we. . . . We know that Daniel was a prophet and that he was greater than all the wise men and magicians of Babylon, yet the Sages said that Daniel erred in his reckoning; and what is simpler than arithmetic?[46]

R. Simeon b. Zemach Duran (1361–1444) is even more direct:

The aharonim—despite their acknowledgment that their hearts were so much narrower than those of the rishonim—were not reluctant to admit that they [occasionally] contradicted the words of the latter. For it is appropriate for every sage and scholar not to favor one who is greater than himself if he finds obvious errors in the words of the other.[47]

Before citing other significant sources on the sensitive question of how distinguished authorities of the Jewish tradition treated the very issue of the authority of their predecessors, it is necessary to make one unambiguous observation: the legitimate challenge to precedent and earlier authority must itself be authoritative. This means that the right to counterpose one's own views or interpretations to those accepted by generations of observant Jewry is reserved for those who assent to the fundamental principles on which the whole structure of halakhic life and community is built, and who, in addition, possess the minimal scholarship necessary to make their own contributions credible. Halakhah is not a game for curious onlookers or untested tyros; amateurs should not be taken seriously in matters of such import.

Let us now return to our sources. Along the same lines as those previously mentioned, we hear the following from the fifteenth-century sage, R. Isaac de Leon of Toledo, author of *Megillat Esther*, a defense of Maimonides against the critique of Nahmanides:

It is possible for the aharonim to know more than the rishonim for two reasons: First, one of the aharonim may have taken it upon himself to specialize in one particular area, working on it in depth and so assiduously applying his intellectual efforts that he understands it better than the rishonim. Second, we of the later generations, despite our lack of adequate industriousness in our studies, attain more in a short time than did [our predecessors] in a much longer time. That is so because in their times [the various branches of] wisdom were unknown or incomplete, and they had to deduce them by dint of great intellectual effort, whereas we find all prepared for us [by them] like a table that is all set.[48]

A century later we read similar sentiments by R. Eliezer Ashkenazi, the famous commentator on the Bible:

Each of us who underwent the covenant which He made with us—and our children and children's children after us to the end of time—are all obligated to inquire into the mysteries of the words of the Torah and to align our faith in accordance with [the Torah] in the most proper way that we can. We must accept the truth, after we have come to know it, from whoever propounded it; and we should not allow the opinions of others, even though they preceded us, to deter us from inquiring. On the contrary, we ought to learn and accept from our predecessors in the sense that just as they chose to accept some of what their predecessors said and not to accept other things they said, so is it appropriate for us to do as they did. There is no doubt that not one of them, when writing his book, intended to say to all his successors: you must accept my opinion. Rather, it is clear that his intention was only to convey to us his view so that those who follow him will see and then choose for themselves; for only by gathering all different opinions can the truth be determined. . . . I have committed all this in writing to you because I have seen that in these generations there are many who follow this path [of unquestioning subservience to the authority of predecessors] because of either [intellectual] laziness or fear—which they consider proper—but you should not choose this path and not come near.[49]

Le Plus Ça Change, Le Plus Ç'est la Même Chose!

Even in modern times, with a more conservative tendency prevailing—as it has since the Enlightenment and its excesses encouraged such a reaction—we find scholars who display remarkable intellectual courage despite their acceptance of the degeneration thesis and their unlimited reverence for the founders and transmitters of the halakhic tradition. Two examples come to mind. First is the famous head of the Yeshiva of Volozhin, R. Naftali Zevi Yehudah Berlin (Netziv), who considers profound investigation into Torah and the discovery of new insights and interpretations as the fulfillment of the commandment "to keep and do all the words of the Torah":

> Just as it is impermissible for a natural scientist to feel complacent about having discovered all the secrets of nature and, moreover, it is even possible that his colleague or [a scientist] a generation later will demolish the results of his investigation—as long as he has no decisive proof—[despite the fact that he is contradicting the] view of a predecessor; so may not the scientist of Torah be complacent that he knows all there is to know of Torah—all the details and distinctions that require serious thought. There is no proof that his explanations conform to the truth of Torah; whatever, we must do the best we can.[50]

The second such example is that of R. Abraham Isaiah Karelitz (Hazon Ish), who writes:

I have taken it upon myself to search in the Talmud as best I can, even though [my conclusions] may go against the *rishonim*. I must rest content with the awareness that the words of our Rabbis are most important, and we are but the orphans of orphans. Nevertheless, one must never desist from clarifying and refining [his views] as best as is possible given his limitations, even to the point of deciding the Halakhah [according to his own interpretation], provided there is no explicit contradictory ruling of the *rishonim*. Were it not so, I would be lacking in the involvement in Torah study.[51]

Perhaps the most outspoken advocacy of intellectual integrity in the face of the necessary reverence for past authority comes to us from the son of Maimonides himself. R. Abraham excoriates those who seek to have the opinions of an authority prevail whether or not they are true:

You must know that it is injurious to strive to cause a certain view to prevail because one reveres the one who propounded it and therefore wishes to accept it without pondering and understanding it, regardless of whether it is true or not. This is forbidden both from the point of view of Torah and the point of view of reason. Reason cannot accept it because it implies a lack and deficiency in understanding that which we are required to believe in. And from the vantage of Torah—because it diverges from the way of truth and departs from the path of integrity. The Almighty said: ". . . you shall not respect the person of the poor, nor favor the person of the mighty; but in righteousness shall you judge your neighbor" (Leviticus 19:15). There is no difference whether we accept an opinion without [adequate] proof or whether we [accept it because we] believe the one who uttered it and respect him and assert that he must undoubtedly be right because he is a great man. . . . Not only is this not [adequate] proof, but it is forbidden.

Our author concludes this simple but powerful argument for honesty and truth by referring to the dispute between Jewish and non-Jewish sages, which R. Judah the Prince, compiler of the Mishnah, decided in favor of the Gentile sages.[52] R. Judah was called "our holy master" specifically because of this: "For a man who casts away falsehood and establishes the truth and decides truthfully, and is willing to change his mind if he is proven wrong—such a person is undoubtedly holy."[53]

This fearless respect for truth and intellectual audacity are not confined to rationalists (and their families!). Thus, the Gaon of Vilna advises against any submission to higher authority when one must render an objective decision. His student, R. Hayyim of Volozhin, decries exclusive reliance upon the *Shulhan Arukh,* the accepted standard code of Halakhah, without investigating the original talmudic sources. He follows his own thinking, and if he finds some other author opposed to his views he neither abandons his own position nor does he necessarily dispute the other authority. He relies, instead, upon his readers to judge for themselves. "For when it comes to Torah, which is called Truth, we look only for truth." He is grateful to the Creator for the fact that people's opinions differ, and he seeks only the truth in every problem that confronts him. "It is forbidden for a student to accept his teacher's words if he finds them deficient, for at times the truth is with the student." When we disagree with a teacher or some earlier authority, we are engaged in a "holy war," a *milhemet mitzvah.* Of course, this passionate search for truth, even in defiance of established authority, must be conducted with humility and respect.[54] There should be no conflict between reverence for predecessors and the pursuit of truth. This is a view that characterizes the greatest of halakhic minds, and it is meant to be normative for all of us—even intellectual and spiritual dwarfs. . . .

For all these reasons, the *nitkatnu ha-dorot* or degeneration-of-the-generations argument cannot be employed uncritically.

Not all questions have been resolved for all time. "Our ancestors have left us space to grow."

Not only is there a place for *hiddush,* but intellectual, scientific, halakhic, and philosophic creativity are positive goods, part of the unending search for truth, a search that—as we have seen—is characteristic of the striving for holiness.

And the right and duty to engage in intellectual exploration is something we most certainly can and should learn from our sacred predecessors, both despite and because of their acknowledged spiritual excellence. It is a tribute to them that we imitate their intellectual and spiritual independence and thus seek to reconcile *kevod hakhamim* with *bakashat ha-emet,* reverence for the Sages with the quest for truth.

Thus, Maimonides was indeed a giant among men, probably the most illustrious Jew and luminous thinker since the close of the Talmud. But the succeeding generations have built upon his historic contributions, and they have developed expertise in numerous areas that gives them insights that were not available to him, even as he had information that was not available to his predecessors. It is no tribute to him that we refuse to act on his advice (in this case, relating to the value of philosophic and scientific studies) because we are dwarfs and he was a giant.

He would, it seems, simply invite us to climb on his shoulders and proceed from there.

Notes

1. The reader may wish to refer to a longer and more comprehensive treatment of this subject in an excellent summary by the eminent Yemenite authority on Maimonides, Rabbi Joseph Kapah of Jerusalem, in an article that appeared in the Israeli halakhic annual, *Tehumin* 2:242–245.

2. *Guide of the Perplexed* 1:34.

3. Ibid., 2:29, and in his *Milot ha-Higayon.*

4. *Guide of the Perplexed* 1:34.

5. Ibid., 3:28.

6. As Maimonides had already codified in his *Mishneh Torah, Hilkhot Yesodei ha-Torah* 2:2.

7. *Guide of the Perplexed* 3:54.

8. See Yehezkel Cohen, *Ha-yahas le'Limmudei Hol be'Yahadut* (Tel Aviv: Hakibbutz Hadati, 1983), p. 68.

9. *Hil. Yesodei ha-Torah* 4:13.

10. *Hil. Talmud Torah* 1:12. In R. Joseph Karo's monumental halakhic code, the *Shulhan Arukh* (Yoreh De'ah 246:4), the author, as is his wont, quotes verbatim from Maimonides' *Hil. Talmud Torah* 1:11, but mentions not a word about *Pardes* from 1:12. R. Moses Isserles, in his gloss, cites RIVaSH and the disciples of RaSHBA prohibiting non-Torah studies; Isserles himself permits such study only on a casual, not a systematic, basis.

11. *Teshuvot ha-Rambam,* ed. Alfred Friemann (Jerusalem: Mekitzei Nirdamim, 1934), p. LX; ed. Yehoshua Blau (Jerusalem: Mekitzei Nirdamim, 1957), vol. 3, p. 57; *Iggerot ha-Rambam,* ed. Dr. Yitzhak Shailat (Jerusalem: Seder Bein ha-Homot, 1986), vol. 2, p. 502. Cf. Maimonides' marital metaphor to a remarkably similar one in Philo, *De Congresso,* trans. and ed. G. H. Whitaker (Cambridge, MA: Harvard University Press, 1932), vol. 4, pp. 74–76, who speaks of his principal loyalty to philosophy, but apologizes for "consorting in early youth with one of her handmaids, Grammar, and all that I begot I dedicated to her mistress." So too for Geometry and Music. "And again of none of these did I make a secret hoard, wishing to see the lawful wife a lady of wealth with a host of servants ministering to her. . . ."

12. See the debate between Rabbi Joseph Kapah and Dr. Yitzhak Shailat in *Studies in Memory of the Rishon Le-Zion R. Yitzhak Nissim* (Heb.), ed. Meir Benayahu (Jerusalem: Yad ha-Rav Nissim, 1984), vol. 2, pp. 235–258. In another letter, of equal or probably superior authenticity, Maimonides casually describes his busy medical practice at the court—including the amusing but not surprising fact that some officials solicited his professional advice without any effort to compensate him—which left him no time during the week to study. "As a result," he writes, "I am unable to find a spare hour to study Torah; I can study only on the Sabbath. But with regard to other [branches of] wisdom—I find no time at all to dwell on them. This causes me great pain" (cited in Dr. Yitzhak Shailat, *Letters and Essays of Maimonides* [Hebrew, Jerusalem: 1987], vol. 1, p. 313).

This is certainly as revealing of his fundamental attitude as is the passage cited in our text.

13. Hirsch, whom we shall presently be discussing, was particularly harsh in criticizing Maimonides on this point. See his *The Nineteen Letters of Ben Uziel,* trans. Bernard Drachman (New York: Bloch, 1942), Letter XVIII. Maimonides, Hirsch maintains, merely "reconciled" Judaism with Greek philosophy, that is, philosophy was superadded to Judaism, distorting it in the process, rather than allowing a philosophy of Judaism to issue from within the Jewish tradition autochthonously. Maimonides was "the product of uncomprehended [*sic!*] Judaism and Arabic science" and "was obliged to reconcile the strife which raged in his own breast" (p. 181). Hirsch blames Maimonides for emphasizing abstract rational principles as opposed to action and deed as the highest expression of Judaism. "This great man is responsible, because he sought to reconcile Judaism with the difficulties which confronted it from without, instead of developing it creatively from within. . . . He entered into Judaism from without, bringing with him opinions of whose truth he had convinced himself from extraneous sources and—he reconciled!" But Hirsch is not really fair in accusing Maimonides of "reconciliation," with the implied derogation of without-ness. Maimonides, like Saadia before him, believed in the common origin of reason and revelation, hence of philosophy and Torah (cf. Julius Guttmann's Introduction to Chaim Rabin's translation of *The Guide of the Perplexed* [London: East and West Library, 1952], pp. 9–31). All discrepancies must then be considered as only apparent, and these are to be "reconciled," but this can hardly be subject to the accusation of stepping out of the realm of Judaism to introduce, subversively as it were, alien ideas. Once the original identity of Torah and Wisdom is granted (see Chapter 7), such a charge is irrelevant. When Maimonides makes use of Aristotelian terminology and methodology, he is no more "without" the pale of Judaism than is Hirsch himself when he employs the dialectical modes of Hegelian thought popular in his day, albeit without mentioning their source (cf. Noah H. Rosenbloom, "The 'Nineteen Letters of Ben Uziel,' " *Historia Judaica* [April 1960], pp. 23–60, especially p. 58, and reprinted in his *Tradition in an Age of Reform: The Religious Philosophy of Samson Raphael Hirsch* [Philadelphia: Jewish Publication Society, 1976], pp. 148–183, especially on p. 182). It is truly ironic that Hirsch, who was so critical of Maimonidean rationalism, was himself enamored of German idealism and culture, now mere intellectual artifacts in the academicians'

museum of philosophical antiquities. See the end of the next chapter.

14. Quoted and translated by Eliezer Goldman, in *Studies in Contemporary Jewry, II,* ed. Peter Y. Medding (Bloomington, IN: Indiana University Press, 1986), pp. 52–73.

15. See Chapter 3, and especially note 12. The theme is widespread in the popular Musar literature of the past few generations. R. Hayyim of Volozhin, without explicitly citing the terms *yeridat ha-dorot* or *nitkatnu ha-dorot,* effectively endorses the idea in his conception of the irreversible constriction of halakhic freedom through the ages; see *Nefesh ha-Hayyim* (Vilna, 1837), Part I, Chapter 22, and my *Torah Lishmah* (New York: Yeshiva University Press, 1989), pp. 75–76 and p. 96, note 98.

16. *Berakhot* 35b.

17. *Eruvin* 53a.

18. Jerusalem Talmud, *Shekalim* 5:1.

19. *Shabbat* 112b, and elsewhere.

20. *Yoma* 9b.

21. *Avot de'Rabbi Nathan* 9.

22. *Yevamot* 39b; and, in another context, in *Hullin* 93b, the same question is asked, implying the obvious impossibility of entertaining a notion of moral progress in time.

23. *Rosh Hashanah* 25b.

24. Ad loc. s.v. *she'ha-yamim.*

25. Rashi's gloss is consistent with the context of the talmudic passage. However, the simple literal meaning of the verse is the reverse: it is unwise to attribute superiority to the past just because it is the past. Cf. Ibn Ezra ad loc., and Mordecai Zer-kavod's remarks in the Mosad Harav Kook edition of Ecclesiastes (Jerusalem: 1973), p. 40.

26. *Hullin* 6b, 7a.

27. Rashi's comment, ad loc.: "If our children who come after us will find nothing to contribute, how will they achieve fame?"—is a radically honest insight into the legitimate ego needs of scholars to put their own imprint on their times in a creative fashion. The subject of creativity from a halakhic perspective deserves more comprehensive treatment. Rabbi Joseph B. Soloveitchik holds that creativity is the *telos* of the Halakhah. "The dream of creation finds its resolution in the actualization of the principle of holiness. Creation means the realization of the ideal of holiness." In the halakhic norms "is embodied the entire task of creation and the obligation to participate in the renewal of the cosmos. The most

fundamental principle of all is that man must create himself. It is this idea that Judaism introduced into the world." (*Ish ha-Halakhah,* translated by Lawrence Kaplan as *Halakhic Man* [Philadelphia: Jewish Publication Society of America, 1983], pp. 108–109; and see Marvin Fox, "The Unity and Structure of Rabbi Joseph B. Soloveitchik's Thought," in *Tradition,* Winter 1989, no. 2, pp. 55–56.)

28. Jerusalem Talmud, *Yoma* 1:1.

29. *Gittin* 5b.

30. Mishnah, *Sheviit* 10:3.

31. *Gittin* 36b.

32. Ad loc., s.v. *li'vetuleih.*

33. This holds true for halakhic authority in succeeding generations too. Thus, Rabbah can surpass Rav Judah; *Taanit* 24a, b, and see in detail in *Kessef Mishneh* to *Hil. Mamrim* 2:2, s.v. *hayah gadol.*

34. *Eduyyot* 1:5. The Moroccan talmudist, R. Abraham b. Mordecai Azulai, sees in this mishnah a challenge to the accepted thesis of the superiority of the earlier authorities, and responds with the medieval parable, to be mentioned presently, of the dwarf riding on the shoulders of the giant. See Dov Zlotnick, "The Commentary of Rabbi Abraham Azulai to the Mishnah," in *Proceedings of the American Academy for Jewish Research* (vol. 40, 1972), p. 163.

35. See Nahmanides' commentary to *B. Kamma,* end.

36. *Kessef Mishneh* to *Hil. Mamrim* 1:1, s.v. *beth din.*

37. R. Isaac Alfasi to end of *Eruvin.*

38. *Ha-Mishpat ha-Ivri* (Magnes Press: Jerusalem, 1973), vol. 1, p. 233.

39. Y. Ta-Shma, "*Halakhah ke'Batrai. . . ,*" in *Shenaton ha-Mishpat ha-Ivri,* vols. 6–7 (1979–1980), pp. 405–423. In note 16, Ta-Shma traces this difference in legal philosophy between the Ashkenazim and Sephardim to the different communal realities that prevailed. Ashkenazi communities were generally decentralized. Scholars in one community did not encroach upon the prerogatives of the scholars of neighboring communities and tended to advocate a large measure of halakhic independence and judicial autonomy. The Sephardi communities were far more centralized and inclined to invest single authorities of eminence with the power to decide for all communities; hence the phenomenon of the outstanding roles played by such personalities as R. Isaac Alfasi, Maimonides, and R. Joseph Karo.

40. See *Lehem Mishneh* to *Hil. Talmud Torah* 5:4 who reads this opinion

into the ruling of Maimonides, ibid., and who cites authority for his view that the prohibition of a disciple ruling on Halakhah in the presence of his teacher no longer applies today, "because we learn from books, and the books are our teachers." The author, R. Abraham di Boton, flourished a century after the printing of the Gutenberg Bible (ca. 1455).

41. Robert K. Merton, *On the Shoulders of Giants: A Shandian Postscript* (New York: Harcourt Brace Jovanovich, 1965), p. 268f. The entire book is an attempt to trace the development of the aphorism. For the history of the aphorism in Jewish literature, see too Dov Zlotnick's article (Heb.) in *Sinai* 77:184-189; Tuvia Preschel's articles (Heb.) in *Hadoar* 53:425 and 55:156; and in *Sinai* 78:288; and Hillel Levine, "Dwarfs on the Shoulders of Giants: A Case Study in the Impact of Modernization on the Social Epistemology of Judaism," in *Journal of Social Studies* 40:63-72. I am indebted to Professor Sid Z. Leiman for these references.

42. *Teshuvot ha-RID* (Jerusalem: Machon Ha-Talmud b'Yisrael, 1967), pp. 301-303.

43. On the verse, "One generation to another shall laud (*yeshabah*) Thy works" (Psalm 145:4), the commentator Malbim writes, "The more each succeeding generation ponders the works of the Lord and the secrets of Nature, it recognizes in them wisdom and wonders that were hidden from the earlier generations, and it improves [probably a play on words: *yeshabah*—will praise/*yashbiah*—will improve] His works by increasing its goodness and wisdom over what prevailed in the past, so that every new generation will see that the generation before it did not properly understand the works of the Lord."

44. *Hullin* 124a.

45. *Teshuvot ha-RID*, pp. 6-7. This streak of intellectual independence is characteristic of the greatest halakhic authorities of all generations. See, inter alia: *B.B.* 130b; R. Asher to *Sanh.* Chap. 4, no. 10; ReMA to *Sh.A. H.M.* 25:1; and my *Torah Lishmah*, pp. 7-9, on this quality in the school of the Gaon of Vilna.

46. See R. Abraham Ibn Ezra's commentary to Ecclesiastes 5:1.

47. For this and other relevant passages in the same vein, see S. Z. Havlin's illuminating article in *Mehkarim be'Sifrut ha-Talmudit* (Jerusalem: Ha-Academia ha-l'eumit ha-Yisraelit l'madaim, 1973), pp. 175-176, especially note 20.

48. This second reason may well refer to the "giant and dwarf" idea discussed above, note 41.

49. In R. Isaac de Leon's *Maasei Hashem*, Chapter 31.

50. Introduction to Netziv's commentary on the Pentateuch, *Haamek Davar.*

51. See note 47.

52. *Pes.* 94b.

53. See note 47.

54. For references to the Gaon and R. Hayyim here cited, see my *Torah Lishmah,* pp. 7–9, 29.

CHAPTER 5

THE CULTURAL MODEL:
SAMSON RAPHAEL HIRSCH
AND "TORAH IM DEREKH ERETZ"

RABBI SAMSON RAPHAEL HIRSCH

The most significant and successful communal–educational effort to integrate the worlds of Torah and worldly culture was that of Rabbi Samson Raphael Hirsch of the nineteenth century (1808–1888) in Germany. Hirsch was a prolific author and a gifted speaker, an accomplished talmudist and a man of broad culture, a visionary and an organizer, an educator and a leader.

Hirsch was personally responsible for the flourishing *Denkglaubigkeit*—"enlightened Orthodoxy"—that survives him, though sometimes a bit limpingly, to this day. Thoroughly Jewish, and also a completely modern Western man, he aspired to bring about a harmony between the two traditions and outlooks. He tried to formulate a Jewish humanism, demonstrating that the humanism so popular in the Europe of his day had Jewish roots. Hence his superman, the *Jisroel-*

Mensch. And hence, too, his great educational program under the slogan of *Torah im Derekh Eretz.*

Torah and Wisdom were not regarded by Hirsch as deadly enemies, requiring from us an either–or choice between them. True, he gave Torah primacy over secular education if a choice had to be made.[1] But from his critique of Maimonides and Moses Mendelssohn, who approached Torah "from without," and from his development of his own autochthonous attitude to Judaism,[2] we get the impression that Hirsch believed in the original identity of Torah and the secular disciplines that now appear but in different forms. Granted that Torah and Wisdom were originally and essentially identical, one cannot posit any substantive conflict between them—but neither can one speak of a meaningful dialogue between them. They can cooperate, even as the limbs of the body cooperate and coordinate; but they cannot interact substantively, even as a sane and balanced person does not interact with or talk to himself. Hirsch does not say this explicitly, but it is an inescapable conclusion and one that will appear more significant when contrasted with the position of Rav Kook. The encounter of Torah and Wisdom as formulated by Hirsch is pleasant, harmonious, and creative. The secular studies help us to understand Torah more deeply,[3] even as the Torah tells us how to contemplate nature and listen to history.[4]

Considering the long estrangement of Jews from secular studies since the Golden Age of medieval days until the Enlightenment some two centuries ago, and the unhappy record of the relations of science and religion in European history, this was a courageous attitude and a refreshing approach. His stature must be assessed from this background, as well as against the then contemporary isolationism of East European Jewry. If indeed there seems to be a publicistic dimension to Hirsch, an attempt to present Torah Judaism without the narrowness or provincialism attributed to it by its critics, the "enlightened moderns,"[5] that attempt must not be dismissed as mere posturing or apologetics. It was a pedagogical necessity if Hirsch's program was to be successfully achieved and implemented.

Equally important for Hirsch in his rabbinate in Frankfurt was taking his *Gemeinde* (congregation) out of the established Jewish community—which was officially recognized by the government and which embraced both the Orthodox and growing Reform movement—and declaring it an autonomous Jewish community (the *Israelitische Religionsgesellschaft*). This strictly segregationist community has lasted to this day in many of the countries to which Frankfurt Jews fled after World War II, particularly the United States.

Although this is not the place for either an exhaustive summary or a history of Hirsch and his movement, it is important to demonstrate the indebtedness of contemporary Torah Umadda to *Torah im Derekh Eretz* and to consider the problems that the latter faced and that the former either has solved or is still grappling with, and the ways in which the two diverge from each other.

DEREKH ERETZ

By *derekh eretz* Hirsch means "culture" in its broadest sense, and most especially the contemporary Western culture. Torah is the fixed element, never changing, the eternal verity; *derekh eretz* is the culture of the day—which was unborn yesterday and will be obsolete tomorrow.

The term itself as used in the Talmud did not indicate anything more than the normal business of life or propriety in manners, dress, custom, conduct, business, domestic affairs, and so on.[6] An earlier source for the use of the term *Torah im Derekh Eretz* as a description of an educational theory is Rabbi Samuel Landau (d. 1834), the son of the author of *Noda*

Bi'Yehuda, who emphasized the need for general studies alongside sacred studies as a necessary evil, considering the demands of the times:

> Parents should see to it that their children succeed in Torah and in *derekh eretz* and the boys should not let go of either one. When he reaches the age of twelve, it will be possible to tell where [the youngster] is heading. If he is deemed capable of continuing his studies, it should be determined what he wants and what he chooses, whether to go into other disciplines or to study Talmud until he receives *semikhah* [rabbinic ordination]. But if he does not seem likely to succeed as a student, he should be directed to study a trade or business, each one according to his own inclinations.[7]

Probably the first to use the term in this restricted sense is R. David Ha-Nagid (grandson of Maimonides). In his commentary to *Avot* he says that *"derekh eretz* includes every activity contributing to the sustenance of the world, including the study of the various branches of Wisdom."

Actually, the term *Torah im Derekh Eretz* appears neither in Hirsch's *Nineteen Letters of Ben Uziel* nor in his *Horeb.* Isaac Breuer explains why: *"Torah im Derekh Eretz* is only a slogan inscribed on a flag . . . a road to practice and not an ideological foundation." The real ideological foundation is "a Judaism which knows itself, a Judaism which does not separate itself from nature or history in its constant changes but affirms life and recognizes itself out of its relationship to life. This is a Judaism which affirms every cultural element, every human creativity, which sees in them values if they pass the test of Torah which is the divine instrument given to us . . . for the knowledge of ourselves and our very being in nature and in history."[8]

HIRSCH'S CRITICISM

Hirsch was an educational reformer who did not suppress his criticism of the prevailing educational norms and institutions, especially as embodied in the vibrant Orthodox culture of Eastern Europe of a century and more ago. Thus, he wrote of the "old" *derekh eretz:* "Removed from life, estranged and strange to the world and to life, the old type of East European yeshiva student yielded his views on world and life and no longer used them . . . in order to understand Torah."[9] Hirsch negated the religious legitimacy of a great deal of traditional life,[10] calling into question the religious legitimacy of certain *minhagim,* ritual customs.[11]

The model community he built in Frankfurt reflected this dissatisfaction with the East European model of education. Indeed, when Hirsch's son-in-law and spiritual heir, Rabbi Solomon Breuer, came to Frankfurt and wanted to open a yeshiva, he had to work very hard until he succeeded in convincing the lay leaders that there was a need for such an institution. Ten years had to pass before local students began to attend the school.[12]

Rabbi Azriel Hildesheimer

It was left to Rabbi Azriel Hildesheimer, a towering rabbinic authority of the times, to dedicate himself to precisely the task of implementing his own version of *Torah im Derekh Eretz.* While Hirsch was interested in the broader community, Hildesheimer strived to prepare the spiritual leadership for the future. Thus, Hildesheimer built a seminary, whereas Hirsch concentrated on elementary and high schools.[13] Hildesheimer's seminary in Berlin did not strive for integration of the two poles, but assigned them to separate institutions—the Rabbinical Seminary and the University. The Rabbinical Seminary, devoted totally to Torah, produced such giants as Rabbis David Zvi Hoffmann and Y. Y. Weinberg. However, the fact that the Torah was studied in a "scientific" method aroused the reservations and suspicion of Hirsch and those in his circle.[14]

Students of the *Torah im Derekh Eretz* movement are in disagreement as to whether Hirsch or Hildesheimer strived for an organic synthesis of Torah and *derekh eretz,* and which one wanted them to coexist separately—even though both were necessary—without combining them. (It is the opinion of the writer, as mentioned earlier, that Hirsch posited a coexistence, not a synthesis.) Similarly, there is some confusion as to whether Hildesheimer considered secular wisdom as significant only for its value in enhancing Torah, or whether he believed it had, from a religious point of view, its own intrinsic value. A descendant of the original Azriel Hildesheimer (by the same name)[15] gives a rather contradictory account of the matter. He repeats Hildesheimer's first report about what he wants to accomplish in his yeshiva, a report written a few years after he set it up. It is rather a restricted view: German language; geography and history; enough mathematics, such as the Pythagorean theorem, to understand problems in Talmud; enough Latin to understand foreign words derived from Latin in Midrash and Talmud—and yet, in the same report, "in addition to this, science for its own sake: If one engages in such labors with a proper attitude toward religious research, it becomes at all times for Judaism an important contribution to spiritual life."

Hence, Hildesheimer appears ambivalent on the issue of whether *derekh eretz* has only instrumental value or whether it is, as well, endowed with inherent significance from a Torah point of view. Indeed, the uncertainty with regard to both Hirsch and Hildesheimer on this point indicates that, in all probability, neither of them focused on the problem or gave it much thought.

In 1868 Hildesheimer issued another report about his yeshiva. In it he said, among other things, "It is most certainly possible to justify the time taken from exclusive study of Talmud in order to devote it to contemporary scientific matters, as long as one keeps the proper relationship between them, and as long as the study of the sciences is clearly *le'shem shamayim* (for the sake of Heaven)." Thus, on the one hand Hildesheimer agrees that *derekh eretz* requires a yielding on Torah, but on the other hand he is sure that this concession is not only justified but necessary if it is done *le'shem shamayim,* that is, if it is not done for its own sake but in order to derive some benefit for the study of Torah. This should be compared with the versions of Torah Umadda that are proposed in later chapters.

East European Criticism of Hirsch

There was powerful opposition to Hirsch from East European Torah authorities, albeit great respect for him personally. His methodology of Torah learning incurred the opposition of the Haredim at the beginning of his career, while he was still the Rabbi of Nikolsburg. The local talmudists would say, slightingly, about Hirsch, "We used to recite Psalms and study Talmud; now [with the advent of Hirsch] we study Psalms and recite Talmud."[16]

In the same vein, in 1934, when one of the luminous alumni of the *Torah im Derekh Eretz* school of thought, Rabbi Y. Y. Weinberg, became head of the Rabbinical Seminary founded by Hildesheimer, he proposed that it be moved from Berlin to Palestine. However, the eminent Rabbi Chaim Ozer Grodzensky of Vilna was against the move, and Weinberg yielded to his authority. In a letter to the son of Azriel Hildesheimer that same year, Rabbi Grodzenski begrudgingly expressed his understanding of why such a seminary was necessary in Germany, in light of conditions prevailing in Central and Western Europe, but said that it clearly had no place in Palestine.[17]

Illustrative of the ambivalent but ultimately negative attitude of East European leaders to Hirsch and his outlook is the charming story reported by Menachem Friedman[18] about the visit of a great hasidic leader, the Belzer Rebbe, who came to a famous spa in the West. On his way back, he stopped off in Frankfurt, in the *Austritt Gemeinde* of Hirsch, where he was shown a school, a synagogue, a *mikvah,* and so on, and it was pointed out how esthetic and clean they were, unlike those of Eastern Europe. Every place he visited, the rebbe commented, was "*gants shein, gants shein*" (quite beautiful, quite beautiful). At the very end, he summed up everything once again by saying, "*gants shein, gants shein,*" but added, "*uber tzu a shiddukh kumt dos nisht*" (quite beautiful, but not enough for a marriage proposal).

Most, but not all, East European Orthodox Jewish leadership felt that for the benighted Jews of Central and Western Europe, *Torah im Derekh Eretz* was a necessary concession, but that a healthy, Torah-learned Jewish organism was in no need of such bitter medicine. Thus, they gave *Torah im Derekh Eretz* partial approval—as *bidi'avad* (*de facto*) and not *le'khat'hilah* (*de jure*) recognition.[19] In an attempt to reconcile their personal reverence for Hirsch with their fundamental antagonism to his ideals, some of them maintained that Hirsch too meant *Torah im Derekh Eretz* as a stopgap for assimilated communities alone and not as an ideal worthy in its own right and universally applicable. That is patently a distortion of Hirsch's intention; Hirsch believed that his theory was reflective of the essence of Torah Judaism and not merely a temporary measure—a *horaat shaah*—designed for embattled Jewish communities.[20]

CRITIQUE OF "TORAH IM DEREKH ERETZ" FROM WITHIN

Both Hirsch and Hildesheimer made enormous contributions, yet they were not without critics in their own camp. Moreover, such criticism has increased in our own day as the very community that Hirsch founded has begun to abandon his ideals and revert to a largely Haredi approach, which, as stated, combines reverence for Hirsch's person with a dismissal of Hirschian thought and program.

THE LACK OF CREATIVITY

Jacob Rosenheim (1870–1965), one of the founders of Agudath Israel and one of the most eminent leaders of Hirsch's separatist community, complained in 1924 about the lack of spiritual productivity of German Orthodoxy. He considered the disciples of Hirsch and Hildesheimer to be sterile and lacking in originality, and believed that they had failed to achieve a synthesis in the realms of metaphysics, ethics, and aesthetics. Rosenheim felt that Hirsch had built an institution but not a school, and had no disciples to whom he was able to transmit the task of developing his ideas. Hildesheimer did build a school, but, according to Rosenheim, it was restricted to communal leadership and historic and philological research. He did not, of course, deny that the disciples of these two had certainly made great contributions, but believed these were not in the realm of *religious creativity*. Neither leader, he felt, had left disciples who continued *Torah im Derekh Eretz* as a religious–philosophical system. The two exceptions, according to Rosenheim, were Joseph Wohlgemuth in Berlin and Isaac Breuer in Frankfort.[21]

HIGHER JEWISH EDUCATION

A second serious shortcoming of Hirsch concerns his neglect of preparing future rabbinic and scholarly leadership, although he did raise a generation of laymen imbued with the philosophy of *Torah im Derekh Eretz*. This was the high price he paid for the overmodernization of the East European ye-

shiva model. This criticism of the Hirschian educational program has been made by, among others, Rabbi Eliyahu
Dessler,[22] one of Hirsch's respectful but persistent East European critics, who maintains that the Frankfurt outlook
succeeded in raising thoroughly observant laymen—even
more observant than the laymen of Eastern Europe—but at
the cost of being unable to develop a single giant in Torah.
Professor Jacob Katz[23] attributes this failure to the absence of
a classical, traditional yeshiva in the Hirsch system. In his
judgment, this is why the *Torah im Derekh Eretz* experiment
remained a mere episode in Jewish history, and why Hirsch
himself remains a singular but marginal figure. Menachem
Friedman and Moshe Arend[24] make a more debatable point:
Torah im Derekh Eretz's success in building a community of
laymen who could sanctify daily life was also its weakness,
because it is almost impossible—except for rare personalities
such as Hirsch himself—to be able to achieve a true synthesis
of Torah and *Derekh Eretz;* to expect anything more is utopian.

THE SCHIZOID EFFECT

Yet a third criticism of *Torah im Derekh Eretz* from within its
own ranks concerns the psychological burden that its adherents experienced. In 1912 Lilly Freimann, a religious teacher
in the Adas Israel Congregation in Berlin, lectured to a group
of religious women in Berlin and pointed out one of the major
criticisms of *Torah im Derekh Eretz:* the dualism of Judaism and
Germanism that brings about internal conflict in a child. The
problem can be solved, she said, only by teachers who are role
models and who would show that Torah and *Derekh Eretz* can
be combined in a harmonic whole.[25] Certainly, the role
models she recommended appear to be the right pedagogical
solution if the question is posed as a purely educational problem. It does not respond, however, to the needs of the serious

adult student or thinker for whom Hirsch's *Torah im Derekh Eretz* may raise as many psychological and existential problems as it offers philosophical and sociological solutions.

One of Hirsch's followers who attempted, on a more substantive level, to overcome this fear of a split personality and dualism was Rabbi Meyer Munk, a scientist and student of the philosopher Hermann Cohen. Munk, in a number of articles and books, tried to heal this internal rift by introducing his readers to the world of Kabbalah.[26]

Sometimes this self-criticism by Hirschians appears more like self-laceration. Thus, the late Rabbi Elie Munk rejected Hirschian thought because he believed that in its essence it was dualistic—it was *kilayim* (the biblically proscribed mixture of wool and linen). He felt that people whose lives were formed by this compound ideal carried in themselves the residue of internal conflicts, and the result was a lowering of their cultural level. People raised on *Torah im Derekh Eretz,* he averred, became neither leaders in Western culture nor, with very few exceptions, *talmidei hakhamim* (authentic talmudic scholars).[27] The charge of a schizoid reaction confirms what others have said, but the accusation of a diminished cultural level certainly seems to be overstated. Frankfurt Jewry was tiny in comparison with East European Jewry, and one should not expect from it as many Torah scholars or cultural giants as arose in Eastern Europe.

EXTRAVAGANT RESPECT FOR CONTEMPORARY CULTURE

Hirsch has been faulted as well for being overly fond and respectful of his contemporary *derekh eretz,* namely, such towering personalities as Kant, Beethoven, Goethe, and Schiller; the humanistic culture and idealistic philosophy he espoused proved incapable of resisting the political and historical developments that originated in his much-admired, "enlightened" Germany and all but destroyed civilization.[28] Others have found him to be a follower of Hegel.[29] The criticism is not without a measure of irony; it was Hirsch who upbraided Maimonides for attempting to reconcile Judaism with a discredited Aristotelianism instead of developing his philosophy autochthonously from within Judaism, which, presumably, Hirsch himself succeeded in doing. Hirsch's criticism of Maimonides, and his own followers' criticism of Hirsch, benefit much from hindsight. One can hardly be expected to be completely successful in emancipating oneself from the particularities of time and space, which define not only one's cultural and psychological milieu but limit one's perspective. One can be faulted only for not making provision for such limitation, not for failing to see one's own time from the perspective of an as yet unborn future.

THE SPIRITUAL DIMENSION

A final point in this summary of the critique of Hirsch: For all his devoutness, there is a lack of a sweeping religious feeling, of an underlying spirituality—not in Hirsch himself, as he comes through in his writings, but in the rather rarefied and desiccated theory that he spins out for us. One waits expectantly for a sense of mystery, of transcendence, of spiritual vision and grandeur—and the expectations remain unfulfilled. In a comparison of Hirsch and Kook, clearly Kook succeeds precisely where Hirsch fails; and it is more than a matter of style. Kook's thought is permeated with *neshamah,* with soul, with religious imagination; Hirsch, despite his efforts, does not succeed in attaining such heights.

Perhaps this is why a number of loyalists of *Torah im Derekh Eretz* found their way to Kabbalah, which was much neglected—if not disdained—by Hirsch himself. Hirsch was critical of East European Jews because of what he considered a tradition of irrationality in the "old" Orthodoxy, especially as it came to expression in eighteenth- and nineteenth-century

Hasidism. He opposed mysticism, or at least consciously and deliberately ignored it; in his *Torah im Derekh Eretz* there is no place for mysticism and no need for it.[30] Mention was made earlier of Rabbi Meyer Munk, who found his way to Kabbalah. One of the other elders among the disciples of Hirsch, Rabbi Pinchas Cohen, took a similar route. He felt that people had become chilled by the rationalistic doctrines of Hirsch, and he wanted to give them some more religious warmth. In 1912 he wrote a novel dealing with this theme. Because of his sense of a spiritual emptiness in the rather austere structure of *Torah im Derekh Eretz,* and hence a thirst for something more spiritual, Cohen developed a kabbalistic tendency in Neo-Orthodoxy.[31]

In the atmosphere of a century ago, when German idealism held sway, such a negative attitude to the mystical element no doubt made *Torah im Derekh Eretz* more attractive to Jews struggling with acculturation (with the exception of the aforementioned Pinchas Cohen and other religiously sensitive souls among his own followers). The same cannot be said, of course, for Orthodox Jews wrestling with the problems of Torah Umadda in the closing years of the twentieth century. Kabbalistic and hasidic thinking have become respectable in enlightened Jewish circles today and are not considered obstacles to the search for a meaningful religious and spiritual dimension in modern life.

Before leaving Hirsch and his *Torah im Derekh Eretz* ideology, it is appropriate to comment on the change in nomenclature from *Torah im Derekh Eretz* to *Torah Umadda*. The reason for this is neither a preference for the term coined in Lithuania over the one favored in Germany, nor simple inertia in continuing a motto already in use and introduced into the United States by Dr. Bernard Revel almost three quarters of a century ago. Neither is it intended to signal any necessary discontinuity between the Hirschian *Torah im Derekh Eretz* and the kind of cultural integration that is taking place at Yeshiva University and related circles. Whereas there may be such differences, the reason for this specific terminology has to do, rather, with its communal and political dimensions. *Torah im Derekh Eretz* for Samson Raphael Hirsch was closely associated with his *Austritt* (self-exclusion from the established community) policy, the segregation of his own *Gemeinde* from the general Jewish community because the latter included non-Orthodox elements. Moreover, Hirsch was antinationalist, and his anti-Zionism has remained largely identified with his school of thought. *Torah im Derekh Eretz* thus has associations that go beyond the cultural–intellectual question per se, and with which we do not wish to burden the concept of Torah Umadda (which term should be kept neutral from the separate question of communal segregation or integration and the question of Zionism or anti-Zionism for the purpose of understanding its specifically cultural–pedagogic dimension).

Insofar as *Torah im Derekh Eretz* as a theory is concerned, Torah Umadda shares with it to a greater extent than it diverges from it. In a later chapter we test these criticisms of Hirsch's *Torah im Derekh Eretz* and see whether they are valid against the models of Torah Umadda that we propose.

NOTES

1. S. R. Hirsch, *Judaism Eternal,* ed. Dayan I. Grunfeld (London: Soncino, 1958), vol. 1, p. 170.

2. See Chapter 4, note 13.

3. Zvi Kurzweil, "Samson Raphael Hirsch," *Tradition* 2:296; and see his *The Modern Impulse of Traditional Judaism* (Hoboken, NJ: Ktav, 1985), pp. 27ff. Cf. the attitude of the Gaon of Vilna in Chapter 8 of this book, especially note 2.

4. *The Nineteen Letters of Ben Uziel,* trans. Bernard Drachman (New York: Block, 1942), p. 197.

5. See ibid., p. xxi.

6. See, for instance, the item *derekh eretz* in the *Encyclopedia Talmudit* (Jerusalem: Talmud Encyclopedia Publishing Ltd. 1947), vol. 7, pp. 672–706, where the term is taken primarily as indicating proper conduct.

7. See Mordechai Eliav, "Gishot Shonot le'Torah im Derekh Eretz—Ideial u-Metziut," in *Torah im Derekh Eretz,* ed. Mordechai Breuer (Heb.) (Ramat Gan, Israel: Bar Ilan University, 1987), p. 47, quoting Landau in his *Ahavat Tziyon* (Prague: 1827), no. 6.

8. Cited in Moshe Arend, "Torah im Derekh Eretz be'Mishnatam shel Dovrei Yahadut Germania ha-Haredit lifnei ha-Shoah," in Breuer, pp. 137–138.

9. *Nineteen Letters,* p. 98.

10. Ibid., pp. 196–197.

11. Aryeh Fishman, "Ha-Musag 'Torah' be'Mishnato ha-Mehudeshet shel S. R. Hirsch," in Breuer, pp. 11–12.

12. Eliav, ibid., p. 54.

13. Ibid., p. 53.

14. Ibid., p. 52.

15. Mordechai Breuer, "Ortodoksia u-Temurah," in Breuer, pp. 77–79.

16. Jacob Katz, "Rabbi Shimshon Raphael Hirsch, ha-Meimin u-Masmil," in Breuer, p. 25.

17. Yaakov Baror, "Torah im Derekh Eretz be'Aspaklariah shel Yahadut Mizrah Eiropah," in Breuer, p. 167.

18. Ibid., p. 173.

19. Ibid., p. 76.

20. Mordechai Breuer, in Breuer, p. 85, and Moshe Arend, in Breuer, pp. 136–137.

21. Moshe Arend, in Breuer, pp. 135–136.

22. See R. Eliyahu Dessler's *Mikhtav Me'eliyahu,* vol. 3.

23. Jacob Katz in Breuer, p. 31.

24. Ibid., pp. 140, 177–178.

25. Mordechai Breuer, in Breuer, p. 87. After the First World War, Lilly Freimann sharpened her criticism and demanded that there be a strengthening of national consciousness and teaching of Hebrew in the Hirschian circles.

26. Breuer, in Breuer, p. 87.

27. Immanuel Jakobovits, "Torah im Derekh Eretz be'Yamenu," in Breuer, p. 284.

28. Jakobovits, in Breuer, p. 284; Mordechai Breuer in Breuer, p. 85.

29. See Chapter 4, note 13.

30. Mordechai Breuer, in Breuer, p. 86.

31. Breuer, in Breuer, p. 88.

CHAPTER 6

THE MYSTICAL MODEL:
ABRAHAM ISAAC HAKOHEN KOOK
ON THE SACRED AND THE PROFANE

Born in Latvia to a family that had both hasidic and mitnagdic roots, Rabbi Abraham Isaac Hakohen Kook (1865–1935) became the first Chief Rabbi of what was then Palestine, an achievement of far less importance than the enormous influence he had, and still has, on religious thinking in all circles of world Jewry.

Rav Kook was a distinguished talmudic scholar and an acknowledged *posek* (decisor of Jewish law), one of the last great creative kabbalists of our time, one of the fathers of religious Zionism, a leader widely beloved by almost all segments of the Jewish people, a masterful poet—a gift that usually served to inspire his readers but sometimes obscured what he meant to communicate—and a seminal thinker who boldly addressed the great problems of his time.[1]

THE SACRED AND THE PROFANE

For Rav Kook, the educational problem of Torah and Wisdom is to be treated not in a cultural but in a mixed mystical–metaphysical frame. The categories within which he operates are those of *kodesh* and *hol,* the sacred and the profane, and the issue transcends, therefore, particular social or cultural issues. Kook speaks of two tendencies of the Jewish spirit. One is directed inward; it is a deepening of the sacred and is represented by the traditional yeshivot. The other is an outward one, relating the within to the without. Just as the intensification of the sacred is embodied in the old type of yeshiva, so is the relating of the sacred to the secular the function of the university.[2] (We must forgive Rav Kook if, despite his courageous criticism and warnings issued at the occasion of the formal dedication of the Hebrew University in Jerusalem, he allowed himself the extravagance of imagining that it would fulfill the lofty religious–spiritual mission he assigned to it; hindsight is always wiser than foresight. But his analysis remains valid.)

It is the second tendency, the centrifugal motion of the sacred to the secular, that is of utmost consequence to us. The interaction or integration of Torah with Wisdom is not meant to make up for some lacunae in Torah, but rather to create something new and original in the world of the spirit through these combinations.[3] Kook tells us that the sacred is not antagonistic to science, but first he reminds us that it vitalizes all; it is that which gives life to the secular disciplines.[4] *Kodesh* and *hol* are functionally and indissolubly related to each other. "The sacred must be established on the foundation of the profane."[5] They are related to each other as matter is to form—the secular is matter, the sacred is form—and "the stronger the secular, the more significant the sacred."[6] Just as the body must be healthy in order for the spirit to flower, according to Kook, so secular knowledge should be of superior quality if the sacred is to benefit.[7]

This intimate relationship of sacred and secular is given its strongest expression when Rav Kook writes that the *yesod kodesh ha-kodoshim* (the element of the "holy of holies") comprises both the sacred and the profane.[8] This implies the significant notion, which Kook later states explicitly,[9] that there is nothing absolutely profane or secular in the world. There is no absolute metaphysical category called *hol;* there is only the holy and the not-yet-holy. Eventually all that is profane (not-yet-holy) is to be found in and sanctified through the Torah, for which reason, says Rav Kook, it is called *de'kullah bah* ("containing everything") and is regarded as the fulfillment of God's blessing of Abraham *ba-kol* ("with everything"—Genesis 24:1). This Kookian version of Torah Umadda is the very antithesis of secularism, which recognizes the sacred only in its insularity. Kook's centrifugal *kodesh* is so overpowering and outgoing that the profane loses its absolute character even before its encounter with the sacred. It is, as it were, fated from its creation to submit to the sacred.

Does this denial of the absolute character of the profane imply a blurring of the distinction between *kodesh* and *hol?* While such antinomian possibilities should never be entirely dismissed, this did not happen in the case of Rav Kook; indeed, he was sufficiently sensitive to the issue as it was raised during the Hasidism–Mitnagdism polemic to avoid it entirely. It is appropriate to recall an insight by R. Isaiah Halevi Horowitz (1565?–1630). In his famous *Shenei Luhot ha-Berit,* he asks why, in the *havdalah* (the prayer that marks the end of the Sabbath and the beginning of the profane week), the distinction between Israel and the nations is mentioned. The other distinctions—between light and dark, Sabbath and weekday, sacred and profane—are all appropriate to the *havdalah,* but that between Israel and the nations seems irrelevant. He answers that there is a significant difference between Israel and the other nations (read: religions) in how they conceive of the distinction between sacred and profane, and so on. The non-Jewish faiths conceive of an unbridgeable abyss between them. Judaism, however, believes that the gulf between *kodesh* and *hol* is meant not to introduce a permanent and irreconcilable dualism, but to allow the sacred to be confirmed in its strength and purity so that it might return and sanctify the nonholy.[10]

So does Rav Kook conceive of the relationship of *kodesh* and *hol,* as his thought emerges from his *Orot ha-Kodesh* and his courageous address at the opening of the Hebrew University in Jerusalem.[11] There is a *havdalah,* in order to allow for the intensification of the sacred in its centripetal motion,[12] and this itself is prelude to its outward, centrifugal movement, where it reaches for the profane and transforms it into the sacred—a transmutation that fulfills the purpose of its existence. The fact of *kodesh* (sanctity) leads to the act of *kiddush* (sanctification).

Hence, it must be fundamentally acknowledged that the secular studies are not inherently and eternally unholy, and that the sacred studies are sterile when they have nothing but the sacred to act upon. There is no blurring of the distinctions between sacred and secular. But there is an appreciation of the function of the sacred in relation to the secular. The secular studies are important, not *despite* the fact that they are not holy, but *because* this is the way in which all life, all knowledge, all existence is ultimately integrated in the great "*yihud* of the Holy One and His *Shekhinah*"—the restoration of the primordial Divine Unity that is one of the fundamental concepts and values of all the Kabbalah.

Hirsch and Kook

This brief survey of Rav Kook's thought on the central issues of Torah Umadda should now be compared with the *Torah im Derekh Eretz* ideology of Rabbi Hirsch. Both men and the *Weltanschauungen* they represent are relevant to our day and to the shaping of Jewish destiny. Each represents a different version of the encounter between Torah and Wisdom. Hirsch, the aristocratic pedagogue, and Kook, the poetic kabbalist, both inspire admiration. Yet basically, Hirsch is the cultural thinker and educator, whereas Kook is the metaphysician and mystic.

Hirsch tried to show, in the words of his translator, Bernard Drachman, that "Orthodox Judaism was not maintained solely by the superstitious or narrow-minded older generation that had never been initiated into the science or the culture of the age."[13]

It is precisely a statement of this sort that makes one wonder about the sufficiency of Hirschian *Torah im Derekh Eretz* for contemporary Orthodox Judaism. For Hirsch it was important to produce a Westernized Orthodox Jew in order to refute the charge that Judaism is a collection of old superstitions. For Hirsch's translator Drachman in the America of his day, at the very end of the nineteenth century, a college education and a Ph.D. were necessary social ornaments lest Torah Jews be classified as narrow-minded. Surely contemporary American Orthodoxy has progressed beyond the stage where it has to prove itself, where an English-speaking Orthodox rabbi with a university education is an unusual phenomenon.

Perhaps the following statement by Hirsch himself will allow the reader to feel the temper, if not the content, of his particular outlook on the engagement of Torah and Wisdom.

> Pursued hand-in-hand, there is room for both [Jewish and general studies], each enhancing the value of the other and producing the glorious fruit of a distinctive Jewish culture which at the same time is "pleasant in the eyes of God and man."[14]

Even after accounting for the highly florid and hortatory literary style that was characteristic of his period, he appears to us to be delighted that he can avoid those intellectually bloody conflicts between religion and science, that he can steer clear of the ragged edges of discord between Torah and Western Wisdom. "Hand-in-hand" they will walk and appear "pleasant" in the eyes of all. There is something placid as well as idyllic and utopian in this vision. It is too easy, too gentlemanly, too cultured—or, if one may say this, too bourgeois.

The slogan *Torah im Derekh Eretz* would not be appropriate to Rav Kook's grand vision of the sacred and the profane. Torah "with" *derekh eretz* implies that they keep a respectable distance from each other, like neighbors who remain courteous as long as they do not become too intimate. Torah "and" *derekh eretz* would be more fitting for Kook. There is a decided difference between these conjunctions.[15] Torah "and" *derekh eretz* suggests a meeting of two powerful personalities, the two of them coming to grips with each other, with the very serious question of whether this engagement will be an embrace or a wrestler's headlock.

Hirsch's view of Torah and Wisdom is one of coexistence and therefore is essentially static. Kook's is one of interaction, and hence dynamic. Hirsch is an esthete who wants Torah and *derekh eretz* to live in a neighborly and noncombatant fashion for the cultural enhancement of both. Kook is an alchemist who wants the sacred to transmute the profane and recast it in its own image. From the point of view of Kook, it is not enough to raise a generation of Orthodox Jews who will also be cultured Western people, admirable as this ambition may be. It is not enough to conceive of the two cultures as parallel lines that can meet only in infinity. It is urgent that there be a confrontation and an encounter between them. For Kook, there must be a qualitative accommodation of both studies, for the secular studies are not inherently unholy, and the *limudei kodesh* must have something not-already-sacred to act upon. The *limudei hol* (secular studies) are part of the drama of *kiddush* (sanctification).

Hence, for Kook, Torah Umadda represents a genuine *synthesis,* with all the benefits and problems—and dangers—associated with that. For Hirsch, for whom the direction of the interaction is from the profane to the sacred—that is, for whom the secular disciplines are employed to order, define, and assist the sacred and place it on a firm scientific basis—*Torah im Derekh Eretz* is a relationship of *coexistence.* For Rav Kook, who demands interaction as the central theme of the relationship, the motion goes in both directions. The less important one is the kind we have just mentioned: the rationalization, explanation, and adornment of the sacred by the profane (essentially assigning to Wisdom the role of "perfumers and cooks and bakers" for Torah, as discussed earlier). Kook calls this a right-to-left motion. Far more significant and consequential is the left-to-right motion: the radiation of *kodesh* toward *hol,* ennobling it, raising it to the loftiest levels, sanctifying it, impregnating it with meaning and purpose.[16] Thus, whatever the engagement between *kodesh* and *hol* in *Torah im Derekh Eretz,* it will be something on the order of using chemistry to clarify a problem in *Yoreh De'ah* or mathematics to settle a problem in the construction of the Jewish calendar. The dynamic relationship demanded by the Kookian sacred–profane axis emphasizes the use of Halakhah in defining for the chemist or mathematician how to shape his approach, his purpose, his significance in the world. It requires the mastery of Torah so as to teach the *ben Torah* how to grapple with the mundane, stubborn issues of ordinary life and make them yield to the light of Torah. The encounter of Torah and Wisdom has as its goal to "create in the world new souls, and give life a new, thriving, healthy form."[17] One senses here a breakthrough of light and life, adding a new and dynamic dimension to what otherwise might be an ordinary pedagogical debate on curricular priorities.

Hirsch's coexistence of Torah and Wisdom is not easily attained, Kook's even less so. Tension is an indispensable concomitant of the interface between two disparate cultures of any variety. Anxiety and doubt and perplexity are necessary side-reactions of the act of encounter. Both Hirsch and Kook recognized this phenomenon, and both thought the benefits worth the mental anguish. Thus Hirsch writes to his fictitious young friend:

> Do not think our time so dark and helpless, friend; it is only nervous and uncertain, as a woman in childbirth. But better the anxiety that prevails in the house of a woman about to give birth, than the freedom from anxiety, but also from hope and joy, in the house of the barren one.[18]

These words of comfort and encouragement strike home to us, a century later and on another continent, who are concerned by the constant self-examination and critical self-evaluation in our ranks. They are signs of creation and birth.

Rav Kook speaks of such anxiety in similar terms.[19] He quotes Isaiah 60:5: "And thy heart shall tremble and be enlarged." The dynamic synthesis of Kook is fraught with danger and risk. Fear and trembling are inescapable. The centrifugal motion of *kodesh,* the sanctification of the profane, suffers from a historical ambivalence, as when it appeared in the controversy surrounding the translation of the Torah into Greek. Whenever there is an encounter of sacred and profane there must be anxiety, for who knows but that instead of the *kodesh* converting the *hol,* the *hol* will master the *kodesh,* as in Anatole France's novel, *Thaïs.* If it is security and freedom from fear that is sought, then it is sufficient to withdraw into hermetically sealed ghettos or vanish into easy assimilation;

the confrontation between Judaism and world culture is thus either avoided or ended. But if neither world is to be relinquished, and if they are to be allowed to act upon each other, then one must accept fear and the sense of crisis and all the neurotic tensions that come with them.

He who enters into this dialogue of Torah and Wisdom must tremble at the risks inherent in it, even while acknowledging that it is his duty to undertake it. Many religious casualties have already resulted from this historic program of Torah Umadda, and there are more yet to come. Rav Kook reminds us that those who approached the encounter without apprehension and trembling were failures—most of their descendants were assimilated and were subsequently lost to our people. Only if there is such fear can there be hope to experience the second part of the Prophet's verse: "and thy heart shall be enlarged"—true joy and exultation.

This comparison between Rav Kook and Rav Hirsch cannot be concluded without observing the greater success of Hirsch in his impact on later generations. Despite the tergiversation of so many Hirschians today in their reversion to the American forms of the East European models criticized by Hirsch, and the lamentations of the remaining Hirsch loyalists, *Torah im Derekh Eretz* remains a living option for numbers of talented and committed Jews and holds a powerful attraction for young people searching for a viable model for integrating Torah and Wisdom. Professionals of German-Jewish descent who observe the mitzvot and regularly study Torah *lishmah,* for its own sake rather than for "professional" reasons, and communities of observant laymen of all geographic origins who are open to the culture of the contemporary world—these are Hirsch's very real legacy. On the other hand, Kook's ruminations on the holy and the profane, profound as they are, have—tragically—had little effect on his followers. His late son, Rabbi Zvi Yehuda Kook, did not openly encourage the study of Madda. The yeshiva that the elder Rav Kook founded does not to this day abide any affirmative attitude toward university studies; its only distinctive trait is its extreme nationalistic character. Rav Kook's thought thus still awaits its redemption. Perhaps jointly with some of its closest ideological relatives (discussed in Chapter 10), Kookian theories of the relation between the sacred and the profane can be implemented in the institutions that are today dedicated to Torah Umadda.

NOTES

1. There is a large and growing literature on Rav Kook, both in Hebrew and in English, too voluminous to mention here. The comments in this chapter are adapted, with some modification, from my book *Faith and Doubt* (New York: Ktav, 1986), pp. 69–82, and my essay, "Harmonism, Novelty, and the Sacred in the Teachings of Rav Kook," in *Abraham Isaac Kook: His Thought and His Legacy,* ed. Lawrence J. Kaplan and David Shatz (New York: New York University Press, expected publication date—1990–1991).

2. See in Kook's *Hazon ha-Geulah* ("The Vision of Redemption"), a collection of his dicta (Jerusalem: Ha-Agudah le'Hotzaat Sifrei ha-Riyha Kook, 1941), pp. 266–273.

3. Kook's *Orot ha-Kodesh* (Jerusalem: Ha-Agudah le'Hotzaat Sifrei ha-Riyha Kook, 1938), vol. 1, p. 63; and my "Harmonism" essay mentioned in note 1.

4. Ibid., p. 3

5. Ibid., p. 145. Compare a striking parallel to this view in Rabbi Joseph B. Soloveitchik's interpretation of the biblical commandment to tithe one's livestock: "And concerning the tithe of the herd or of the flock, even of whatsoever passeth under the rod, the tenth shall be holy unto the Lord" (Leviticus 27:32). But why could not the shepherd simply set aside a tenth of his livestock without going through the procedure of counting them by rod and specifying the tenth as "holy unto the Lord"? The answer: Holiness requires a substratum of the profane; without going through the nine that remain profane, the tenth cannot be accounted sacred (in an article for *The Jewish Week* [Yiddish], 10 Shevat 5719 [1959], p. 5). I

am indebted to Dr. Leo Landman for this reference.

6. Ibid., p. 145; also p. 64.

7. Ibid., p. 685.

8. Ibid., p. 64.

9. Ibid., p. 143.

10. The interrelationship of *kiddush* and *havdalah* is evidenced in the Halakhah, too. Thus, Maimonides (*Hil. Shabbat,* Chap. 29) defines *havdalah* as the *kiddush* performed at the end rather than the beginning of the Sabbath. Similarly, the *kiddush* of Friday night implies the element of *havdalah* or separation of Sabbath from the preceding profane days. See especially Maimonides, *Sefer Hamitzvot,* Positive Commandments, #155; and cf. Chapter 11 in my *Halakhot ve'Halikhot* (Jerusalem: Yeshiva University Press and Mosad Harav Kook, 1990).

11. See note 2.

12. This requirement for the sacred to deepen within itself before it undertakes the venture of sanctification of the nonsacred has certain practical consequences. It necessitates, for instance, the existence of the "old-fashioned" yeshivot that are fully devoted to Torah study, alongside the "modern" yeshivot where the actual interaction takes place. Cf. the remarkable letter by Rav Kook in *Iggerot Re'iyah,* vol. 1, pp. 206–207, also quoted in Rabbi Binyamin Efrati's *Ha-senagoryah be'Mishnat ha-Rav Kook* (Jerusalem: Mosad ha-Rav Kook, 1959), pp. 105–106.

13. *The Nineteen Letters of Ben Uziel,* trans. Bernard Drachman (New York: Bloch, 1942), p. xxi.

14. Samson Raphael Hirsch, *Judaism Eternal,* ed. Dayan I. Grunfeld (London: Soncino, 1958), vol. 1, p. 170.

15. Cf. the difference between the two kinds of conjunctions in *Guide of the Perplexed* 2:22.

16. *Orot ha-Kodesh,* vol. 1, p. 68f.

17. Ibid., p. 63, and see my "Harmonism" essay, note 1.

18. *Nineteen Letters,* p. 201.

19. See note 8.

CHAPTER 7

Sources for New Versions
of Torah Umadda

The three models of Torah Umadda described in the preceding chapters, and the three models that remain to be offered, share certain fundamental presuppositions. It is these underlying ideas that lead eventually to some form of positive orientation to Torah Umadda. These notions must be explicated and understood if we are to appreciate the aspirations of Torah Umadda and vindicate the faith that the encounter between the two can be fully creative.

BASIC PREMISES

The most important element that the various versions of Torah Umadda share is the tenet that the two, Torah and Madda, are fundamentally compatible; perhaps, in an ultimate sense, they can be said to have once constituted a unity. Hence, in seeking to bring the two together, we are not endeavoring to combine two disparate entities *de novo*.[1] We are not in metaphoric violation of the biblical prohibition of harnessing a mule to an ox, or sowing the seeds of the vine with those of other fruit, or weaving wool with linen. The enterprise of Torah Umadda is that of *reestablishing* a primordial harmony. This ancient harmony can be discussed on two levels—the historical and the spiritual. We begin with the former—the harmony that was shattered when the Temple was destroyed, Judea ravaged, and our ancestors carried off into captivity among the nations of the world.

As an independent people living in its own homeland—and even when that homeland was continued spiritually and intellectually by the creators of the Mishnah and the Talmud despite the political vicissitudes visited upon them—Jews perforce engaged in the mundane aspects of the then contemporary Madda. They learned the techniques of agriculture and commerce, they studied architecture and military science, they wrote poetry and explored animal husbandry, they investigated the orbits of the spheres and the intricacies of human anatomy, and they planned the channeling of rivers and the building of bridges. All this was consonant with their uniqueness as a people covenanted by God to lead a life of Torah and mitzvot. There is an old Jewish tradition that Greek philosophy was borrowed from the Jews, that all its wisdom had Mosaic roots.[2] The historical truth of this tradition, much embellished in legend, is irrelevant. What is most germane is the undeniable kernel of truth it contains: Israel was originally a thriving, dynamic civilization in which Torah and Madda were aspects of one central reality—a people wholly covenanted as both a natural and a supernatural polity.

It was only when this wholeness was broken, when the covenanted people was torn away from its covenanted land, that the primordial integrity of Jewish civilization became problematic. As the scope of our Madda involvement was restricted by outside forces and the adverse conditions of exile, and we retreated deeper into Torah as the sole channel to our divine source, the fissure between Torah and Madda grew ever stronger and more pronounced. It is this artificial abyss, the product of exile and its harshness, that placed a question mark over the nonsupernatural, "civilizational" aspects of our lives.

It is thus not surprising that Torah Umadda as a problem arises whenever external conditions allow Jews to feel relatively free—religiously, politically, socially, and economically. At such times, when life more closely approximates the conditions of national wholeness, Jews inevitably contemplate the reunion of the two halves of their severed spirit. When such external conditions deteriorate, Jews flee in one direction or the other and despair of the sense of covenantal-civilizational wholeness.

The efforts at restoration are risky. The process of reunification requires a finer sense of balance than did the maintenance of the original wholeness, which was natural and fairly effortless. The reestablishment of that original harmony involves the danger of overemphasis on the natural, profane elements, and the consequent reaction of a return to the status quo of limiting Judaism to the realm of the sacred alone and declaring all profane pursuits in the intellectual sphere as out of bounds for a covenanted people.

Such a flowering of Torah Umadda took place during the Spanish Golden Age, and also during the Renaissance. It reappeared in the nineteenth century in Germany, when Hirsch and Hildesheimer and the others developed and implemented their *Torah im Derekh Eretz* approach, a movement that later began to disintegrate during the miserable economic and political conditions in Germany following World War I and in the unrelieved horrors of the Holocaust years and the aftershocks that we experience to this day. Rav Kook flourished in the heady atmosphere of an incipient independence

about to be regained as the precursor to the State of Israel, and
thus began to anticipate the question of Jewish wholeness as
the promise of national redemption appeared on the Eastern
horizon. American Jewry during this past one hundred years
has enjoyed the freedom and prosperity necessary for it, too,
to consider the possibility of Torah Umadda.

An example of imbalance in the attempt to reintroduce
Torah and Wisdom to each other, under the new conditions of
freedom and reentry into the larger world, is provided by the
critical events of two centuries ago, events that proved revolutionary in Jewish history. The fracturing of soul from body,
of Torah from Madda, of the spiritual and mundane dimensions of national existence from each other, was exacerbated
by the two historical forces of the Enlightenment and the
Emancipation. Yehudah Leib Gordon's slogan, "Be a man
abroad and a Jew at home," signaled the Enlightenment's
bifurcation of Jewish experience between Jewishness and hu-
manness and the need to choose one and reject the other.
Gordon's solution—a form of voluntary Marranoism—was
functionally the method adopted by those Jews whose assimilation ended only a step before the baptismal font. "Orthodox" Jews, acquiescing to the *force majeure* of both Napoleonic
edict and massive social–historical forces that encouraged
such fragmentation of the wholeness of Jewish life and experience, and wary of the blandishments of modernity, opted for
Torah, for an intensive Jewishness, and the abandonment of
the Madda element, as the price of survival. In the course of
the years, this bifurcation, like the ghetto clothes that were
forced upon them and later became a badge of honor, was
accepted as natural, and the separation of Torah from Madda
was viewed as necessary, a positive virtue.

Thus, advocates of Torah Umadda do not accept that Torah
is fundamentally at odds with the world, that Jewishness and
Jewish faith on the one side, and the universal concerns and

preoccupations of humanity on the other, are fundamentally inapposite, and that Torah and Madda therefore require substantive "reconciliation." Rather, whereas it may be true that effectively Torah and culture have become estranged from each other—both as a result of the religiously negative forces unleashed by the Enlightenment, and the political and socio-economic factors that caused Jews to lose touch with the progress of general cultural thinking while they immersed themselves in Talmud and Kabbalah—in essence they are part of one continuum. Hence, the motivating mission of Torah Umadda must be to reunite and restore an original harmony. In other words, the exclusive concentration on one of these two poles to the detriment of the other is a sign of *galut* (exile), the one-sidedness that results from the need to respond to an artificial distinction (Jew/human) that carries the weight of established doctrine while being inherently invalid. The arguments and rationales we marshal in defense of Torah Umadda are therefore unfortunate necessities.

To turn now from a historical to a spiritual or theological perspective, it may be said that, in a sense, we are here dealing with an anthropological form of the Lurianic "breaking of the vessels." In this kabbalistic scheme, Creation begins as an act of destruction. The primeval wholeness of the Deity is shattered, and divine "sparks" inhere in the dumb and profane "shells," giving birth to the natural world. The sparks of Divinity await their "redemption" by man and lead to the reunification of the *Sephirot* (the structure symbolizing the unfolding of the divine life as it turns outward from its absoluteness in the *Ein-Sof*—the ineffable One *sans* attributes or name), and the restoration of the ultimate divine harmony at the End of Days. So, too, in our current unredeemed state, we seek reasons of all kinds—halakhic, kabbalistic, philosophical—for the merging or synthesis of dimensions that once were part of an organic religiocultural unity and whose *re*conciliation is an act of reunion, reintegration, and restoration.

Our starting point is the conviction that when we speak of Torah *and* Madda, it is not because of practical economic necessity or because we impute any imperfection or inadequacy to Torah unintended by its divine Author, but because *we affirm that both Torah and Nature are the results of divine revelation;* and even as God is One, so is there no split between His self-revelation in Torah (His word) and His self-disclosure in Nature (His world). Hence the study of Torah is the contemplation of God's self-revelation as *Teacher* (as in the blessing *melamed Torah le'amo Yisrael,* "He who teaches Torah to His people Israel"); and Madda is the study of Him as *Creator.* God as Creator is the focus of Genesis, the first Book of the Torah, whereas God as Teacher is the focus of Exodus, the second Book. And both "are given from One Shepherd" (Ecclesiastes 12:11).

The celebration of Nature as divine handiwork, and therefore as creation implying the glory of its Creator, is common throughout the literature of many peoples. The point is not at all philosophical—whether the design we discern in Nature "proves" God's existence—but religious and spiritual; that is, that the intuitive response to the marvels and wonders of Nature inspire one to worship its Creator who is thus "revealed" in His creation. To cite but two examples:

> . . . .Beauty is God's handwriting—a wayside sacrament. Welcome it in every fair face, in every fair sky, in every fair flower, and thank God for it as a cup of blessing.
>
> —Ralph Waldo Emerson

> God Himself is the best Poet,
> And the Real is His song.
> —Elizabeth Barrett Browning

One can find hundreds of other such examples in world literature and, of course, Jewish literature. One particular parallel to the Browning couplet from the Kabbalah comes to mind at once. The *Zohar Hadash* (one of the major parts of the Zohar, the classic work of Jewish mysticism), commenting on the first word of the Torah, *beresheit* ("in the beginning"), divides its six Hebrew letters into *shir ta'ev,* ("a song it yearns")—"that is to say, [the creation] yearns to offer a song for His wonders in [creating] heaven and earth."[3]

This does not necessarily imply the equal value or significance of the two forms of revelation—of His *logos* and His *cosmos,* His Word and His World. Clearly, the revelation of Torah is directly a disclosure of the divine Will; the revelation of His creative office is not. But the unity of God does imply the fundamental oneness of the Revealer and, hence, the affinity of both forms of revelation to each other.

These two elements are parallel to the first two blessings that precede the *Shema,* the great proclamation of divine Unity in both the daily morning and the daily evening services. The first, *birkhat yotzer,* acknowledges Him as the Creator of Nature; the second, *birkhat ahavah,* as the Teacher of Torah. (Thus, the Halakhah considers the second blessing as a form of *birkhat ha-Torah,* the blessing to be recited prior to the study of Torah.) This unity of both aspects of Divinity is reflected in the *Shema* itself: *Elohim* ("God") denotes God's creative office as the Sovereign of Nature (hence, e.g., "In the beginning *God* created . . .") and *Ha-Shem* ("Lord") refers to Him as the Teacher of Torah (thus, e.g., "And the *Lord* descended upon Mount Sinai . . .").

That both Torah and Nature manifest the Creator is evident throughout the Book of Psalms, which contains some of the most beautiful nature poetry ever written, praising the Maker for the magnificence of His handiwork. Equally so, there are whole psalms devoted to the glorification of the Torah, of God who revealed it, of those who study it and observe its precepts.

Both themes are joined in Psalm 19, which is equally divided between the two. The first half proclaims that "the heavens declare the glory of God" and soundlessly reveal the divine wisdom (knowledge) of the Creator. Nature, however, has its dangers. The very sun that so promisingly rises in the morning, like a bridegroom emerging from the wedding canopy or an athlete about to run his course, can become a source of woe: "Naught is hidden from its heat." Man who benefits from the generosity and opulence of Nature is also in peril from the cruel indifference of its mindless powers.

The second half begins with the asseveration that "the teaching (Torah) of the Lord is perfect, restoring the soul." The righteous precepts make man's heart rejoice; they are enlightening, true, enduring, and infinitely precious. But the spiritual law, like that of Nature, has its dangers for man, for just as natural forces can be a threat to him physically, so do the Torah and its teachings challenge his moral fortitude. "Who can discern his errors? Cleanse Thou me from hidden faults. Yea, keep back Thy servant from willful sins; let them not have dominion over me, then I shall be blameless and clear of great transgression."

Thus, both Torah and Nature speak of God and remind man of his Creator-Teacher. Because the psalmist is realistic as well as rhapsodic, he recognizes that each of his two ways of relating to God brings danger as well as opportunity (what Paul Tillich called existential anxiety and moral anxiety). He thus concludes his brief but rich psalm with the plea, "May the words of my mouth and the meditation of my heart find grace before Thee, Lord, my Rock and my Redeemer." As Creator of Nature, the Lord appears as a Rock; as the Teacher of Torah, He is the Redeemer.

While a sensitive reading of the psalm reveals these nuances that distinguish between the two aspects of man's perception of the Deity, there is no clear indication of a qualitative difference between them in the sense that one is preferable to the other. However, such a value judgment, to which we referred a few paragraphs ago, is found in an interesting Mishnah that clearly sets Torah, the direct revelation of the Lord, over Nature, which is but emblematic of Him:

> R. Jacob used to say: One who is studying Torah as he walks by the way, and who interrupts his studies to say, "How beautiful is this tree," or "how beautiful is this furrow," it is as though he is guilty with his life.[4]

This is not by any means an anti-esthetic statement. It is a ruling on the relative merits of seeking the Creator through His handiwork (Nature) and through His revelation (Torah).

Both *cosmos* and *logos* are legitimate sources of religious inspiration; both point to Him. But there is no contest when it comes to making a choice between them. The Sages do not condemn a man for admiring Nature and thus appreciating its Maker. They do not criticize him for interrupting his nature appreciation in order to study Torah. They do excoriate him for turning from study of Torah to indulge his bent for admiring the beauty of Nature, even if such appreciation leads him back to its Creator.

The song of David, sharpened and refined by the wisdom of R. Jacob, lies at the heart of our view of Torah Umadda as its most fundamental axiom: Nature, the world, must not be neglected, and it must be studied and explored as part of man's relationship with his Maker. But Torah, as more than a creation of God but His very Word, ever remains supreme. MaHaRaL, who generally supports the study of Wisdom, similarly distinguishes between Torah and Wisdom.[5]

These reflections on the primordial unity of Torah and
Madda as revelations of God, albeit of different levels of
significance and sanctity, underlie most if not all theories of
Torah Umadda in their various configurations throughout
the centuries.

However, there is a respectable body of opinion, most
explicitly articulated by R. Hayyim of Volozhin, theoretician
and spokesman of Mitnagdism (the traditional rabbinic Judaism in opposition to Hasidism), which dissents from this
view and asserts a far more profound qualitative difference
between Torah and Nature. We discuss this dualistic view
presently, and test whether it allows any form of Torah
Umadda based upon its major premise of the dissonance and
disjunctiveness or inappositeness between Torah and the
world, or whether it must inexorably lead to a "Torah only"
position and a necessary rejection of Torah Umadda.

The East European Matrix

In the following chapters, three additional models of Torah
Umadda are proposed. The first two are not altogether unprecedented, and may be found in different forms in the
writings of both Maimonides and the German school. The
third, which is based upon a fascinating hasidic notion, has
not, to the author's knowledge, been proposed before, although it is functionally closest to that of Rav Kook.

What makes these three versions of Torah Umadda different and novel is their point of departure, which is neither
the rationalism of the medieval Sephardi world, nor the
thought and programs of Frankfurt where traditional Judaism
first encountered modernity, nor the kabbalistic world of Rav
Kook, even after it is stripped of its esoteric terminology.
Rather, their source is the competing ideologies and theolo-
gies that abounded in the fertile cauldron that was eighteenth-

and nineteenth-century Eastern Europe. Here, profound and exciting issues occupied the attention of the Ashkenazi world, where there flourished such giants as R. Elijah, the Gaon of Vilna (1720–1797) and R. Hayyim Volozhiner (1749–1821) on the mitnagdic side; and R. Israel Baal Shem Tov (ca. 1700–1760), R. Dov Ber, the Maggid of Mezeritch (d. 1772), R. Shneour Zalman of Lyadi (1745–1813), founder of the HaBaD movement, and countless other luminaries in the hasidic world.

For a variety of reasons, secular education was anathema to most groups in the Eastern Europe of the seventeenth and early eighteenth centuries, and hence the religious thought of this era has not usually been considered in connection with Torah Umadda. However, these reasons were primarily sociological and cultural. They were historically conditioned— they had to do with the rise of the Haskalah (Enlightenment), which was inimical to the millennial Jewish tradition and hence evoked an antagonistic reaction from the traditionalists; and also with the hermetically closed conditions in which most East European Jews lived—and thus these reasons do not go to the essence of Torah Judaism in either the hasidic or the mitnagdic version. But normative halakhic Judaism, as taught by both the mitnagdim and the hasidism, contains a wealth of material that, if its implications are spelled out imaginatively but respectfully and responsibly, can support alternative versions of Torah Umadda. This is true despite the fact that Torah Umadda did not actually flourish in this era and this area, from which the majority of today's American Orthodox Jewish community stems.

This demographic fact is not the only reason for this effort to probe East European Jewish sources for opportunities to support a Torah Umadda viewpoint. More important is the very fact of the almost splendid isolation from external cultural influences in which this remarkably rich Jewish subculture flourished. That it was not altogether immune from external intellectual and cultural influences, at least on an unconscious level, goes without saying; at least *some* interaction with the environment characterizes every living organism, whether individual or collective. But relative to other great Jewish communities—medieval Spain, Renaissance Italy, nineteenth-century Germany, contemporary America—it was the least acculturated to the surrounding environment and the most intellectually and religiously autonomous. Hence, two advantages accrue to searching in East European Jewry for a source for Torah Umadda: First, this Jewry, protected as it was from infiltration by alien ideologies, is most authentically Jewish in the sense that its vision drew its sustenance from internal sources of the Jewish tradition. Second, since this Jewry was most emphatic (apart from some significant exceptions noted earlier) in its espousal of "Torah only," extrapolation from its own sources to Torah Umadda reveals that its "Torah only" stance was at bottom one of prudence rather than principle or philosophy.

In order to derive such conclusions, it is necessary first to sketch in the larger ideational context of the divergence between Hasidism and Mitnagdism on certain fundamentals.

Judaism posits both the transcendence of and immanence of God—His closeness to and withinness in the world, and His total otherness and infinite remoteness from the mundane spheres. Two familiar terms from both the Torah and the liturgy may be said to represent these two facets of Divinity: *kedushah,* holiness, implies transcendence, and *kavod* or "glory" indicates immanence.

However, in assessing the relative importance and significance of these two dimensions of Divinity, we find a substantial difference between the mitnagdim, represented by the Gaon of Vilna and R. Hayyim, and the hasidim, especially of the school of the Maggid, most forcefully expounded by R. Shneour Zalman.

For Mitnagdism, man relates to God primarily through His transcendence. In His transcendence, He spoke to Israel and gave them the Torah and the commandments. Because of this, it is possible for man to grasp the divine Will both intellectually and spiritually; whereas divine immanence, which is uniformly present in all creation, and which man must be aware of and acknowledge, is uncognizable. We can know *about it,* but cannot know *it.* Now, since we do not relate to God's immanence via the Torah and its mitzvot, the world as such (in which Divinity is immanent) fails to achieve the level of holiness. Nature has no special claim on religious value. There seems to be no plausible rationale, therefore, for the study of the world in a Torah context.

Hasidism, however, took the diametrically opposite view. It placed the greatest emphasis on divine immanence and on our relating to Him through that immanence. Its literature is laced with quotations from the Bible and the Zohar that are invoked in defense of its immanentistic position: "Thou givest life to them all" (Nehemiah 9:6); "The fullness of the whole earth declares His glory" (Isaiah 6:3); "There is no place that is empty of Him,"[6] and so on. We must acknowledge divine transcendence but can have no personal relationship with it. Torah and mitzvot are the expression of divine immanence as they deal with this-worldly matters. Thus, while transcendence is inaccessible, this material, phenomenal world is the stage on which the drama of man's encounter and dialogue with his Creator takes place. Hence, the stories of the Baal Shem Tov communing with Nature, learning the language of the beasts, and deciphering the rustle of the leaves. And hence, too, the narrowing of the gap between the sacred and profane, with the consequent idea that Nature is pregnant with spiritual potential.[7]

For the mitnagdic world, the element of holiness is reserved for Torah alone, which is the exclusive channel for relating to God. This principle was enunciated by R. Hayyim as a foundation of his (mitnagdic) outlook and was a consequence of his assertion of a vast qualitative difference between the supernal origin of Torah and that of the other "worlds." Nature has its origin in God, of course, but it is the result of long *hishtalshelut,* a kind of reverse or down-sloping evolution, whereas Torah is a direct and unmediated manifestation of the Deity and hence preserves its primordial sanctity. He *created* Nature; but He *is in* Torah.[8]

The question of the holiness potential of Nature is ultimately dependent on whether one takes an emanationist or creationist view of the origin of the cosmos. A created world essentially means a desacralized cosmos, the handiwork of the Creator that does not, however, share in His holiness; whereas an emanated world implies that Nature retains, albeit in highly diminished form, ontological traces of the sanctity of the Source. In this connection one cannot help but feel that R. Hayyim would much have preferred a creationist view, but could not because he was operating within the Lurianic (and hence emanationist) context. He does his best to avoid accepting the sacredness of Nature by positing an abyss between Nature as the product of long development and Torah as an unmediated manifestation of the *Ein-Sof.*

Now, the fact that Nature is, according to the mitnagdic view, utterly profane, does not mean that Madda-study is necessarily prohibited or inherently evil. It may, however, be in violation of the injunction to avoid *bittul Torah,* the illicit waste of time better reserved for the study of Torah. That has been discussed in Chapter 3.

Is there any way to formulate a more vigorous role for Madda—as a spiritual good in Judaism rather than as a concession to human weakness or economic need—within this mitnagdic framework?

In order to discover such an assertive role, it is necessary to understand the two ways of analogizing the relationship be-

tween Torah and Madda (or Nature) according to the mitnagdic view.

NOTES

1. See Chapter 4, note 13, and the beginning of Chapter 5, on this
theme as it relates to Maimonides and Hirsch.

2. See Salo W. Baron, *A Social and Religious History of the Jews* (New
York: Columbia University Press, 1952), vol. 1, pp. 198f. Not only Jews,
but non-Jews too shared this conviction. Thus, Ambrose and his student
Augustine held that the ideas of Plato and the Pythagoreans came to them
from the Jews; similarly, some held (while others denied) that Plato was an
"Attic Moses"—see E. G. Weltin, *Athens and Jerusalem* (Atlanta, GA:
Scholars Press, 1983), Chapter 1.

3. *Zohar Hadash,* Genesis 5b.

4. *Avot* 3:9.

5. In R. Loewe's *Netivot Olam, Netiv ha-Torah* (Prague, 1596), Chapter
14.

6. *Tikkunei Zohar* 57, p. 91b.

7. See my *Torah Lishmah* (New York: Yeshiva University Press,
1989), pp. 9–18 and 82f., and my "The Phase of Dialogue and Reconciliation" in *Tolerance and Movements of Religious Dissent in Eastern Europe,* ed.
Bela K. Kiraly (New York: Columbia University Press, 1975), pp.
115–129.

8. Hillel Zeitlin, in *Pardes ha-Hasidut ve'ha-Kabbalah* (Tel Aviv, 1960),
pp. 22–24, wrote that while others believe in "Torah from Heaven"—the
standard term for the Jewish belief in the Divine origin of the Torah—
Hasidism believes in "Torah that is Heaven." The epigram is, however,
more appropriate for R. Hayyim and the Mitnagdim than for Hasidism.

CHAPTER 8

The Instrumentalist Model: Perfumers, Cooks, and Bakers

"Hekhsher Mitzvah"

The simplest and most direct way of constructing a model of Torah Umadda based on the mitnagdic assertion of the Torah/Nature dualism is by viewing Madda as *hekhsher mitzvah*, the preparation for a mitzvah. This is a halakhic term that denotes an act devoid of innate religious value, but one that derives its significance from its utility in making possible or enhancing a mitzvah. This approach thus envisions Madda as having *instrumental* value.

Torah, as said, always possesses holiness. Nature, while it never attains that level, does have the potential for endowing its study with the rank of *hekhsher mitzvah* if it is pursued with the intention of leading to an act of mitzvah, specifically, in this case, that of *Talmud Torah*; for any profane act can be ennobled if it is performed *le'shem shamayim*, "for the sake of

Heaven." This is the conventional interpretation of the talmudic dictum, "Let all your acts be for the sake of Heaven."[1]
Just as eating or drinking or working can be ennobled if
performed "for the sake of Heaven," in the sense that it is
intended as a spur to a mitzvah to be executed at some later
time, so can secular studies be viewed as ancillary to the life of
mitzvot and the study of Torah; and in that sense it is an
expression of performing all one's deeds for the sake of
Heaven.

This accords with the view of the Vilna Gaon, who
encouraged his disciples to translate the masterpieces of
secular knowledge into Hebrew so that they could be used to
enhance Torah learning. It is worth repeating the words of
the Gaon as cited by his disciple, R. Baruch of Shklov: "To
the degree that one lacks in his knowledge of other [branches
of] Wisdom, he lacks a hundredfold in the wisdom of Torah,
for Wisdom and Torah are intertwined."[2] The corpus of
"other [branches of] Wisdom" or Madda thus helps one
better to understand the depths of Torah. It is a *hekhsher
mitzvah* (although from the final clause in the quotation from
the Gaon, "for Wisdom and Torah are intertwined," one
would grant far greater value to Wisdom or Madda than, for
instance, to earning a living).

Now if, as stated, we accept the premise that the study of
Madda has positive value, in the instrumental sense of *hekhsher
mitzvah,* it is not open to the charge of *bittul Torah*—even without the excuse of earning a livelihood. Nevertheless, it is obvious that Torah and Madda do *not* have equal value. In the
passage just cited, the Gaon is approving, in a limited sense, the
study of "Wisdom" as an aid to the better comprehension of
Torah, not as an independent good. One must be cautious in
reading too much into this statement of the Gaon, as has indeed
been done since it was first recorded by R. Baruch in the Gaon's
lifetime. It may by no means be taken to imply a blanket en-

dorsement of secular studies in their own right as having intrinsic religious value, but it most certainly does support the
view of Wisdom as a legitimate auxiliary of Torah study, having the instrumental value of *hekhsher mitzvah*.[3]

This view is not very different from that advanced by
Maimonides in a responsum.[4] He said that all forms of
Wisdom are "perfumers and cooks and bakers" for Torah,
which remains the superior mistress over all Wisdom. It is,
essentially, the view of Samson Raphael Hirsch as well. Moreover, as it emerges from the matrix of Lithuanian Rabbinism
or Mitnagdism, its formulation is appropriate to the substratum of halakhic thought prevalent in mitnagdic circles. As
such, it completely fulfills Hirsch's requirement that the approach to Wisdom (*derekh eretz,* in his language) issue from
within Jewish sources and not be imposed as a "reconciliation" from without. What such an approach lacks in Western
sophistication it more than compensates for in its unquestioned validity as reflective of an independent and organically
Jewish orientation.

This important, albeit restricted, version of Torah Umadda
has ample historic precedent. For instance, in Chapter 2 we
gave a brief history of the Yavneh educational system in
Lithuania following World War I. The curriculum included
instruction in general or secular education and in Jewish
philosophy and history as well as in Talmud. The secondary
school in this system was even called "The Universal School
for Torah Umadda." And it received not only the approbation
but also the active participation and leadership of such universally acclaimed luminaries as Rabbi Abraham Duber Kahana
Shapira of Kovno, Rabbi Joseph Leb Bloch of Telshe, and
other dignitaries. A number of the graduates of Yavneh went
on to study in universities, their faith unimpaired. The dom-
inant theme of the enterprise was undoubtedly the instrumentalist version of Torah Umadda.

Variations on the Instrumentalist Theme

Another way of looking at this theme of Madda as an instrument for the enhancement of Torah is by referring to Torah and Madda respectively as *hayyei olam* (eternal life) and *hayyei shaah* (temporal life), a pair of concepts known to us from the Talmud.[5] Madda, in its most comprehensive definition, is a matter of temporal life, for one is engaged in it as long as he lives, but it does not survive him to the world-to-come, for in the world of utter spirituality there is no need for this kind of wisdom. Not so, obviously, for Torah, which is considered eternal life as in the concluding blessing over the reading of the Torah that describes it as such.

Furthermore, Madda may be identified as temporal life because the subject matter of Madda—namely, the world—is finite. It may take another thousand years to unravel all of nature's secrets, but the secrets are no more infinite than the created world itself. Torah, however, is eternal, and therefore the study of Torah is endless (thus, the Talmud's magnificent and characteristic portrayal of the world-to-come as the place where the righteous study Torah in a celestial yeshiva forever). This articulates nicely with R. Hayyim's distinction between Torah and Creation.

But if, indeed, Torah and Madda are equivalent, respectively, to eternal and temporal life, how can we assign any innate value, even of an instrumentalist rank, to Madda alongside Torah? The answer is, of course, that temporal life too is of value. The Talmud, comparing prayer with Torah, refers to the former as temporal life and the latter as eternal life. So, while this inequality guarantees the subordination of temporal life to eternal life, and hence Madda to Torah, it does affirm a place of honor for Madda alongside prayer.

The eternal/temporal metaphor for an instrumentalist model of Torah Umadda is capable of yet a third definition, this one offered by Rav Kook.[6] He defines temporal life as that which gives life and meaning to the ephemeral aspects of existence, and eternal life as that which contributes life force and energy to eternity. This highly interesting definition has its roots in the teaching of R. Hayyim, for whom the study of Torah empowers and vitalizes the highest mystical or spiritual worlds. Hence temporal life, in turn, must mean the vitalization of and the endowment of meaning on this phenomenal, empirical, mundane sphere of existence, what in kabbalistic terminology is known as the *olam ha-asiyah* ("The World of Action"—the lowest of the quaternity of mystical worlds that mediate between the Ein-Sof and our phenomenal world)—a lower world, but a world nonetheless, and no less a creation and thus expression of the Will of the Creator.

Madda, from this perspective, means not only the (passive) study of secular wisdom, but it implies the need for creativity and leadership in Madda—the infusion of "life" into such studies—as a meritorious religious act. By the same token, Torah implies not only learning, but actively expanding and energizing Torah and the universe of Torah, putting one's heart and soul into it as the *summum bonum* of one's existence.

NOTES

1. *Avot* 2:17.

2. See the introduction to his Hebrew translation of the Book of Euclid (Hague: 1780).

3. See the illuminating article by Emanuel Etkes, "The Gaon of Vilna and the Haskala: Image and Reality," in *Studies in the History of Jewish Society in the Middle Ages and in Modern Times* (Hebrew) (Jerusalem: Magnes Press, 1980).

4. This was quoted and discussed in Chapter 4. Note that this is not to be taken as representative of Maimonides' "mainstream" view.

5. As in *Shabbat* 10a and 33b and elsewhere.

6. Quoted by Rabbi Shelomoh Yosef Zevin in his *Ishim ve'Shitot* (Jerusalem: Zioni, 1958), p. 213.

CHAPTER 9

THE INCLUSIONARY MODEL:
MADDA AS TEXTLESS TORAH

The second model of Torah Umadda that may be constructed on mitnagdic sources also makes use of a characteristic mitnagdic view, one enunciated by R. Hayyim Volozhiner with a generous helping of support from Maimonides. Indeed, it is functionally the Maimonidean model of Torah Umadda, except that it is based on East European halakhic ideas along with the views of Maimonides instead of being based exclusively on the rationalistic metaphysics adopted by Maimonides.

The kabbalists pointed out that *olam,* "world," comes from *he'elem,* "hiddenness," because the world is a disguise of God; He is hidden, as it were, within it. Now, if indeed the world is an emanation or disguise of God, although far lower and more indirect than Torah, then may not the study of this world under a certain set of conditions be considered a form of Torah study, albeit of a much lower rank than the study of actual halakhic texts? If "the heavens declare the glory of God," as

161

the psalmist put it (Psalm 19:2), is not astronomy or astrophysics a form of *intellectual worship* of God, and does not such intellectual worship imply a form of *Talmud Torah,* so that the study of Madda may be included in the study of Torah?

LEVELS IN THE STUDY OF TORAH

R. Hayyim posits a hierarchy of texts and their values within *Talmud Torah.* He approvingly quotes from *Midrash Tehillim* (1:8) that David pleaded that learning his Book of Psalms should be considered on a par with learning the mishnaic tractates of *Nega'im* and *Ohalot,* that is, regular halakhic study. Since there is no indication that his plea was granted, R. Hayyim assumes that the divine response was negative. Hence, the highest value is assigned to the study of Halakhah. Thus, while *Talmud Torah* includes a variety of subjects and texts, including such things as the recitation of Psalms, they do not have equal rank with the study of Halakhah.[1]

Interestingly, R. Hayyim also asserts that just as each verse, indeed each letter, in a Torah scroll is equal in holiness to any other, so is all of Torah of uniform and equal sanctity and one may not make invidious distinctions within Torah. Thus, for instance, he considers the study of arcane and apparently irrelevant sections of the order of *Kodoshim,* dealing with the preexilic laws of sacrifices, to be as holy and significant as the study of *Shulhan Arukh Orah Hayyim,* which is the standard code of law for contemporary daily living.

Now, this seemingly contradicts what we just said in R. Hayyim's name concerning the Book of Psalms. However, I believe there is no inconsistency if we accept that what he is saying is that there is a hierarchy of values in the various branches of Torah, so that Halakhah is superior to Psalms—indeed it is preeminent among all such branches of Torah—but that within each branch one may not assert priorities in value and sanctity.

Thus, if one studies Agadah, he is credited with the reward for the study of Torah, although not on the same level as Halakhah.[2] What of, let us say, the ethical literature, the *sifrei musar?* Clearly, if such works contain quotations from Bible and Talmud, they too are considered *Talmud Torah;* but if not, is such study to be designated as *bittul Torah,* an invalid waste of time that ought to have been dedicated to Torah study, or may such study be categorized as satisfying the requirements of the mitzvah to study the Torah?

R. Hayyim himself does not touch on this question directly in any of his own writings, that is, his *Nefesh ha-Hayyim* and the few responsa of his that have survived. But there is ample oral testimony from his disciples indicating that he did indeed regard such efforts as *bittul Torah.*[3] Hence, we shall call upon Maimonides for assistance in this matter. With his help, and according to R. Hayyim's hierarchical view of *Talmud Torah,* we may find a role for the study of Madda within the realm of Torah.

MAIMONIDES ON TEXTLESS TORAH

Maimonides, as we pointed out in Chapter 4, holds that Madda has *Talmud Torah* value. Although, as stated, R. Hayyim himself does *not* subscribe to this view, we may proceed to integrate the Maimonidean position into the framework of R. Hayyim's hierarchical view of *Talmud Torah.* We may then say that just as R. Hayyim envisions a hierarchy of *texts* of *Talmud Torah,* so is there a category of *Talmud Torah* that is *textless,* a form of Torah study that calls for intellection but has no formal, canonized text upon which such thinking is focused. Madda is that textless subject of *Talmud Torah.*

Now, if Madda is to be accepted as included in *Talmud Torah,* we are presented with some immediate questions, namely: Should one recite a *birkhat ha-torah* (the blessing mandated for the formal study of Torah) upon studying organic chemistry? Or, equally absurd, may one study calculus all day and thereby be halakhically exempt from all other *Talmud Torah* that day?

The first question can be answered quite simply. The Torah blessing is restricted to *texts* of Torah and the review, explication, and analysis of such texts, Written or Oral, and is not to be recited in the absence of a specific text or its derivatives. Nevertheless, the study of matters that Maimonides classifies as *Pardes,* or what we call Madda, remains a case of *Talmud Torah.*[4] Hence, the study of physics, for example, done in the proper manner, is an act of study of Torah but requires no blessing.

The second question, about the division of one's time, can be dealt with similarly. Maimonides' teaching about dividing one's time into three equal parts holds true, he says,[5] only for the *early* part of one's career in studying Torah; but once a student has made reasonable progress, so that he has learned all of Scripture and no longer has to spend much time in the Oral Law, he ought to set aside a certain amount of time for these branches of Torah "so that he does not forget any of the laws of the Torah"; and then he ought to spend the rest of his time in Gemara "according to the breadth of his mind and maturity of his intellect."

Thus, after one has learned Scripture well and has made an earnest start on Mishnah, he can devote larger amounts of time to Gemara which, according to Maimonides, includes not only original creative thinking in Halakhah but also *Pardes* (which, again according to Maimonides, means natural science and speculative philosophy). Hence, for the more advanced student, the learning of Scripture and Oral Law is meant not only to fulfill the mitzvah of *Talmud Torah* but also to avoid violating the commandment not to forget Torah. But the fulfillment of the commandment of *Talmud Torah* comes equally in the area of Gemara, which now includes what we would today call Talmud, and, as well, the subjects that properly belong in the category of Madda, especially the sciences and humanities.

Hence, if we define academic studies as primarily career preparation, the time so spent is not at all to be included in the schedule of *Talmud Torah;* and all the rest of one's time—the hours spent in the "sacred studies"—ought to be divided according to the subjective criterion proposed by Maimonides: namely, in addition to Scripture and Mishnah, the Madda courses, "according to the breadth of his mind and maturity of his intellect." But if we define our secular subjects (excluding clearly vocational ones such as accounting) as fitting into the category of Gemara, then Madda should be formally included in the time allotted to Torah, and our division of time should arouse no special criticism. So long as we continue to learn Scripture and Oral Law to acquire new knowledge and to refrain from forgetting what we know, then the study of the sciences and humanities is, in effect, the study of Gemara and thus a fulfillment of the study of Torah, with the division of time for the two curricula depending on the subjective criterion of "according to the breadth of his mind and maturity of his intellect."

Hence, the proposal that Madda might be assigned *Talmud Torah* value under certain conditions is not really that revolutionary, or even that novel.

IN FEAR AND TREMBLING

Of course, the view of Madda as included under the rubric of Torah study depends on the attitude that informs such study. The Talmud teaches that Torah must be studied "in fear and awe and trembling and reverence," the same emotions that possessed Israel when the Torah was first given at Mount

Horeb (Sinai).[6] For Madda, this is critical in determining if study has any *Talmud Torah* value, no matter what its position on the scale. If such awe and reverence are present, then this subjective attitude converts a neutral or indifferent cognitive exercise into *Talmud Torah,* albeit of a rank considerably below that of Halakhah. In the absence of such fundamentally religious emotions, Madda remains a profane activity, completely devoid of any sacred value as *Talmud Torah.*

We cannot leave the subject of Madda as textless Torah without clarifying two points. First, we must reiterate that although we have included it in the Torah Umadda models based on East European (especially mitnagdic) thought, it owes more to Maimonides than to R. Hayyim. The latter's contribution to this inclusionary model is the assertion of a hierarchy of subject matter in the mitzvah of *Talmud Torah* (which was a major ploy in establishing the preeminence of halakhic–talmudic studies in Judaism), but the essence of the idea that secular studies can be integrated into a *Talmud Torah* framework owes more to Fostat than to Volozhin.

The advantage of this inclusionary model, which draws upon both sources, over the pure rationalist model of Maimonides, lies in the former's independence from any specific philosophic doctrine, such as rationalism itself. This is the major weakness of Maimonides' model, in seeking to adopt it as a basis for Torah Umadda. The inclusionary model is, as it were, content-neutral with regard to the nature of the Madda involved. It salvages from Maimonides the extremely significant teaching that Madda may indeed be included as *Talmud Torah,* but without identifying any specific doctrine and, moreover, without commenting on the Maimonidean definitions of *maaseh bereshit* and *maaseh merkavah* as, respectively, natural science and philosophy, or physics and metaphysics, definitions that would be hard to sustain or justify today.

The second point is that the strength of this model is also its weakness. The subjective attitude to Madda can convert it into an act of *Talmud Torah,* but the minute that attitude fades from one's consciousness, the Torah dimension vanishes, leaving Madda a strictly profane enterprise. As we shall see, the model discussed in the next chapter, which also relies on a subjective approach, avoids this pitfall by positing a broader fundamental commitment of one's entire personality in his orientation to the totality of life and experience, and thus is not contingent upon subtle and momentary shifts in one's moods or thoughts.

NOTES

1. R. Hayyim of Volozhin, *Nefesh ha-Hayyim* (4:2).

2. R. Hayyim identifies Halakhah as the *Will* of God and Agadah as the *Word* of God, and while the study of each is equally an act of automatic *devekut* or communion, Agadah is subordinate to Halakhah in the fulfillment of the study of *Torah lishmah.* See *Nefesh ha-Hayyim* 4:6, and my *Torah Lishmah* (New York: Yeshiva University Press, 1989), pp. 280 and 297, note 33.

3. See ibid., p. 289 and p. 305, note 95 for documentation.

4. In halakhic terminology, the *kiyyum mitzvat Talmud Torah* is executed through the intellectual service of God, *avodat ha-Shem al yedei ha-sekhel,* whereas the prescribed form it must take, the *ma'aseh mitzvah,* is restricted to formal texts of the corpus of the Written and the Oral Laws.

5. *Hil. Talmud Torah* 1:11, 12.

6. *Ber.* 22a.

CHAPTER 10

THE HASIDIC MODEL:
MADDA AS WORSHIP

A hasidic model for Torah Umadda? The suggestion itself, the very conjunction of the two terms, seems implausible if not incredible.

Indeed, hasidic masters have been virtually unanimous in banning "alien studies," in the rare event that the issue arose at all, and some have been sharply critical of their more intellectually inclined colleagues for submitting too quickly to the temptation of "philosophy." Faith is sufficient without "investigation," and Torah is whole and self-sustaining without the help of the world's Wisdom.

R. Nahman of Bratzlav (1772–1810), great-grandson of R. Israel Baal Shem Tov, the founder of Hasidism, and himself one of the most important figures in the history of the movement, maintained that faith is inapplicable when the intellect understands, and therefore intellectual speculation is irrelevant to faith.[1] He believed the medieval Jewish philosophers were wrong, even "evil," in declaring that knowledge is the

purpose of existence, that "the essence of the attainment of
one's purpose is by means of speculations and secular
sciences."[2] The purpose of life is Torah and piety, and this
purpose is attained by simplicity and artlessness—and not by
studying "the books of [secular] wisdom, Heaven forbid."[3]
Amalek, the biblical archetype of wickedness, was an in-
quirer, a philosopher, and R. Nahman wrote that in each of the
sciences there lies ensconced something of Amalek that causes
man to stumble and fall and fail to reach his goal in life; hence,
none but the *Zaddik* (the hasidic master, who has steeled
himself against the temptations of Amalek) may venture into
that perilous domain.[4]

Pure faith—faith that comes to us through holy tradition
alone—is akin to "hearing," whereas faith that relies upon
speculation partakes of the nature of "seeing," and we hold
the former to be superior to and more enduring than the latter.
So teaches R. Zvi Elimelech Shapira of Dinov (1783–1841).[5]
Those who feel a need for independent rational or intellectual
verification of their faith are of suspect genealogy, according
to this belief, for true descendants of Father Abraham, like
their biblical progenitor, are possessed of "natural" faith.

That same formulation unquestionably applies to Torah
Umadda. Our task thus is a formidable one.

We turn, therefore, to the hasidic world, so rich and original
in religious thought, to see if—despite the explicit rejection of
independent sources of religious knowledge and thus by implication all of Torah Umadda—we can mine some of its
treasures for nuggets of guidance in this area of Torah
Umadda. Our conclusion will be that it yields probably the
most potent confirmation of the legitimacy of Torah and
Wisdom.

WORSHIP THROUGH CORPOREALITY

We pointed out earlier the emphasis of Hasidism on divine
immanence, God's closeness to man and "withinness" in the

world. Far more than did the mitnagdic approach, this vision invested the world with the possibility and promise of holiness. The ordinary, trite, mundane, natural world was suddenly opened up to the creative spiritual energies of hasidim brimming with a divine enthusiasm, an unquenchable flame of faith.[6]

The religious energies released by this new form of *avodat ha-Shem,* the worship of God, carried with it the dangers of antinomianism, of overrunning the Halakhah, which insisted on fundamental distinctions between the sacred and the profane, the forbidden and the tolerated and the mandated. But its fires were banked and its excessive enthusiasm dampened, and Hasidism remained within the fold of normative Judaism.

A corollary of Hasidism's emphasis on immanence that became one of the most significant and characteristic contributions of the Baal Shem Tov and was elaborated on by such greats as the Maggid of Mezeritch (d. 1772), R. Yaakov Yosef of Polonnoye (d. 1782), R. Elimelech of Lizensk (1717–1786), and R. Nachum of Chernobyl (1730–1798), is the concept of *avodah be'gashmiut*—serving God with and through our very corporeality, worshiping Him in our material, physical situations.

The concept of *avodah be'gashmiut* is that God's immanence in all creation—in Nature as well as in Torah—means that the mundane, physical order represents a legitimate avenue of approach to God. An oft-quoted source for this theory is to be found in *Midrash Talpiot* to the effect that the biblical Enoch was a cobbler, and over every stitch he would recite the words, "Blessed is the Name of His glorious kingdom forever and ever." *Avodat ha-Shem* can be expressed not only through the formally sanctioned means of *Talmud Torah,* mitzvot, and prayer, but also informally by involving oneself with certain specific attitudes in the whole realm of creation and the corporeal world. Thus, we have two forms of *avodat ha-Shem: avodah be'ruhaniut,* serving Him through the spirit, the standard halakhic means; and *avodah be'gashmiut,* the informal, extra-halakhic way of "worship through corporeality." Each is a legitimate way of serving the Creator.

In elaborating the idea of "worship through corporeality," Hasidism insisted that the perimeters of divine worship be expanded to include *all* life and all times so that the Jew be pervasively God-conscious.

R. Zvi Hirsch of Zhydachov (d. 1831), more than most other hasidic thinkers, puts into bold relief the truly innovative aspect of Hasidism's doctrine of *avodah be'gashmiut.* The classical rabbinic view, he tells us, is represented by the medieval *dayyan,* philosopher, and ethicist, R. Bahya, in Chapter 5 of his classical *Hovot ha-Levavot* ("Duties of the Heart"). There he speaks of *yihud ha-maaseh,* the dedication of all one's activities to divine service. All bodily functions, all one's mundane occupations, must be pursued with the thought that they somehow lead to divine worship by strengthening the body, achieving economic sustenance, and so on, so as the better to serve Him. It is this thesis that is codified in the standard halakhic code, the *Shulhan Arukh.*[7] (We recognize this, of course, as the instrumentalist approach, whereby the profane is the means to attain the sacred—"perfumers and cooks and bakers" for Torah.)

Now, says the Zhydachover, while that certainly is commendable, it is not ultimate. There is a yet higher category, that of *avodah tammah,* "perfect service." The Talmud declares this to be the highest form, beyond which there is no greater. The kind of service proposed by R. Bahya, however, cannot be that ultimate service, for while one's activities are ennobled by regarding them as necessary for *avodat ha-Shem,* they are not now in and of themselves of any significance, as are, for example, prayer or study of Torah; they are of instrumental, not intrinsic, value—*hekhsher mitzvah,* not mitzvah itself.

Hasidic teaching, however, does provide that highest form

and derives it from the Lurianic doctrine that all existence is sustained by the holy sparks of divinity that are the vehicles of divine immanence. When one is involved in any worldly matter, he has it in his power, by virtue of his thoughts and intentions, to liberate those sparks, returning them to their divine Source. This act of the redemption or elevation of the divine sparks is, in and of itself, an act of the greatest religious significance, not merely an instrument for some later fulfillment. (It is irrelevant for this thesis that Hasidism changed the nature of the thought processes that Luria recommended, from mystical meditations to ecstatic enthusiasm.) The point is that one can perform genuine *avodat ha-Shem* by engaging in the corporeal realm, here and now.[8]

As mentioned, nature, natural acts, or the study of nature can attain significance as an act of *hekhsher mitzvah* according to the mitnagdic view, though it possesses only instrumentalist, extrinsic value. For Hasidism, however, a profane act performed for the sake of Heaven is considered *in and of itself* as worthy. If it is so consecrated, its value is intrinsic, it is a worthy fulfillment of the divine Will, and it is not merely propaedeutic to some other good.

WORSHIP THROUGH INTELLECTUALITY

It should by now be obvious that there is a very small step from *avodah be'gashmiut* to Torah Umadda, from worship through corporeality to worship through intellectuality, from the service of God with the body to service of God with the mind. If Hasidism can find the promise of holiness in eating, why not in studying the chemistry of carbohydrates and the physiology of ingestion? If in working with a hammer and a chisel or a cobbler's awl, why not with a theory and a hypothesis? If in conjugal relations, why not in the contemplation of the relations of the business cycle to various arcane mathematical models? The religiously inspired study of Madda is the cognitive equivalent of *avodah be'gashmiut,* worship through corporeality.

Indeed, it is a fact that hasidic rebbeim have been far more open to their followers developing their talents in music and art than have been their counterparts in the yeshiva or the mitnagdic world. Madda, on the basis of *avodah be'gashmiut,* thus appears, in a new dimension, as an authentic and autonomous form of worship, of *avodat ha-Shem.* In this light, Madda is important not only because it helps one to understand Torah, although it most assuredly does that; it is not so much a "perfumer, cook, and baker" as a helpful co-wife to Torah. And Madda's significance is established not only because we can assign it a value of *Talmud Torah* on a lower level, as in the inclusionary model we suggested, but because it is, *in its own right,* a sacred activity—provided, and *always* provided, that it is pursued *as an act of avodat ha-Shem,* and not merely for career reasons, cultural curiosity, or because it is socially expected.

Surprisingly, therefore, this extrapolation of basic hasidic doctrine yields a much more affirmative and dynamic vision of Torah Umadda than is otherwise available once its implications are properly spelled out. This is not merely a dispensation for Torah Umadda. It is a Divine imperative, a charge to seek inspiration in the broadest realms of the intellect and imagination.

Just as Hasidism succeeded in expanding the realm of the sacred to cover the profane—the very opposite notion from contemporary secularism, which is antagonistic to the encroachment by the sacred on the public domain and seeks to restrict the sacred—by making available the *adiaphora* (religiously neutral) world of ordinary physical and natural activity to the movement of sacralization, so may this area of *adiaphora* include the previously nonsacred areas of cognition and culture as candidates for the worship of the Creator.

In its highest, most necessary, and most successful application, this cognitive or intellectual variant of *avodah be'gashmiut* leads us back to the sublime insight of Hasidism: that all of creation, in all its incredible complexity and fantastic richness, is only an illusion, a disguise for the Ein-Sof, a mask for the Divinity that pulsates through all of existence. This ontological radicalism, which crosses all borders and annihilates all distinctions only to regenerate them in new form, allows us to see all of creation, whether Torah or Nature, as conducive to *avodat ha-Shem,* the service of the One Shepherd who both created Nature and revealed Torah.

As attractive and spiritually edifying as this doctrine of worship through corporeality is, it is quite dangerous too. It can be overstated and vulgarized. Perhaps that is why it was originally restricted by Hasidism to the spiritual elite. It is replete with antinomian possibilities; taken too far, it can undermine the Halakhah. Thus, skirting the edges of such peril, R. Nachum Chernobyler writes that *avodah be'gashmiut* is as significant as the mitzvot of *tefillin* and *tzitzit!* A similarly bold statement is made by his contemporary, R. Elimelech of Lizhensk, founder of Hasidism in Galicia:

> For the *Zaddikim,* there is no difference between the study of Torah and prayer [on the one side] or eating and drinking [on the other]. All are . . . [forms of] the service of the Creator, and it is merely a matter of switching from one form of service to another.[9]

Unquestionably, there is more than a little exaggeration in these statements, and the hyperbole underscores the fact that we here face the troubling antinomian conclusion that, for instance, tying one's shoe-laces or eating one's breakfast cereal "for the sake of Heaven" is of equal importance with performing one of the 248 positive commandments. If doing one or the other is merely a matter of "switching from one service to another," then who needs mitzvot altogether? If one can come close to the Creator by *any* act if it is accompanied by the right *kavvanah* (intention), then *all* formal mitzvot are superfluous. Of course, in keeping with the hasidic tendency, manifested so often in its brief history, to skirt the edges of antinomian heresy and pull back before tumbling into the abyss of spiritual lawlessness, neither the Lizhensker nor the Chernobyler ever came to that conclusion; however, they do come uncomfortably close to such explosive, radical consequences.

This is one reason why the early masters of Hasidism preferred to reserve worship through corporeality for *Zaddikim* only, not for *hoi polloi;* spiritual brinksmanship is not a sport for the masses. They feared that spiritual amateurs would abandon the formal mitzvot in favor of seeking religious thrills in the realm of the corporeal—an apprehension quite plausible for those who lived so close to the Sabbatean heresy. Nevertheless, later Hasidism no longer focused on *avodah be'gashmiut* as a major issue on their ideological agenda, certainly not to the extent that the earlier generations did. There is reason to believe that this was not because of the reclaiming of *avodah be'gashmiut* by the *Zaddikim* and its denial to the common folk, but rather for two related reasons: First, it was felt that the crisis had passed and the movement was safe: the anti-halakhic consequences that were so feared had simply failed to materialize. Second, worship through corporeality became "naturalized" in the hasidic community. It had become the accepted norm for thoughtful hasidim, even if they were not themselves *Zaddikim*—the spiritual leadership elite—and there appeared to be no danger of the radicalization of the concept.[10]

We accept this caveat as well as the encouraging lesson from hasidic historical experience for the purpose of worship through intellectuality—the hasidic model of Torah Umadda that we are now proposing. There is no need to limit it to the spiritual aristocracy and the halakhic *cognoscenti* who alone may be entrusted with such perilous doctrine. There is little danger of antinomian exploitation of this interpretation of Torah Umadda; those interested in Torah Umadda in the first instance have opted out of the assimilatory and religiously indifferent majority of Jews who care for neither law nor spirit. What they seek is a way that accommodates the two apparently incongruous cultures to which they are heir, a way of broadening their spiritual outlook so they can comprehend both worlds in one framework. They are not furtively ferreting out esoteric means of expressing halakhic abandon. But the caveat is nonetheless important, lest this doctrine lead to the substitution of Torah by Madda under a pseudoreligious guise.

Hence, it should be made clear that when we propose the hasidic or Madda-as-worship model of Torah Umadda based on this tenet of *avodah be'gashmiut,* we rule out any equality between *avodah be'gashmiut* and a formal mitzvah, and between Torah and Madda. *Avodah be'ruhaniut* (worship through spirituality), the performance of a halakhic act informed by the proper intention, remains superior and absolute; *avodah be'gashmiut* or Madda is subordinate to and also contingent on it. That is, to invoke the talmudic principle, "one who is commanded and does" always takes primacy over "one who is not commanded and does."[11] Indeed, it is *worship through spirituality* that legitimates worship through corporeality and, consequently, Torah that legitimates Madda. The pursuit of Madda without Torah is devoid of any innate Jewish significance. Hence, in addition to requiring that Madda be pursued "for the sake of Heaven"

and in the spirit of awe and reverence recommended by the
Talmud for *Talmud Torah,* the religious legitimacy of Madda
would require that one spend a significant portion of his time
in the formal study of Torah, the *Talmud Torah* component of
avodah be'ruhaniut. With Torah, Madda has not only instrumental but also intrinsic value, but never without it. With
Torah, Madda rises to the unbelievable heights of worship
through corporeality (or, more specifically, worship through
intellectuality). It is the two of them in conjunction that give
our religious experience, our *avodat ha-Shem,* both breadth
and depth. To vulgarize this concept of worship through
corporeality in its proposed contemporary cognitive form by
looking on it as an excuse to minimize the study of Torah or
to deny its centrality, either theoretically or functionally, is to
distort it most deplorably.

Perhaps an appropriate and helpful analogy is the difference
between the required sacrifice (*korban hovah*) and the good-
will offering (*korban nedavah*). The former, legally mandated
and independent of the volition and good will of the worshiper, retains formal superiority as the act of "one who is
commanded and does," for it embodies the heteronomous
value of a divine commandment. The latter, originating in the
conscience and generosity of the worshiper as an act of faith
and good will—"one who is not commanded and does"—
becomes sacred by virtue of a special and conscious act of
sanctification by man. In Judaism, doing the required is considered more meritorious than doing the voluntary out of the
goodness of one's heart.[12]

It must be emphasized again that there is here no hint
whatsoever that, historically, hasidic leaders approved of secular studies. On the contrary, the fear of the contamination of
pure faith by the dark forces unleashed by modernity at all
times overcame what otherwise might have been a more
positive accommodation of Madda as part of Hasidism's en-

deavor to sanctify all life, even beyond the strict requirements of the Halakhah. What we have here attempted is to spell out the implications of certain of its key principles and values—implications that hasidic thinkers themselves failed to spell out because of extraneous considerations, such as those mentioned.

It is important to reiterate what was said at the end of Chapter 9: The inclusion of Madda in the category of the corporeal, which we can exploit as a medium for the worship of God, is not meant for an occasional spurt of sanctification, when one is moved by the spirit. Such sporadic acts of consciousness are necessary for the treatment of Madda as a textless form of *Talmud Torah,* as in the inclusionary model. *Avodah be'gashmiut,* however, is not an act or an isolated event but a permanent state of mind. It is the expression of a spiritual *Weltanschauung,* a comprehensive world-view in which all natural activity, cognitive as well as corporeal, is accepted as the normative framework within which the growth and progress of sanctification and worship are carried out. The very term for worship is *avodah,* the primary signification of which is servitude. The bondsman who is in service to his master is not hired by the hour; he is not a part-time worker. His servitude defines his status as a whole. So, too, for the hasidic model, or the Madda-as-worship form of Torah Umadda: "worship" characterizes the existential situation and is pervasive, not sporadic and episodic. Madda as worship requires an orientation of mind and spirit permanently fixed in one's psyche, so that the drama of sanctification comprehends all of life in all its marvelous richness and variety, whether or not we are specifically and explicitly aware of each individual act in the ongoing process.

Of all the versions of Torah Umadda mentioned, this hasidic model is most closely allied to the mystical model suggested by Rav Kook. The similarities are self-evident. How-

ever, there are differences, too, and these are discussed in the
coming chapter.

NOTES

1. R. Nahman of Bratzlav, *Likkutei Etzot, Emet ve'Emunah* (Warsaw,
1875), sec. 4.

2. R. Nahman of Bratzlav, *Likkutei MoHaRaN* (Lemberg, 1826), vol.
2, p. 19.

3. Ibid.

4. Ibid.

5. R. Zvi Elimelech Shapira of Dinov, *Benei Yisaskhor,* Adar 3, Derush
2.

6. A particularly interesting passage demonstrating the intimate relationship between Torah and Nature in hasidic thinking may be found in
the work of R. Zadok Hakohen of Lublin (1823–1900), *Tzidkat ha-Tzaddik*
(Lublin: Schneidmesser and Hirschenhorn Printers, 1902), # 216. He
heard, says the author, that the world is a book written by God (and hence
the source of Abraham's discovery of God, presumably the forerunner of
the argument from design—the teleological proof of God's existence) and
that the Torah is the commentary on that book. Moreover, the renewal of
creation daily by God finds its echo in Torah: thus the *hiddush* in Nature is
occasioned by the *hiddushei Torah,* novellae or creative thinking in Torah.
See also his *Peri Tzaddik* (Lublin, 1933), *Be'midbar, Rosh Hodesh Tammuz.*
This leads to further development of the possibility of religious sanc-
tioning of the "secular" study of the world.

7. *Orah Hayyim* 231.

8. See R. Zvi Hirsch of Zydachov, *Sur Me-Ra va-Aseh Tov* (Tel Aviv,
1969), pp. 116 ff. This is a faithful summary of the Beshtian doctrine on
this subject; see R. Yaakov Yosef of Polonnoye, *Toledot Yaakov Yosef*
(Vilna, 1868), to *Bo,* s.v. *Dabber,* and in *Ben Porat Yosef* (Pietrokow, 1883),
p. 46b. Actually, a much earlier, pre-hasidic source for this very idea may
be found in *Derashot ha-Ran, Derush* 6, p. 103.

9. *Noam Elimelech* (Warsaw, 1881), *Korah,* s.v. *Ve'neheshav.*

10. This naturalization of the *avodah be'gashmiut* theme in later Hasidism is borne out by a personal experience of the writer. My revered
grandfather of blessed memory, Rabbi Yehoshua Baumol, was a distinguished halakhist and *posek* (decisor) and author of two very important

volumes of halakhic responsa. At the same time, he stemmed from a Galician hasidic background and was himself immersed in hasidic lore and experience. Shortly before his death in New York in 1948, while he was critically ill with the disease to which he ultimately succumbed, he penned a short list of the principles by which he lived and which, together with another and similar document, constituted his ethical will to his family. The following is the second item on the list. The reader will note the unconscious repetition of the theme of R. Elimelech Lizhensker and its vitality—without any radical consequences—a century and a half after the issue came to the fore in early Hasidism:

> You [must] know clearly that the will of the Creator is to act kindly towards us, and every act we perform, to do good for others or for ourselves, is a fulfillment of His will. Hence, even when we are engaged in [such things as] eating and drinking and other enjoyable activities, in keeping with the laws of the Torah—and even when we are occupied in such activities to improve our condition so that we might live in greater peace of mind and the like—we are in communion with Him, may He be blessed, by carrying out His will, *just as we do when we lay the tefillin or perform other mitzvot; for what is the difference between them, since both are His will.*

The phrases that are so reminiscent of the Lizhensker view—indeed, an almost verbatim repetition of the *Noam Elimelech* passage by someone who composed the list of principles in a hospital bed without the benefit of a library or books—are italicized to show the persistence of the *avodah be'gashmiut* theme even in contemporary hasidic thinking. And all this, without any untoward antinomian results.

11. Such is the conclusion of the Talmud's disquisition in *Kiddushin* 31a.

12. See *Kiddushin* 31a.

CHAPTER 11

THE HASIDIC MODEL COMPARED

We have had occasion to compare the views of Rabbis Kook and Hirsch. In this chapter we evaluate the hasidic model of Torah Umadda in relation to the mystical and cultural models.

THE HASIDIC AND THE MYSTICAL MODELS

It is self-evident that the hasidic model, based on the theory of Madda-as-worship, has the greatest affinity for the drama of sanctification of the profane proposed by Rav Kook as the model for the relationship of Torah and Wisdom. This is no accident, given the fact that Madda-as-worship is based on hasidic doctrines and that Rav Kook drew heavily, albeit in his own terminology, on kabbalistic and hasidic sources. It is appropriate at this point, therefore, to compare the two Torah Umadda structures—hasidic and mystical—to see where they agree and where they diverge.

Both see Madda as possessing religious potential, and

therefore view the Torah Umadda enterprise as a religious good, not as a compromise or concession. It must be pursued with spiritual élan and psychological vigor and without apologies.

Both accept an affirmative role for "Torah only" within the perimeters of a Torah Umadda outlook for the total community, with Torah Umadda proponents considerably more tolerant of "Torah only" institutions than was Rabbi Hirsch himself.

Both are based upon a monistic view and consider the primordial unity of all knowledge, indeed all existence, as reflective of the Unity of God.

The differences are more subtle, but substantial enough to warrant the elaboration of Madda-as-worship as a new model of Torah Umadda alongside that of Rav Kook. They include the following four elements.

First, Kook's version is more ontological, whereas the hasidic is more existential. The sacred and the profane, the protagonists in the Kookian drama, are objective spiritual entities which, although they are used and activated by the *Homo religiosus,* are possessed of their own autonomous existence. In the hasidic model, the focus is not on the sacred and the profane as such, but on the *Homo religiosus,* the worshiper or *oved ha-Shem* whose thought processes and spiritual strivings, emerging from the totality of his life experiences, are the stuff of which the sanctification drive is constituted. In this sense, the Kook model reflects more the kabbalistic outlook that informs so much of Rav Kook's thinking, whereas the Madda-as-worship model mirrors the hasidic background out of which it is constructed. The latter model of Torah Umadda is thus less esoteric and more accessible.

Second, and following from this, the Kookian mystical

scheme requires a more focused consciousness in the process of sanctification than does the hasidic model, which relies more on the substratum of a generalized approach of the psyche, as mentioned in the preceding chapter. Here again, the Hasidism-based approach appears more accessible and practicable than the Kookian mystical model.

A third difference is akin to what has been mentioned at the end of the last chapter when distinguishing the hasidic from the inclusionary model. More specifically, the mystical model is atomistic: it focuses anew on each contact between the sacred and the profane, demanding a fresh exercise of the religious imagination in the course of the sanctification process. Each triumph of the sacred is separate and distinct from every other. The hasidic model, however, is holistic: it requires the training of one's consciousness to acquire a generalized attitude to *all* profane activity, to approach all one's corporeality (which in this sense includes intellectuality) as an act of worship. The focus of the spiritual exercise is, in the Kookian mystical model, on the particular area of the secular that is being dominated and sanctified. In the hasidic version, the focus is on the self, the subjectivity of the worshiper, for whom this act of sanctification is but one illustration among the many that befall him in the course of daily life.

Fourth, the mystical model must by necessity result in an interaction between the sacred and the profane, especially by the sacred *on* the profane. The question then arises as to the nature of this interaction, or action, and the concomitant problem of the integrity of the secular, especially its methodology. This problem never arises for the hasidic model, because there the center of attention is not the objective encounter of Torah with Wisdom but the subjective consciousness of the worshiper/student. Hence, what the mystical model gains in possible spiritual cognitive creativity, it stands to lose in intellectual integrity. The reverse is true for the hasidic model.

The Hasidic and the Cultural Models

What does an *avodah be'gashmiut* (Madda-as-worship) foundation accomplish for Torah Umadda that makes the hasidic version more viable and responsive than the Hirschian cultural model, *Torah im Derekh Eretz?* Let us respond by referring back to the critique of Hirsch (mentioned in Chapter 5).

However, before reacting to those criticisms *seriatim,* we must address a problem referred to earlier: the question of the nature of the interrelationship between Torah and Wisdom. Is it to be a synthesis or a plan of separate coexistence—peace or an armed truce?

Synthesis or Coexistence?

Professor Zev Falk argues for a genuine synthesis between Torah and Madda (or *Derekh Eretz*).[1] Applying a Hegelian structure, he sees exclusive Torah learning as the thesis, general culture as the antithesis, and *Torah im Derekh Eretz* as the synthesis. But such synthesis is not merely the combination of thesis and antithesis; it is something *new* that transcends both thesis and antithesis. In the present case, it must lead to an integration or interaction of Torah and culture so that a genuine change takes place in the nature of Torah study as well as the study of general culture, resulting in a distinct and observable difference between the Torah study of those who advocate *Torah im Derekh Eretz* and those who follow the traditional modes of Torah study.

However, Falk accuses Hirsch of not carrying this synthesis through to its logical conclusion; had he done so, he would not have had to be defensive about the relatively low level of Torah learning in his movement, but he could have pointed to its qualitative superiority over the traditional forms of learning. Using historical examples, Falk points to Maimonides as one who used his philosophical understanding to offer a new interpretation of Torah. Hirsch, however, gave preference to such Sephardi scholars as Yehuda Halevi and Nahmanides, who kept to the traditional modes of the study of Torah. Hence, Hirsch did not, for instance, agree to give a new interpretation of the creation of the world in Genesis according to the view of geology or evolution. For him, therefore, general culture served only the purpose of "perfumers and cooks and bakers" for Torah. (Indeed, the Hirschian cultural model is at bottom instrumentalist, as mentioned earlier.) This accounts for the failure of *Torah im Derekh Eretz* to raise generations of scholars or rabbis in any significant number.

We noted earlier that Hildesheimer was interpreted by some as favoring synthesis, and by others as advocating coexistence. Not surprisingly, therefore, another writer in the same volume, Professor Mordechai Eliav,[2] sees Hirsch in exactly the opposite way from Falk. Eliav compares Hirsch with Hildesheimer and tells us that one of the major differences between them is in the nature of their conception of *Torah im Derekh Eretz:* Hirsch wanted an absolute and organic synthesis of Torah and general studies, whereas Hildesheimer saw them as cocurricular necessities, but separate categories incapable of ultimate merger. Eliav quotes Mordechai Breuer, approvingly, who says that the difference between Hirsch and Hildesheimer was that Hirsch saw *Torah im Derekh Eretz* as a chemical synthesis, whereas Hildesheimer saw it as a physical mixture! Eliav continues by pointing to Hirsch's early curriculum plans in his *Nineteen Letters of Ben Uziel,* according to which the synthesis of Torah and *Derekh Eretz* was not meant to be a compromise or a concession as a necessary evil, and not as two value systems that were coexistent with each other; rather, while the poles were not equal in value—for Torah remains constant whereas *Derekh Eretz* always changes—they nevertheless merge so that they can no longer be separated, thus conforming to Hirsch's educational ideal of *Jisroel-Mensch*. The ambiguities, or at least the lack of clarity, on such a critical issue by the two major figures of the *Torah im Derekh Eretz* school is certainly puzzling and indicates that they never gave it sustained attention. The question is thus left to students, interpreters, and historians of the movement to decide.

While Falk does not quite spell out what he regards as the ideal synthesis, it appears that for him the ultimate goal of *Torah im Derekh Eretz* is the development of *Wissenschaft des Judentums,* or the academic study of Judaica. If this is indeed Falk's criticism of Hirsch, then it is disappointing. Undoubtedly, academic Jewish studies make a significant contribution—all the pious objections to academic Judaica notwithstanding—but to identify this as the glorious end-product of the encounter between Torah and Western culture is an instance of the proverbial mountain bringing forth a mouse. It is illustrative, moreover, of the truth of the Yiddish saying, *"Yeder darshan darshent far zich,"* every preacher preaches for himself. Plato thought a philosopher should be king; the Sages conceived of the Almighty poring over a tome of the Talmud in the heavens; Albert Einstein once said that God is a mathematician; playwrights love to write about playwrights, and writers about writers; and distinguished academic Judaica scholars *know* that their craft is the ultimate desideratum enabling them to drink the heady brew of the cultural cocktail known as *Torah im Derekh Eretz*. While such a Hegelian synthesis may be beneficial, its benefits are reserved for a small coterie of fine scholars working in only one esoteric area of research. Where does that leave the rest of the Jewish people—

should they decide to accept the basic doctrines common to Torah Umadda and *Torah im Derekh Eretz?*

Moreover, there is serious question as to the other pole— what is to be the fate of the antithesis (secular studies) in a Hegelian synthesis? Surely, intellectual probity calls for some measure of symmetry and reciprocity between the two. If Torah is to emerge changed from its encounter with Wisdom, must not the reverse be true as well? Are we now to have Jewish molecular biology, Jewish differential equations, Jewish macroeconomics . . . and Catholic organic chemistry, Protestant music theory, and Islamic English literature?

Merely phrasing the issue in this manner is enough to reveal its absurdity, in which case simple intellectual equity calls for sensitivity to the probable inauthenticity of the synthesized Torah pole. This points to perils in the process of synthesis: the confusion of methodologies and the consequent obfuscation of content, and the lack of acknowledgment of the integrity of each domain which—while they all derive from a common origin and aspire to a common destiny—is different from and has developed differently from the other one, and should have such differences respected.

Both Falk and Eliav leave us with only two alternatives: either a genuine synthesis or mere coexistence. We shall leave it to the historians to decide who is right in the exegesis of Hirsch. As we have indicated, the point is moot with regard to the evaluation of Hirsch and Hildesheimer; the very existence of so many conflicting interpretations of both men leads one to conclude, as we did earlier, that they never formulated the problem definitively or, indeed, paid much attention to it.

The problem before us, in seeking to elaborate a Torah Umadda vision, is the essential question itself: What kind of relationship between Torah and Wisdom do we envision? Is the kind of Hegelian synthesis advocated by Falk as the highest expression of *Torah im Derekh Eretz* too radical, too specialized, too perilous for the future of Torah, which must survive to face another order of challenges in yet other eras? Is mere coexistence, without interaction, too conducive to a cultural schizophrenia (about which more anon) and more indicative of a curricular scheme than a religious philosophy? Better yet: Who is to say that we have here a forced option, that no other choices exist, that—to quote Mordechai Breuer again—we must emerge with either a chemical synthesis or a physical mixture? Is it not possible for there to be mutual enhancement without radical change? Referring again to Breuer's metaphor, there certainly are intermediate stages between the two extremes of chemical synthesis and mere physical mixture; colloidal suspensions, for instance, allow a thorough intermingling without the essential loss of chemical properties by either ingredient. Or, to use an even better and more appropriate analogy from biology, can we not speak of *symbiosis* instead of *synthesis* or *coexistence?* This third option in the scientific metaphor deserves to be considered by all supporters of Torah and Wisdom, and most especially by the practitioners of the "Science of Judaism."

The author admits, with appropriate professions of shame and inadequacy, that he has not (yet) come to a firm conclusion on the matter. His excuse is that his vision of Torah Umadda as based on *avodah be'gashmiut*—what we have called the hasidic model—does not require of us to make that decision. This vision or construct allows us to undercut the synthesis–coexistence question. It gives us a structural framework without committing us exclusively to either version of Torah Umadda. By stepping back from the dilemma of the nature of the objective encounter between Torah and Wisdom and viewing it from the larger perspective of *avodat ha-Shem,* insisting only that this spiritual element predominate and suffuse any Madda activity, every individual is free to follow his or her own judgment, talent, and inclination in choosing either genuine synthesis or coexistence. If the failure to commit Torah Umadda to a specific mode is a major flaw, then we have not improved over *Torah im Derekh Eretz*. But that is not necessarily the case. This particular model of Torah Umadda locates the fulcrum of the entire enterprise in the individual, as a subjective servant of God, and not in the corpus of either Torah or Madda per se. The question of synthesis versus coexistence is therefore certainly of interest, but the solution is relatively irrelevant, and thus the flaw, if such it is, is not fatal because the engagement in Torah Umadda is fueled by a subjective awareness of the ultimate purpose of one's engagement in Madda—indeed, in all of life, whether in the intellectual realms and the flight of the mind and imagination or in the daily struggle for existence and the thousand distractions, worries, and anxieties that so sorely need the unifying theme of dedication to *avodat ha-Shem*.

CREATIVITY AND CONTINUITY

The criticisms of Hirsch by Jacob Rosenheim—that his Frankfurt school left no true disciples, no one to continue *Torah im Derekh Eretz* as a religious philosophy, and that it lacked creativity—are overly harsh. Often, one man's creativity is the next man's banality. The term *creativity* is not susceptible to easy definition, and one feels that Rosenheim, a genuine religious personality, may have been hypersensitive and therefore overly self-critical as he cast envious sidelong glances eastward at the thriving and flourishing yeshivot of Russia, Poland, and Hungary. But the kinds of creativity evoked in a hermetically sealed, homogeneous society are different from those that develop in communities faced with a clash of cultures, with their charged atmosphere of conflicting values, premises, and aspirations.

Moreover, if indeed Torah Umadda as functionally practiced in the United States and elsewhere represents a continuation of *Torah im Derekh Eretz,* even if in different form as a mutated species, then the shared ideal of both forms has been developing for well over one hundred years; and that is enough, in this frenetic age, to qualify as continuity.

EDUCATING TOWARD GREATNESS

This last point is relevant to the criticism by Rabbi Dessler and others that while Hirsch succeeded in educating laymen, he failed to raise up a corps of learned rabbis and scholars. Although it appears that this was a failure in educational strategy by Hirsch, rather than an integral weakness in his ideology of *Torah im Derekh Eretz,* the fact remains that he did indeed fail in this respect.

It is here that American Torah Umadda has succeeded where German *Torah im Derekh Eretz* has failed. The communal loyalty, in-group cohesiveness, and shared ideals of Hirschian laymen are probably as much the result of Hirsch's *Austritt* policy as of his religious philosophy; but they are superior to that attained by Torah Umadda which, by its very cultural and social openness, loses opportunities to reinforce such inner communal strength. However, Yeshiva University, the institution that most expressly embodies Torah Umadda, has far outdistanced the Frankfurt school in its successful educational achievements. It has not only raised several generations of rabbis as well as Torah-educated laymen, but has produced an impressive number of talmudic scholars, many of them *talmidei hakhamim* of the first rank, who would have been esteemed in the best of the pre-World War II East European yeshivot. This is so because Yeshiva University has affirmed the significance of Torah education in depth as the touchstone of Torah Umadda and of Jewish religious legitimacy by modeling the development of its yeshiva (the Rabbi Isaac Elchanan Theological Seminary) largely on the Lithuanian yeshivot, and by the Seminary's preeminent role in the galaxy of schools that constitute or are affiliated with Yeshiva University.

Whether consciously or not (and it most assuredly has been the latter), Yeshiva has functionally adopted the hasidic Madda-as-worship model, and, equally, Rav Kook's program—the latter better than it is practiced by his disciples, followers, and protégés in Israel. Kook, as mentioned in Chapter 6, spoke of two simultaneous movements as part of the educational dynamic: one is directed outward (the sanctification of the profane), and one is directed inward as the sacred develops, expands, and deepens its own resources of holiness. The first represents the encounter of Torah and Wisdom—or the sacred and the profane—and the second represents the traditional yeshiva model of intensification.

Moreover, this comprehensive Torah education is not restricted to those seeking a career in the rabbinate or those wishing to devote their lives to professional scholarship, those who consider *toratam umanutam* (their Torah as their craft). It is equally available to those who are preparing for careers in the arts and sciences or in business, but for whom Torah Umadda means that one must remain a student of Torah and Talmud throughout his life. That Yeshiva is not successful in all cases is beside the point; which school can claim complete success? The relevant facts are that this is the ethos of the institution and its ideology, and that it has indeed succeeded in an impressive number of cases.

This is therefore the empirical response to the animadversions of both Rosenheim and Dessler to the Hirschian school. The array of creative scholars, *geonim* and *gedolim,* who have taught and are teaching at Yeshiva—preeminent among them Rabbi Joseph B. Soloveitchik, himself the greatest exemplar of Torah Umadda—and the aspirations of so many of its current students to devote their lives to scholarship (whether as Roshei Yeshiva or as academic Judaic scholars) testify to the presence of creative and flourishing Jewish scholarship in the flagship of Torah Umadda. And the fact that the majority of today's Talmud faculty at the Rabbi Isaac Elchanan Theological Seminary are alumni of Yeshiva points to the ability of the school to perpetuate itself and guarantee its continuity. That many faculty members may have more limited definitions of Torah Umadda is not germane to this argument; the basic concept of the legitimacy of Madda, even if only for the purpose of earning a living, is assented to by all of them, with a good number accepting the instrumentalist theory, and some committed to even more affirmative models of Torah Umadda. We return to this theme in the final chapter when we discuss Torah Umadda pluralism in greater detail.

CREATIVE TENSIONS

The charge that *Torah im Derekh Eretz* encourages schizoid reactions, a split in one's own personality, must be carefully evaluated, for, in a way, it is a criticism that might be directed against all models of Torah Umadda.

However, here too the criticism is overstated. Undoubtedly, the attempt to embrace two disparate cultures and value systems, with all their associated emotional dimensions and nuances, contributes to a life of tension. No one who is serious about his intellectual and religious commitments, whether of the *Torah im Derekh Eretz* or other Torah Umadda schools, is without tensions between the two poles around which his inner life and practical existence revolve. Such anguish is the tribute that faith pays to integrity. But the following must be stated not so much in rebuttal as in modification of this criticism.

First, intellectual and spiritual tension is a great source of creativity. Without questions there are no answers, and without problems there are no solutions. Transition, change, conflict, tension—these are the working conditions for the production of great art, literature, and philosophy. Freud was right when, in his *Civilization and Its Discontents,* he argued that neurotic tensions and discontents are responsible for the greatest advances of civilization. Eight centuries earlier, Maimonides noted that if not for the neurotics (he called them, in Hebrew translation from the Arabic, the *meshuga'im*), the world would cease to exist. Religious tensions caused by the confrontation of Torah and Wisdom can be and must be transmuted into a new and higher level of creativity. Both Hirsch and Kook spoke movingly of such tensions as the necessary concomitants of the creative and mutually fructifying encounter between Torah and Wisdom.

Second, the existence of tensions, as one's psychic life is polarized about the two ends of this magnet, should not necessarily be identified with a schizoid ideology and a torn soul. The normal and the abnormal are part of one continuum on the spectrum of the psyche. Inner tensions can make life difficult—who said that religious life must be easy?—and may even develop into a neurosis of sorts, but that is a far cry from the spiritually split personality of which some of the critics complain. Schizophrenia, even if used only analogically, is a psychosis, and therefore an inappropriate metaphor for the spiritual suffering that is all but inevitable in the struggle to embrace both poles.

That this is so is attested to by the late Rabbi Yitzchok Hutner, one of the most thoughtful leaders of the Haredi yeshivot in New York. Head of Brooklyn's Mesivta Chaim Berlin, he had studied in the famous yeshiva of Slobodka and then became one of the best students at the yeshiva in Hebron; he spent several months studying in the University at Berlin as well. He writes in response to one of his students, who had

inquired whether pursuing a secular career meant that he was
leading a double life (essentially echoing the complaint of
disenchanted *Torah im Derekh Eretz* followers):

> Indeed, if you rent a room in which to live a settled life, and then rent
> another room in a hotel in order to live as a tourist, you are certainly
> leading a "double life." But if you rent two rooms in one apartment,
> you have not a double life but a broad life. A multitude of diverse
> points, one above the other, certainly implies [an undesirable] multi-
> plicity, but when all the points are arranged around one central point,
> you have a circle. That, my dear friend, is your obligation in the world:
> to place in the center of your life the "One" . . . and every new point
> that you acquire will simply serve to broaden the circle, and this will in
> no wise injure your sense of unity.[3]

A final point in response to this worry over a double or split
life: a Torah Umadda approach based on the hasidic concept
of *avodah be'gashmiut* is better equipped to handle such intellectual anguish. The reason is, quite simply, that since the
locus of the religious condition is situated in the person, rather
than in the two objects involved in the encounter, and since it
is the *avodat ha-Shem* of the person that is critical to the process,
a sense of unity and cohesiveness is preserved in one's psychic
and spiritual life even as he grapples intellectually with the
collision of the two worlds. To put it another way, without a
grounding in the hasidic notion of *avodah be'gashmiut,* the
disjunctiveness between Torah and Wisdom is perceived of as
an ontological conflict; with such a grounding, it is reduced to
an epistemological problem.

A PERSPECTIVE ON THE CONTEMPORARY

The same can be said in response to the concern that Torah
Umadda may be as vulnerable to overestimation of the virtues
of modernity, as perceived in the closing decade of the twen-

tieth century, as *Torah im Derekh Eretz* was to the modernity of a century earlier. That is not, or need not be, the case. With all his perceptivity in criticizing the East European Orthodoxy of his time for being fixated on a *Derekh Eretz* or cultural milieu that had passed into oblivion, Rabbi Hirsch repeated the same error by venerating the German humanism of his own day. Again, without the ultimate grounding outside the two conflicting entities, and inside the soul of the subject (the *gavra,* as we would term it in talmudic jargon), one is largely without the ability to exercise the requisite perspective. With such a grounding for one's Torah Umadda outlook, however, the exact content of the Madda or *Derekh Eretz* pole is of no ultimate consequence; and the resolution of the conflict, or even the sharpening of it, as the case may be, can be carried on with the spiritual composure and psychological serenity that can only add to one's intellectual courage and perspicuity. This hasidic model of Torah Umadda, therefore, insulates one against the tendency to be overabsorbed in the particulars of the Wisdom pole; moreover, it holds the promise of serving future generations as well when, without doubt, our present perspectives will have become obsolete and new problems have arisen to plague the religious and threaten to rob them of their intellectual equanimity.

An Overarching Religious Vision

This selfsame element of Madda-as-worship as the bedrock of the hasidic model of Torah Umadda protects it against the charge leveled against *Torah im Derekh Eretz* that it lacks an adequate spiritual dimension. The Frankfurt school, as we noted, was roundly criticized by its own adherents for the absence of an overarching religious vision, of a sense of majesty and transcendent grandeur. It is precisely that which is provided by the hasidic immanentistic vision of a world bursting with the potential and promise of holiness, yearning for the redemptive touch of the sanctifying soul, and the consequent bending of all one's talents, propensities, physical deeds, emotional fulfillments, and cognitive gestures to the service of the Holy One, so that every single facet of one's total being becomes an offering of love to one's Maker.

Finally, an important advantage of the hasidic model is that while it is proposed as a solution to an intellectual problem, it far transcends the cognitive realm. It serves the purpose of informing the student of both Torah and Madda, but its sweep covers all of existence in all its rich variety—for, indeed, such was the original intent of those who formulated the concept of *avodah be'gashmiut*. Torah Umadda thus becomes just a specific application of a much broader religious principle. What the implications of this broadened hasidic model are for Jewish communal, cultural, and religious life beyond the Torah Umadda issue is a fascinating question, but one that is beyond the scope of this work.

NOTES

1. Ze'ev Falk, "Torah im Derekh Eretz be'Yamenu," in Mordechai Breuer, ed.,"*Torah im Derekh Eretz*" (Heb.) (Ramat Gan, Israel: Bar Ilan University, 1987), pp. 264–266.

2. Breuer, ibid., pp. 48–49.

3. Published in the *Sefer ha-Zikaron le'Maran ha-"Pahad Yitzhak,"* ed. Yosef Buksbaum (Jerusalem: Makhon Yerushalayim, 1983), p. 6.

CHAPTER 12

EDUCATIONAL IMPLICATIONS

What are some of the practical consequences of the hasidic Madda-as-worship model relative to the other models?

None of the major models described in the preceding chapters would dictate a radical change in the practice of Torah Umadda as reflected, for instance, in the curriculum of Yeshiva University. The unquestioned centrality of the study of Torah would continue to be affirmed under any model. But we would be left with certain noticeable consequences, depending on the model of Torah Umadda that we accept as normative.

First, however, we must dispose of two erroneous attitudes toward Torah Umadda that we have not included in our list, the first because it is a misinterpretation and the second because, although it is a legitimate interpretation of a talmudic view, it does not qualify as Torah Umadda, a term that takes Madda seriously and should be reserved for a truly existential encounter.

CURRICULAR MINIMALISM

The misinterpretation is the notion that a standard university education with a sprinkling of Judaic Studies courses satisfies the minimum requirements for a Torah Umadda education. It does not. Torah Umadda claims to be an authentic Torah view, not a convenient stamp of kashruth approval for curricular Torah minimalism. It must never be regarded as dispensing with Torah as a satellite of some other core value or experience. A smattering of Jewish history, a survey of contemporary American Jewish fiction, and "Holocaust 101" may be better than nothing, but it certainly does not qualify as *Talmud Torah* and therefore not as Torah Umadda. Such an attitude does not take the *Torah* of Torah Umadda seriously, and any attempt to validate it as Torah Umadda is an illegitimate pretense.

Indeed, we here touch on an existential core problem far more fateful than the intellectual issue of Torah Umadda. Can the Jewish people survive without Jewish learning? To put it another way: Can Jews survive without Judaism, and is Judaism conceivable without Torah, without Jewish learning and engagement with the Jewish sources? The answer to both halves of the question is a resounding *no*.

Indeed, Torah, as the source of all forms of Jewish learning, is necessary to the survival of Jews as a distinct group, and more critical to the flourishing of Judaism in an open society than in a closed one. To be a Jew in a ghetto requires no knowledge, not even much commitment. An insulated society communicates and enforces its own rules, and its walls not only ward off alien ideas and values but also guarantee conformity with the prevailing norms within that community. However, an open society is, by definition, one in which the citizen is subject to all kinds of competing ideas and ideals and is free to engage in the commerce of values, concepts, and life-styles. Ignorance of Judaism in such an environment—ignorance of our people's history and faith, its dreams and fears, its literary texts and its sacred customs, its visions and its aspirations—ensures that Jews will melt into the majority and disappear, for genuine freedom of choice requires informed choice. In the absence of adequate Jewish learning, a Jew cannot make such choices as to his sense of belonging, his destiny, and his ultimate commitments.

Without Torah, therefore, there can be no Jews—a condition that has already seized a frighteningly large number of American Jews—and ignorance will have done more to "solve the Jewish question" than did the Holocaust. There have appeared recently a number of works purporting to find reason for great optimism for the future of American Jewry, assuming that it continues along its present path. Such starry-eyed Pollyannaism is most remarkable coming from sophisticated and liberal-minded writers who would argue passionately for the right to all levels of education for all Americans lest the whole society be impoverished, and yet find that a Jewish community can get along perfectly well with a level of Jewish learning that is patently pathetic.

"Torah only," as we have been arguing, threatens to reduce the Jewish people from a people to a sect, given the open society in which most Jews of the world today live. But at least it ensures a continuation of Jews as Jews into the future. Such cannot be said of Madda without Torah. No number of Jewish Nobel laureates, no impressive statistics about the high percentage of Jews in the learned professions, can have any positive bearing on the ability of this people to survive the test of freedom. Without Torah there can be no Judaism, and without Judaism there can be no Jews; and hence the syllogistic conclusion: no Jews without Torah.

But, again as we have been arguing, the choice is not only between, on the one side, the end of the history of the Jews as a people and their survival as a sect, or on the other side, their total disappearance by assimilation. There remains the most promising option: Torah Umadda, the struggle for both worlds, the refusal to give up either on Torah or on Madda, either on authentic Jewish wholeness or on participation in the wider society. The balance may often prove precarious and the interface between them onerous, but it is the tension of creativity, of life itself.

The "Torah" in such Torah Umadda must be real, intensive, and rooted in the Jewish sources. It dare not be superficial, lest it suffer by comparison with the high level of secular learning attained by most Jews today. Such Jewish learning should not be confused with preparation for specifically Jewish vocations. It is the pride of Jewry that its religion has obligated study for all its communicants, not reserving it for a special professional class of priests or scholars alone. Torah Umadda requires that Torah be studied at least as seriously as Madda.

Even more than seriousness and depth in the study of Torah is the axiological dimension: for Torah Umadda to be religiously meaningful, it is imperative that Torah be acknowledged as possessing central value and primacy over all else. Only when such centrality is affirmed does the enterprise of Madda become pregnant with meaning and the promise of sanctity. Writing of the righteous, the psalmist says, "Those who are planted in the house of the Lord shall flourish in the courts of our God" (Psalm 93:14). Indeed, only if one is firmly planted within, in the inner precincts of Torah, will he or she spiritually flourish in the outer courtyards of Madda as well.

VOCATIONALISM—EDUCATIONAL PRAGMATISM

The second misconception, which this writer holds to be Jewishly legitimate on its own terms but unacceptable as

Torah Umadda, is the belief that Madda is to be studied only for vocational or preprofessional reasons. Such a view gives far less credence to Madda than do any of the instrumentalist views,[1] and it essentially gives begrudging approval to Torah Umadda only because of necessity (*bi'de'avad*) and not because it is right (*le'hatkhilah*). To return to the Maimonidean metaphor, the pragmatic outlook does not even grant to the various branches of Madda the rank of "perfumers and cooks and bakers" to the mistress Torah, but rather equates them with footstools and chairs and tables. One cannot speak of the study of retailing or programming or insurance-selling as an instrument for the understanding and enhancement of Torah except in the most limited economic sense.

The warrant for a vocationalist program is the view of the Tanna R. Ishmael in *Berakhot* 35b. (This was discussed in some detail in the last section of Chapter 3, where we explained why Torah Umadda does not feel inhibited by this Tannaitic view because of the weight of contrary opinion.) Now, if this vocational approach is to be adopted and no other motivation is to be considered acceptable, then the secular curriculum for conscientious and believing contemporary Jews must be restricted to vocational courses only (following the advice of Rabbi Eliyahu Dessler).[2] All sciences, humanities, and liberal arts would have to be abandoned, save those deemed ideologically harmless and absolutely prerequisite to a career track. Indeed, consistency and courage require that those who advocate this minimalist or economic version of Torah Umadda leave university studies altogether and enroll in a trade school.

This position does not reflect the kind of Torah Umadda that is practiced by most of its protagonists today, and that is expressed in the undergraduate curriculum of Yeshiva University. Even in its Sy Syms School of Business, Yeshiva insists on a liberal dose of the liberal arts. Moreover, the business courses are presented in an academic fashion so that

they become intellectually challenging and culturally edifying. Torah Umadda must of necessity go beyond economic
and vocational dispensations if it is to be a philosophy and not
a scheme—a way of life and not just a way of earning a living.

The problem of the study of humanities in the scheme of a
Torah Umadda education needs to be addressed. There exists
a body of opinion that approves of the study of the natural
sciences but disparages the study of literature, art, philosophy,
languages—indeed of all that comes under the banner of the
humanities. This has been partly treated in Chapter 3, where
we discussed the fear of heretical notions as a motivating force
for the "Torah only" school.

It is true that a large number of authorities opposed to
Torah Umadda have exempted either medicine or the natural
sciences from the prohibition of "alien studies." Effectively,
they are in the same camp as those who advocate Torah
Umadda but restrict it to vocational training. In this camp are
those who invalidate all the humanities—even the study of the
language of the host country in which Jews may find themselves—and those who target specific disciplines, such as
philosophy or psychology or literature.

Leo Levi has performed a valuable service in listing the
categories, arguments, and personalities involved in the polemic against the humanities in talmudic circles through the
ages.[3] He notes that there are widely differing opinions, as
well as inconsistent remarks and decisions often made by the
same authority. However, he avers that further study indicates that there is practically no disagreement among them,
because of the distinction between the natural sciences and the
humanities: the former are permissible, the latter not. Thus,
the matter is resolved.

But the matter is not really so easily resolved. The talmudic
method of reconciling conflicting texts is not always transferable to other situations. It is not legitimate to reconcile dif-

ferent views expressed by authorities separated by continents and centuries in the same way talmudists reconcile two contradictory decisions in the same code of Maimonides. In *Weltanschauung* no less than in Halakhah, different opinions exist and are to be respected. Unlike Halakhah, they need not be reconciled in order to arrive at a practical decision for the sake of uniform behavior.

Furthermore, the distinction between science and the humanities is not as absolute as Levi would have us believe. The "two cultures," as C. P. Snow dubbed them, are not totally separated from each other, and there is no giant abyss yawning on the borderline. There is a continuity that binds them even as they stand counterposed to each other, and that continuum is the human mind, which seeks both to discover and to create. To say, as does Levi, that the natural sciences are objective, whereas "in the humanities we lack all objective criteria and, when left to ourselves, must resort to arbitrary standards,"[4] is to overstate the case. One does not need to be a philosopher of science to question the absolute objectivity of natural scientists. In 1989, the press reported the wildly conflicting results of experimenters throughout the world who were attempting to duplicate the "cold fusion in a bottle" reported by two electrochemists, one from Utah and the other from Great Britain, and commentators were sagely describing the "new face"—anguished, perplexed, competitive, envious—of so many distinguished natural scientists. Ultimately, the "cold fusion" report was discredited, but the "new face" will not go away so quickly. Other problems remain unresolved—the "Big Bang" versus the "Steady State" theories in cosmology; the question of the symmetry of the subatomic world; the rival theories in evolutionary science, and so on.

Nor are the humanities as arbitrary as we are told. Linguistics is quite scientific and therefore presumably as objective as many of the natural sciences. The same holds true, although in lesser measure, for anthropology and psychology. Art lends itself to the most personal treatment, but that does not mean that it has no standards; except for the most radical nonrepresentational forms that explicitly eschew any standards, there are ways of judging good from bad art—as there are ways of distinguishing quality literature from junk.

And while so much literature is indistinguishable from smut, so much of it is genuinely edifying. Literature, the product of the creative human imagination, is as worthy of study and analysis as are buildings and tunnels and other human artifacts, the product of the technological capacity of humans. Quantifiability does not create worthiness.

More to the point is the problem of the liberal arts and humanities posing theological dangers for the unsuspecting tyro. Indeed, one should not expose immature students to readings that will overwhelm them and rob them of their faith, their most precious possession. By the same token, one ought not attempt to introduce eight-year-olds to differential equations, and thus poison them to the beauties of mathematics forever, or immerse ten-year-olds in the study of abnormal psychology and thus confuse them before they have had a chance to learn normal ways.

Moreover, the natural sciences are not immune to the virus of heresy. The various theories of evolution and geology pose serious problems for those who have not yet resolved for themselves a proper reading of Genesis, as proposed by sophisticated Torah sages of recent generations who met the problem head-on without resorting to simple denial. Even more distressing to religious folk are the challenges thrown up by the deterministic bent of the natural sciences; how many can successfully cope with the threat to freedom of the will by neurophysiologists who question the existence of mind?

Despite these exceptions we have taken to Levi's approach,

we must applaud the very last comments in his book, in which he offers a defense for the inclusion of the humanities in the purview of recommended study. In a "Postscript," our author concludes:

> Our situation differs from pre-Emancipation conditions in that a major portion of our people has become estranged from their Torah heritage—and this fact has specific halakhic implications. The *arevut* principle, which makes every Jew responsible for every other, obligates us to draw close even those who have fallen prey to total heresy and this, in turn, requires us to have a common language with them: "I doubt that anyone today knows how to admonish (effectively)." Since in today's culture, concepts of history and literature have become key elements in the language of the man-in-the-street, the duty to develop a common language would seem to call for some familiarity with history and literature.[5]

This is a welcome statement, but its approbation of the study of humanities is far too limited. It is reminiscent of the instrumentalist model of Torah Umadda. One would have preferred the inclusion of the humanities with the natural sciences as part of Madda, which ought to be studied as an attempt to sanctify the profane (the mystical model) or as part of the individual's drama of *avodah be'gashmiut* (the hasidic model).

CURRICULAR CONSEQUENCES

We now may analyze the different implications, both personal and curricular, of the various models proposed.

If one adopts the cultural or the instrumentalist model, he must recall, every now and then, that the purpose of an academic education lies beyond itself, in the enhancement of his study of Torah, in order better to understand the Creator's revelation and his role in it, and in order to be able for the rest of his life to study Torah in a systematic and regular fashion.

The failure to do so later in life retroactively vitiates whatever religious value one's Madda studies may have had during one's student days. And one may then run afoul of the halakhic injunction against *bittul Torah,* the wanton disregard of *Talmud Torah.*

If the model adopted is the rationalist or inclusionary model, then most especially the impractical, noncareer disciplines have to be studied with great respect and reverence (*be'yirah be-eimah u-ve'retet*) because such Madda is a fulfillment of the commandment to study Torah, and demands the requisite subjective orientation and appropriate frame of mind. Additionally, for the same reason, one must study Madda *le'shem mitzvah,* as the performance of a mitzvah, which means to understand it, to master it, and to appreciate it because such is the will of the Holy One.

If the pursuit of Madda is conducted according to the mystical and especially the hasidic model, then *all* one's learning and all one's deeds—whether Torah or Madda, whether accounting or philosophy, woodwork or calculus—must be undertaken with a keen awareness that one is thereby engaging in *avodat ha-Shem,* the worship of the Deity—and that the stage on which the encounter between Torah and Wisdom takes place is not "out there," but within the soul, in the most private chamber of one's heart and consciousness where direction and orientation is given to all matters of one's inner life, great or small; hence, one must take special care to avoid any of those activities banned by the Halakhah, such as gossip, tale-bearing, foul language, deception—indeed, any form of irreverence or any intimation of the lack of probity in the course of one's secular studies no less than in one's Torah studies, for all of them are pregnant with holiness and touched by divine grace.

How may such consciousness of the transcendent dimension of Madda in a Torah Umadda scheme be implanted in students? Perhaps we ought to consider a technique spawned by the Musar movement of the nineteenth century and modified by some of the giants of the Halakhah who were not altogether sympathetic to Musar. The musarites, endeavoring to reinforce the moral and spiritual aspects of Jewish life, set aside major parts of the day for introspection and self-analysis in a rather somber mood. The halakhists felt that too much time was devoted to these sessions and recommended, instead, the interspersing of the day's work with very brief sessions of inspiration to remind the student of the reasons and ultimate meaning of his scholarly labors and the larger vision into which he must integrate them. Might we not adapt this to a Torah Umadda pattern? The success of such a venture would depend almost entirely on the person charged with this task: his effectiveness as a role model, his inspirational abilities, and the scholarly competence necessary for the credibility it would give him in a community of students and scholars.

If this holds true for the first two models—the instrumentalist and the inclusionary—how much more so for the mystical and the hasidic, where much more is called for: the adapted quasi-Musar technique must be expanded to a fullfledged ideological and psychological orientation of the student and a radical revision of the student's attitudes and even values.

A Dream:

The Master of prayers—the One to Whom all petitions are directed—has touched my lips and opened my heart and granted me the gift of prayer. Though I am unworthy, He has instructed me to compose words of praise and petition to Him Who is both Creator and Lawgiver, words to be recited daily before opening my books or entering a laboratory to pursue the goal of Madda.

Haltingly, the words come:

רבונו של עולם, נותן התורה ומקור החכמה!

הנני מוכן ומזומן לקיים מצות עבודת הבורא בכל מאדי כמו שכתוב
"ולעבדו בכל לבבכם ובכל נפשכם," וכתוב "בכל דרכיך דעהו." ובזכות
עסקי בחכמה אזכה ללמוד תורה לשמה ולעבוד את ה' אלקי עבודה תמה,
בחומר וברוח, ולצרפם זה לזה לעשות נחת רוח ליוצרי, וכמו שאמרו
חכמינו, "וכל מעשיך יהיו לשם שמים." ויהיו לרצון אמרי פי והגיון לבי
לפניך, ה' צורי וגואלי.

אמן, כן יהי רצון

Master of the World, Revealer of Torah and Fount of Wisdom!

*I am ready and prepared to fulfill the commandment to serve my
Creator with all my being, as it is written, "to serve Him with all your
heart and all your soul" (Deuteronomy 11:14), and it is written, "in
all thy ways acknowledge Him" (Proverbs 3:6). In the merit of my
involvement in Wisdom, may I deserve to study Torah for its own sake
and serve the Lord in perfect service, with both matter and spirit, and
bring them close to each other so as to please my Creator; as our Sages
said, "and let all your deeds be for the sake of Heaven" (Avot 2:17).*

*May the words of my mouth and the meditation of my heart be
pleasing before Thee, O Lord, my Rock and my Redeemer.*

Amen, and so may it be His will.

NOTES

1. See Chapter 8.
2. Cited in Chapter 3.
3. Leo Levi, *Torah and Science: Their Interplay in the World Scheme*
(Jerusalem: Feldheim Publishers, 1983), pp. 119–148.
4. Ibid., p. 121.
5. Ibid., p. 131.

CHAPTER 13

TORAH UMADDA
AND RELIGIOUS GROWTH

Having spoken of Torah Umadda as a problem in a Torah *Weltanschauung,* and as related to the religious vision and experience of the devout practitioner of Torah Umadda, we must now consider what this can mean to us personally—existentially and psychologically—as citizens of both "Athens" and "Jerusalem."

WHOLENESS

This issue is raised here largely because of autobiographical reasons. When the author came to Yeshiva University as an 18-year-old freshman, the concept of Torah Umadda proved enormously attractive to him (as mentioned in the Preface). He saw before him a number of outstanding role models, and he yearned to understand and perhaps some day emulate their remarkable integration of such apparently disparate worlds. Torah Umadda became for him not, as so many of its critics aver, a source of spiritual and religious schizophrenia but, quite to the contrary, an opportunity—*because* of all its creative tensions—for ultimate inner harmony, a way to unite his deepest Torah commitments with his growing experiences as a modern person living in a scientific technopolis, in an open and democratic society, and in a culture that, despite all its terrible failings, is vibrant and progressive. He could not accept the position of the critics of Yeshiva who nimbly accepted the idea of Jewish students going to college for vocational or career reasons but were horrified at the thought of their actually getting a liberal education. He was unimpressed by these critics' easy, unquestioning acceptance of a high school education, while objecting on halakhic or theological grounds to education on the university level. He felt that if it was forbidden to indulge in the secular disciplines at the university level, then we should desist from them even on the elementary level and suffer the consequences, if any, for our principles. For him, that would be the way of inner dissonance and self-delusion. It was Torah Umadda that held for him then, as it does now, the promise of spiritual healing, of inner reconciliation, of a cohesive life.

Could it be, as well, a way to religious growth?

Religious Growth

It is difficult to determine the origin of the term *religious growth,* or to know when it first achieved its current degree of popularity. An educated genealogical guess would identify it as the progeny of a common-law liaison between pop psychology and modernist theology. Yet behind this fashionable neologism lies a reality that is well known, if not quite clearly defined.

In the tradition of the yeshivot, the heads of the schools and the religious supervisors (*mashgihim*) would speak to their students of *shteigen* (ascending) in one's learning of Torah and in the refinement of his character. One who had experienced a notable degree of success in such ascent was considered a *baal-madregah,* "master of a level"—that is, one who has attained a high level of moral excellence. Drawing on much earlier sources, the idea developed that one's spiritual status could never be static: one had to move either up or down the ladder that connects Heaven and earth. Only angels are *omed,* stationary; humans are *mehalekh,* always on the move. In the realm of pure Spirit there is only Being; in that of man—spirit ensconced in matter—there is Becoming. Thus, R. Menachem Mendel, the hasidic rebbe of Kotzk, in commenting on the verse, "The righteous shall spring up like a palm tree; he shall grow tall like a cedar in Lebanon" (Psalm 92:13), said that "it is in the nature of righteousness (or piety) to spring, to grow." The religious life does not abide stagnation. It flourishes only when challenged, and if unchallenged it withers.

The term of preference for the end goal of such aspiration is *shelemut,* perfection or wholeness. The process of attaining it, or at least striving for it, is what we mean by religious growth.

The word *shelemut* (as well as the related terms *shalem* and *shelemim,* the singular and plural, respectively, for those who have attained *shelemut*) was used throughout the medieval Spanish period, in both the philosophical and ethical–didactic literatures, by such thinkers as Yehuda Halevi, Bahya, and Maimonides to describe the ideal state and the ideal man.

Maimonides, as might be expected, was the most analytic in his treatment of *shelemut.* He sees not one but four distinct categories of such an ideal state, arranged hierarchically. At the bottom is the perfection of possessions, followed by the *shelemut* of one's physical attributes. From wealth and health we proceed upward to the perfection of *middot* or moral character. The final *shelemut* is that of intellectual perfection, which expresses itself in the grasping of truth, especially the true perception or knowledge of God. It is this last *shelemut,* the rational or cognitive one, that represents the highest state of ideal man.

The notion of *shelemut* has been nurtured in Jewish tradition ever since. The lowest of Maimonides' four types, that of possessions, was, of course, dropped—both because of economic conditions throughout much of Jewish history, and, even more, because this was posited as a form of *shelemut* for analytic or morphological reasons only, and certainly had little else to commend it. The second, physical perfection, similarly fell into desuetude. Whether this happened because conditions of exile made good nutrition inaccessible and hence ignored, or because of the medieval and mystical penchant for seeing the spiritual and the physical as fundamentally antagonistic, its omission was most unfortunate. The third, moral perfection, was both intensified and broadened, with piety ("fear of Heaven") and punctiliousness in the performance of the mitzvot included along with refinement of character as a most desirable level of human–Jewish perfection. The highest level, that of intellectual perfection, was narrowed to the knowledge and understanding of Torah, with a concomitant downgrading of the knowledge of God and the philosophical, and especially metaphysical, infrastructure that such knowledge presupposed.

Hence, the conventional concept of *shelemut* and religious growth to which we are heir today consists largely of piety, moral character, and the study of Torah.

OPENNESS

As the ideal of *shelemut* is understood and accepted today in many of the yeshivot, it is thus an intense, inward-looking enterprise, often requiring an almost monastic dedication.

This aspiration is unquestionably a noble one, especially in this narcissistic era of unbridled hedonism and unbuttoned ego display, and hence is deserving of the greatest admiration and approbation. But is there no place for Madda to be integrated in the goal of *shelemut* in a substantive manner? Can we not conceive of a *shelemut* that is outgoing as well as inward-looking, one not limited to one's own psyche and moral character, embracing rather than confining, open rather than closed?[1] Can we not, for example, exploit the varied backgrounds of the *baalei teshuvah* (Jewish newcomers to Judaism) instead of forcing them into an unnaturally narrow framework?

It is our conviction that Madda certainly ought to be incorporated in the *shelemut* ideal, and that, indeed, it gives it new breadth.

At first blush, "openness" is alien and even antithetical to religious growth, especially in its currently accepted form. The demands of devoutness apparently contradict the principles of openness and of tolerance of ideas that might be considered heretical, and the imperative of intense Torah study apparently leaves no place for other disciplines that are integral to the very notion of openness. At bottom, what we have is the clash of two antonymous orientations: a penetrating depth versus a blanketing breadth as most expressive of the ideal of *shelemut*.

Openness can be integrated into religious growth only if we redefine the concept of *shelemut* in a manner compatible with the fundamentals of Torah Umadda. This means moving from the current restricted and constricted conception of wholeness to a more comprehensive vision. In essence, it means returning to a notion of the ideal that is closer to the Maimonidean view of *shelemut* than that developed in the eight centuries since.

THREE SOURCES

There are several sources for this proposed redefinition, not all of them mutually compatible, and they range from contemporary California to medieval Cairo to ancient Canaan.

The West Coast of the United States has a well-earned reputation as the womb and cradle of the most exotic, extravagant, and usually irrational movements or "life-styles" to afflict the nation. Of particular note, as the basis of so many of the "therapies" spawned in California, is the ethos of the "human potential" school: the expression of all latent talents, potencies, and aspirations that the self possesses. This concern with the self usually conforms with the pervasive narcissism, hedonism, and solipsism of contemporary life, the need to taste every dish on the menu of the banquet of life. Everything must be tried and experienced at least once—even if it is corrupt or decadent or perverse—lest one pass through life on this planet only to leave it with the ego untried, hungry, unfulfilled. However, a kernel of genuine moral value lies buried somewhere in this pile of droll dross: the harnessing of all life and experience, and the actualization of all potential contained in the human personality: in short—existential comprehensiveness, containing the promise of a life that is coherent, cohesive, consistent, and comprehensive.

This leads us to our second source: Maimonides. This sage of Fostat (medieval Cairo) declared that for perfection or wholeness to be attained, it is imperative that all potential be realized, all promises fulfilled.[2] Maimonides makes this comment in a rather different context—in his discussion of divine *shelemut,* as part of his "negative theology"—but the concept is transferable to human perfection. The ideal person is not one who merely possesses great possibilities, but one who has expressed these potencies in reality. Religious growth, to put it colloquially, is a bottom-line business that does not offer rewards for a high I.Q. only. Indeed, the very word "growth" implies the movement from the potential to the actual.

(For the sake of completeness—not an irrelevancy in this chapter advocating wholeness—it should be mentioned that classical Greece, too, is a source for the same notion, and probably had an influence on Maimonides. Goethe, following Friedrich Schiller, considered the striving for many-sidedness a principle of the Greek heritage. Matthew Arnold [in his *Culture and Anarchy*] declared that human perfection, as the Greeks understood it, requires listening to all the voices of human experience and working toward the harmonious expansion of all the powers contained in human nature. Yet we should not conclude that this idea is "borrowed" from the Greeks—a common fallacy of academicians who assume that chronological priority by one party automatically excludes originality by all others. Clearly, Judaism stands on its own in its celebration of *shelemut,* and the emphasis on this comprehensiveness should not be looked on as an alien graft, even if it is true that the reemphasis on this particular theme may well arise in reaction to its currency in the outside world.)

Granted, then, that *shelemut* requires the mobilization of the entire personality and the actualization of all potencies within it, we still must add the teleological element: the harnessing and realization of personality must be guided by a purpose beyond itself, one that will provide direction to the entire process, as well as the critical function of avoiding the growth of noxious propensities of the personality.

That purpose was enunciated by the founding Father of Israel. The Lord revealed Himself to Abraham in ancient Canaan, saying, "Walk before Me and be whole" (Genesis 17:1). The original Hebrew for "whole" is *tamim,* which Onkelos translates into the cognate Aramaic as *shelim,* from the same root as *shelemut.* The goal of such total involvement of the self and the actualization of all its potential is to achieve *shelemut* by "walking before" God. It is, in fact, religious growth.

THE COMMENTATORS ON SHELEMUT

It is instructive to see how the classical Jewish exegetes dealt with this key verse. Rashi regards both halves of the verse as essentially two commandments to attain one end: Abraham must possess such mighty faith that he can successfully endure all trials visited upon him by God and remain unshaken in his commitment, walking before Him and staying whole in his belief. The "wholeness" is thus an intense one, one that is attained by rejecting the external threats, dangers, and distractions, and building up one's inner spiritual resources.

Ibn Ezra, reminding us that this verse introduces the revelation in which Abraham is commanded to circumcise himself and his household, similarly sees wholeness as the intensification and internalization of faith: " 'Be whole'—by not questioning [God] concerning [the reason] for circumcision."

However, Nahmanides rejects Rashi's and Ibn Ezra's glosses. He relates *tamim* in this verse to the same word used in Deuteronomy as the culmination of a passage prohibiting Israel from engaging in idolatrous practices relating to magic, sorcery, necromancy, and so on: "Thou shalt be *tamim* with the Lord thy God" (Deuteronomy 18:13). In both cases, says Nahmanides, the intention is the same: wholeness means to attribute everything to God, and nothing whatever to extra-divine sources—not to demons or magic or whatever idols may be popular at the time. Having accepted the commandment to "walk before Me," Abraham must "be whole," committing himself to God wholly and exclusively—but equally: totally and comprehensively—in a manner that is coextensive with every aspect of his unique personality, his experience, his conception of his destiny. This interpretation by Nahmanides thus results in a *shelemut* that is extensive and comprehensive, broadly rather than narrowly focused.[3]

It is this latter explanation of our verse that lends itself to the alternative notion of religious growth here proposed. *Shelemut* thus implies a wide net: the amassing of all one's attributes—intellectual and psychological, spiritual and esthetic, practical and moral—and all one's experiences—sacred and profane, profound and superficial, positive and negative—and their actualization and elevation toward the Holy One, as we worship Him both through our spirituality and our corporeality. And, it should be added, while all models of Torah Umadda can subscribe to this orientation, it is the hasidic model that has the most affinity for it.

A DYNAMIC CONCEPTION

Because of the comprehensive scope of this definition of religious growth, it must of necessity result in a dynamic rather than a static conception of *shelemut*. An intensive view can be more eclectic and selective, choosing only those aspects of personality that are compatible with each other, avoiding conflict and internal contradictions. Such is not the case with the extensive version of *shelemut,* for it is inevitable, given the range and variety of human experience, that internal inconsistencies will develop. My musical aptitudes, if they are to be fully developed as part of my religious growth, may well conflict with the commandment to study Torah whenever time is available. For the narrower, conventional version of *shelemut,* there is no problem whatever: the esthetic element has no standing, and the commandment to study Torah prevails. (It is understood that we are speaking of Torah study beyond the minimum required by the Halakhah, as mentioned in Chapter 3. Otherwise, both views would agree that Torah must perforce take precedence.) The broader conception must

make judgments based on the unique personality of the ques-
tioner, the benefit of either route to the development of his full
religious personality: How good a scholar can he be? How
serious a musician will he become? Will an artistic career be
used by him to enhance his spiritual *Gestalt?* Of what relative
benefit will he be to Israel and to the community of believers
in either case? Such examples can be multiplied manifold. The
solution for the extensive view of *shelemut* is to keep all such
forces in a dynamic balance and exercise a kind of utilitarian
calculus in order to come to a proper decision.

A metaphor that comes to mind immediately for such an
approach is the Platonic one, adopted by R. Yehuda Halevi,
the immortal Spanish-Jewish poet and philosopher, in his
Kuzari—the metaphor of the person of *shelemut* presiding over
his character like a prince ruling a city. He must allot to each
attribute its due, assign to each its duty, see to it that none of
them overdoes or overreaches, while making sure that the
totality functions smoothly with all interrelated parts
working cooperatively and responsibly. An even more appealing metaphor might be that of the conductor of an or-
chestra who must make optimum use of every musician and
every instrument, allowing no sound or combination of
sounds to be more or less than is necessary for the total effect
of the emerging symphony.

The concluding words of the Book of Psalms are: "Let *kol
ha-neshamah* praise the Lord, Hallelujah." The two Hebrew
words are usually translated as "every soul." With equal
fidelity to the text, and with additional support for our thesis,
they might also be translated as, "let the *entire* soul"—all of it,
every aspect, every facet, every talent, every potency—
"praise the Lord, Hallelujah."[4]

OPENNESS AND GROWTH

With these definitions of religious growth, the principle of
openness to the world—which consists largely of Torah

Umadda and the cluster of subjective attitudes that pertain to it—is certainly compatible with the ideals of *shelemut*.

In Chapter 3 we cited a number of examples from Geonic and medieval times to illustrate the compatibility of Torah and Madda. Perhaps the most striking such case is that of Ma-HaRaL, who lived during the Renaissance period, and from whom we quoted earlier at some length. These examples are, equally, illustrations of the possibility of an extensive vision of *shelemut* that includes an openness to the world.

If we accept the possibility of this alternative model of *shelemut,* one that requires breadth as well as depth, then openness is not only permissible but inescapable and admirable. The dazzling galaxy of Torah Umadda personalities mentioned in this book, and the many more who remain unmentioned, come closer to the ideal of *shelemut* because of, not despite, their Madda involvements. The knowledge of medicine did not detract from Maimonides' sense of wholeness; indeed, the *Hilkhot Deiot* of his immortal Code, where he discusses the formation of character, benefits enormously from the medical theories he had learned from the Greeks. Don Isaac Abravanel was no less a full personality because of his financial prowess and diplomatic skill; those acquainted with his commentary on the Bible can attest to the life experiences as a man of Madda that he draws upon in his exegesis. Grammar did not impoverish Abraham Ibn Ezra; philosophy did not diminish the stature of Hasdai Crescas; secular poetry did not reduce the wholeness of either Solomon Ibn Gabirol or Yehuda Halevi; literary style and grace did not chip away at the well-earned fame of Judah Messer Leone; mathematics did not make the Gaon of Vilna any less a *gaon;* and general philosophy has not lessened the greatness of Rabbi Joseph B. Soloveitchik. On the contrary, the Madda development of each contributed not only to his intellectual greatness but also to his *shelemut,* which would have suffered without the development of those gifts.

Wholeness is enhanced by many-sidedness, and fullness by openness.

A caveat must be entered here. Openness applied uniformly is openness applied mindlessly. Doing everything, trying everything, tasting everything, with no thought to discriminating between the more and the less valuable, is sure to lead to dilettantism, and this is hardly the *shelemut* we seek. The primacy of Torah must be recognized as unchallenged; in the language of hasidic thought, *avodah she'be'ruhaniut* is superior to *avodah she'be'gashmiut.* This broader conception of *shelemut,* therefore, is meant to modify and expand rather than to supplant the narrower view.

SHELEMUT AND THE ARGUMENTS FOR GOD'S EXISTENCE

Let us attempt to sharpen the definition of how this form of open *shelemut* attains a truly spiritual end. In order to do so, let us turn to a rather unlikely source, one that is nowadays usually consigned to scholarly antiquarians with little relevance expected for contemporary religious people.

Some of the most famous *rishonim* offered various proofs for God's existence. This includes such eminences as R. Saadia Gaon, Maimonides, Gersonides, and even R. Bahya and R. Yehuda Halevi. Why did they engage in such metaphysical speculations? Surely their own inner faith was strong enough to resist what we today recognize as obsolete heresies, and they did not need these philosophical proofs to reinforce their own faith. Was it, then, to strengthen the spiritual weaklings among their students, or the wavering faith of the defecting masses?

Not at all, answers Rabbi Yaakov Moshe Charlop, the famous disciple/colleague of Rav Kook, and author of *Mei Marom.* The reason for indulging in these efforts to prove the existence of God was to enhance *giluy Elohut ba-olam,* to reveal

God through the medium of intellect. We make Godliness manifest by acts of *hesed* (love) or mitzvot, for example. But we must also reveal Him through the most precious and distinctive property of the human species: the mind.[5]

This "revelation" must not be understood as a function of religious proselytism. While it certainly is valid to preach and teach the existence of God to the world, that is not what motivated the *rishonim*. Rather, the goal was primarily to reveal Godliness, even if only to one's self, through the medium of intellect; to place all one's potencies, including the intellectual, at the service of God; to rise to more exalted levels (*madregot*) in one's knowledge of God—and thereby to grow religiously and spiritually. This is a form of growth that leads to an intellectual *kiddush ha-Shem* (sanctification of the divine Name).

This is indeed a hint of what Torah Umadda can mean, especially if it is structured on the basis of the hasidic model. Grasping a differential equation or a concept in quantum mechanics can let us perceive and reveal Godliness in the abstract governance of the universe. An insight into molecular biology or depth psychology or the dynamics of society can inspire in us a fascination with God's creation that Maimonides identifies as the love of God. A new appreciation of a Beethoven symphony or a Cézanne painting or the poetry of Wordsworth can move us to a greater sensitivity to the infinite possibilities of the creative imagination with which the Creator endowed His human creatures, all created in the divine Image.

In a word, the purpose of marshaling all areas of experience, of using all one's talents toward this sacred goal, is the attempt to achieve *shelemut*. For the broader one's intellectual horizons, the higher one's spiritual reach and the deeper one's religious commitment. The more comprehensive and inclusive the domain one attributes to the Holy One, the closer one approaches the asymptotic ideal of *shelemut,* of being *tamim* with the Lord God. This is *shelemut* with a wide-angle instead of a zoom lens.

THE MIKVEH OF ISRAEL

This view of religious growth, which necessarily involves openness, is one that, if properly pursued, constitutes a life-long process of *avodat ha-Shem,* the service or worship of the Creator. It accords with Nahmanides' commentary on "be whole," and it articulates nicely with our hasidic model of Torah Umadda, the model based on the doctrine of *avodah be'gashmiut,* because it brings everything, without exception, into the realm of the faith in and worship of God.

The prophet Jeremiah (14:8) refers to God as the *mikveh* of Israel and its Savior in the times of its distress. The Hebrew word lends itself to two equally valid interpretations: "hope" or "pool." Hope, in this context, is self-explanatory. By the latter term is meant the *mikveh* or the gathering of natural waters used to effect *taharah* or purification from defilement. This interpretation is accepted by the hasidic master, the Kotzker Rebbe, who explains: According to the Halakhah, the *mikveh* can effect purification only if the body is *totally* immersed in the water. If any part of the body at all, even a solitary hair, remains outside the waters, the *mikveh* is ineffective. And that is true of man's relation with God. The Creator is Israel's *mikveh.* Faith, trust, worship—all are meaningful if all of man, in his entirety, every facet of his person and every aspect of his personality, is immersed in such faith, trust, and worship. Anything less than such a total and comprehensive commitment frustrates the salvific effects of Torah and faith. God is the Savior in times of distress only if He is for us the *mikveh* of Israel.

"For the earth is the Lord's and the fulness thereof" (Psalm 24:1).

NOTES

1. An interesting variation on the ideal of *shelemut* in quite another direction is that of R. Yehiel Nissim of Pisa, the sixteenth-century author of *Minhat Kenaot,* for whom "wholeness" or "completeness" implies the inclusion of the body in the framework of spiritual perfection. This leads him to emphasize the behavioral mitzvot at the expense of an expanded intellectualism. See Isadore Twersky, "Talmudists, Philosophers, Kabbalists: The Quest for Spirituality in the Sixteenth Century," in *Jewish Thought in the Sixteenth Century* (Cambridge, MA: Harvard University, 1983), p. 446.

2. *Guide of the Perplexed* 1:55.

3. See, too, R. Obadiah Seforno, ad loc.

4. Cf. the interpretation of the word *kol* in another context by R. Elijah, the Gaon of Vilna, in his *Shenot Eliyahu* (Vilna, 1832) to *Berakhot,* end of Chapter 1.

5. Remarkably, just about the time I was reading this insight by Rabbi Charlop, several decades ago, I chanced upon an article by the late Professor Charles Frankel of Columbia University, who said the identical thing about *all* the philosophers of the Middle Ages—Moslem and Christian as well as Jewish—who undertook similar enterprises.

CHAPTER 14

A PLURALISTIC
TORAH COMMUNITY

It is worth repeating that, while disagreeing with the exclusivity of the "Torah only" approach, the thesis here presented does not preclude considering it as a live option alongside other options that affirm some form of Torah Umadda. In other words, we are arguing for a pluralistic vision of Torah in its encounter with the environing culture.

AS A MATTER OF PRINCIPLE

Such a pluralistic attitude is appropriate not only for pragmatic reasons but also as a matter of principle. In an analogous situation, that of educating one's son, we find two opinions among the Tannaim. R. Meir holds that one ought to teach his son a trade that is "easy and clean." (Maimonides includes *hokhmah*, the study of "Wisdom," along with *umanut*, a trade.) R. Nehorai adds, "I put aside all occupations in the world and teach my son only Torah."[1] This debate is highly problematic in the light of the Talmud's identification, elsewhere, of R. Meir with R. Nehorai![2]

A solution proposed by the late Rabbi Yitzchak Ze'ev Soloveitchik ("Reb Velvelle Brisker"), a powerful antagonist of modernist tendencies in Judaism, is that each of these presents an equally valid *middah* or point of view, and therefore they are not to be considered in conflict with each other.[3] He attributes this pluralistic solution to the Gaon of Vilna.

Consider, too, the following enlightening interpretation of a beautiful talmudic text that is even more directly related to the issue of pluralism within Torah. The Talmud relates:

> Ulaah Biraah said in the name of R. Eliezer: In the days to come the Holy One, blessed be He, will hold a *mahol* for the righteous and He will sit in their midst in the Garden of Eden. . . .[4]

The word *mahol,* which is translated by Soncino as "a chorus," more accurately means a chorus of both singers and dancers, with the dancers forming a circle.

The eminent talmudist Rabbi Akiva Eger (1761–1837) is quoted by his grandson[5] as explaining: In this world, every righteous person (*zaddik*) worships God in his own manner, and the way of one *zaddik* is unlike that of another. But in the Messianic future, it will be revealed that all these ways are really one, that all revolve about one central point, as does a circle. This is the *mahol* that the Holy One will make for the righteous—that they will revolve in a circle about one point— the Holy One—which is the Truth.

It is this kind of dialectical pluralism that ought to prevail in the matter of "Torah only" or Torah Umadda: they are both acceptable, depending on one's ability and disposition, societal need, and, above all, how one genuinely feels he can best discharge his responsibility for *avodat ha-Shem,* serving the Lord in the particularities of time and place in which he was placed by his Creator.[6]

Of course, the matter of pluralism within the Jewish community cannot be disposed of quite so quickly. This is especially so at a time when the term has been enshrined as the ultimate principle of goodness, democracy, and progressiveness, and used as a battering ram against those who fear its misuse as an excuse for ethical and religious relativism, reducing all religious and doctrinal differences to mere matters of taste.[7] The pluralism here recommended reflects, in a manner of speaking, the pluralism that is inherent in the Halakhah itself. This halakhic pluralism is that which asserts that halakhic judgments are multivalued, that halakhic questions usually admit of more than one solution—and yet acknowledges that the halakhic decision, by its very nature, is a limiting one: this is right and that is wrong, this is obligatory and that is forbidden.[8] This is not an across-the-board pluralism that declares everything equal to everything else (a situation that, mathematically speaking, obtains only when the value of each of the elements is zero!); this is, rather, a pluralism that respects self-evident limits—in this case, commitment to the integrity and inviolability of the Halakhah and the halakhic method—while recognizing the variety and plurality of views intrinsic in halakhic decisions.

Within the framework of such a pluralism a person may accept one particular way as Jewishly legitimate and yet objectionable on a variety of grounds, and another as not only legitimate but far superior and preferable. The debate, in other words, is carried on without the threat of mutual delegitimation.

As a Matter of Facts

It is this perspective that we have here adopted in arguing for certain versions of Torah Umadda, and in objecting to a "Torah only" stance if the latter is proposed as the sole or even main dish on the menu of Torah education. For, in addition to all the other cogent criticisms of the "Torah only" school,[9] one must add the fear that scholars who emerge from such a restricted and highly specialized education and shielded environment will eventually become the *posekim,* the halakhic decisors or judges, for large numbers of Jews; and it is inevitable that such judges' ignorance of the facts, the realities, and the temper of contemporary life—the social, political, economic, and cultural as well as the technological—will distort the knowledge base that goes into proper halakhic decision-making and thus mislead their followers. Theory applied blindly or by hearsay can only corrupt the truth of Torah, and any faith that the *gedolim* or acknowledged rabbinic leaders will invariably issue a true decision, guided by Providence, is misplaced.

Of course, those who will eventually occupy positions of importance as decisors in the halakhic community must perforce devote the great majority of their time and effort to the intensive study of Torah, as must any specialist in any field, lest the community be left at the mercy of cultured amateurs when they need authentic scholars of Torah.

With full cognizance of the incongruity between the study of Torah and of art, an analogy between the two may be instructive. The composer Gian Carlo Menotti recently wrote:

Art becomes a very demanding and jealous mistress who, from her lover, requires undivided attention and blind dedication. The artist's work never ends, never leaves him. He never closes the office and forgets about his job until the next morning. He eats, sleeps, travels, makes love and all the while, in the back of his mind, the demon gnaws at his brain.

Everything in life becomes secondary; any artist's spouse knows well what I am talking about. The social life of an artist becomes marginal,

even eccentric. Often, he is cruelly indifferent to the people surrounding him or else incredibly naive. He must be, first of all, an artist;
time dedicated to his public life is time necessarily robbed from art.[10]

These lines strike a most responsive chord in the mind of
anyone who ever attended a serious yeshiva. He can hear the
loving and encouraging rebuke of his *mashgiah* (spiritual
counselor) admonishing him to concentrate on his study of
Torah with relentless, almost superhuman dedication. Substi-
tute "Torah" for "art" and add the dimension of *kedushah*
(holiness), and the ethos of the yeshiva and its single-minded
emphasis emerges.

Alfred North Whitehead, certainly no cultural philistine,
once remarked that an education has got to be narrow if it is to
penetrate; breadth alone, uniformly applied, may leave one
educated and cultured but hardly competent.

Nevertheless, the *posek* must have some basic acquaintance
with the realities of life outside his own discipline, as, indeed,
we expect of the physician or scientist or economist. He who
accepts for himself the responsibility of leadership of the
community, even if only a community of scholars (no matter
how reclusive), must have good and correct knowledge of the
world his charges come from, even if they seek to escape it.
Certainly one who pretends to the role of halakhic guide for
large numbers of laymen who are perforce engaged in commerce with the culture of the times, in greater or lesser measure, must have a thorough understanding of that culture.

This concept of a pluralistic Torah community, in which
both Torah Umadda and "Torah only" have their rightful
roles, extends both to the amicable coexistence of "Torah
only" and Torah Umadda, and to the variants of Torah
Umadda itself. The simultaneous development of both a traditional yeshiva and a Torah Umadda educational system was
already presaged by Rav Kook, as was mentioned earlier. A
skeptic might argue that this is but an instance of making a

virtue of necessity. But the skeptic, in this case as in so many others, would thereby reveal his own shallowness. The mystical and hasidic models of Torah Umadda must be understood as advocating a more complex and sophisticated approach to the ultimate unity of existence, whether the harmonistic vision of Rav Kook or the subjective coordinate of the unity of God as reflected in the immanentism (if not acosmism) of the hasidic thinkers. Either way, we assert the harmonious blending of the diverse and the resolution of antonymous forces.

As a Matter of Matter

Such an approach has its analogue in the conception of matter and energy in contemporary atomic physics, especially Niels Bohr's theory of complementarity. Bohr, the distinguished founder of quantum theory, noted that puzzling situations arise in man's efforts to comprehend a universe where various approaches to reality appear mutually exclusive and yet are each legitimate—surely a problem for epistemology. Bohr emphasized that the findings of nuclear physics are complementary: they cannot be described without using expressions that are logically irreconcilable. This holds true, as an example, for the paradoxical nature of the atom which, according to some experiments, is undulatory, seeming to possess the continuous nature of waves, while according to other experiments it consists of discrete particles or quanta. Each set of results is opposite to the other, yet reality indeed possesses opposite properties that complement each other. Similarly, the quantum or energy state of an atom evanesces when it is observed by an intrusive probe designed to locate the exact position of the electron. The original state of the atom is restored when the atom is left alone. These aspects, the quantum state and the location, are said to be complementary to each other, and the two apparently contradictory aspects are necessary to grant us a full understanding of atomic reality.

Bohr has maintained that this multiple approach to truth holds not only for subatomic physics, and not only for science, but for all areas of human cognition and creativity. Thus, science and art, compassion and justice, neurophysiology and psychology, action and thought—these and many other such pairs are complementary. His student, Victor S. Weisskopf, has developed Bohr's ideas in a more generalized fashion. Concerning the complementarity of science and art, he writes:

> There are several contradictory, mutually exclusive approaches to reality. The scientific approach to a phenomenon is complementary to the artistic approach. The artistic experience evanesces when the phenomena are scientifically explored, just as the quantum state is temporarily destroyed when the position of the particle is observed. We cannot at the same time experience the artistic content of a Beethoven sonata and also worry about the neurophysiological processes in our brain. But we can shift from one to the other.

"One view complements the other," he adds, "and we must use all of them in order to get a full experience of life."[11]

This is not an easy idea to accept. We tend quite naturally to favor clear-cut, precise, and universally valid answers that exclude all alternative approaches. We resist the assertion that there are complementary aspects to reality, to truth. But what atomic physics teaches us is to liberate ourselves from the prejudice that reality must necessarily conform to the contours and biases of our limited minds. There are, it holds, two kinds of truth: superficial truths, the opposite of which are falsehoods, and deep truths, the opposite of which are also true. Each conflicting proposition may be true, reflecting an aspect of an ultimate truth about a reality too large and too complex to be contained in the simple logic to which we have become accustomed.

There is a good deal of precedent for this in classical Jewish thought. For instance, we affirm simultaneously the divine attributes of justice (*middat ha-din*) and compassion (*middat ha-rahamim*), and Judaism has always fought against separating the two—because of their apparent irreconcilability—into two gods, one of compassion and one of malice and evil. The daily morning prayer of Jews affirms both contradictory qualities in paraphrasing Isaiah that God "forms light and creates darkness, makes peace and creates evil." Each of the two is ascribed to a different divine Name and both are merged in the Unity of God: "Hear O Israel, the Lord (= compassion) is our God (= justice), the Lord is one."

Indeed, the readiness to accept and affirm contradictory sets of descriptions of the Deity is indispensable to the kabbalistic understanding of Divinity. Thus, the affirmation of the One God who is both Ein-Sof (Absolute) and yet self-revealing in the Ten Sephirot is central to the whole kabbalistic enterprise. Both ideas, that of absoluteness and that of relatedness, may be said to be complementary. The same may be said of divine transcendence and divine immanence, as well as a host of other pairs of seemingly mutually exclusive predicates we use in speaking of God.[12] Perhaps the boldest and most useful understanding of the complementary notions about God is the one formulated some four hundred years ago by the great Safed kabbalist, R. Moses Cordovero, who distinguished between the divine and the human points of view (*mi-tzido/mi-tzidenu*).[13] Here we have the notion of complementarity in all but name.

Not only in theology and mysticism but also in law does Judaism presuppose that reality requires apparently conflicting outlooks in order to grasp the underlying truth. Thus, the Halakhah speaks of twilight (*bein ha-shemashot*) as possessing the qualities of both day and night with regard to their legal implications; an androgynous individual may halakhically be considered, at different times and for different purposes, both male and female; a slave owned by two masters and manumitted by one of them may be said to be both slave and freeman; certain kinds of converts to Judaism may be presumed[14] to be both legitimately converted and non-Jewish at the same time. Other examples abound.

Probably the first to articulate an intuitive grasp of the complementary nature of halakhic controversies, and hence the halakhic perception of reality and its underlying epistemology, was the hasidic master R. Zadok ha-Kohen (Rabinowitz) of Lublin (1823–1900). R. Zadok proposed that every original talmudic dictum (*hiddush*) is invariably accompanied by its opposite. Whereas in speech, as in practice, two contradictory propositions are untenable, in the realm of thought it is not only possible but well nigh inevitable.[15] This has become the basis for a recent sophisticated attempt to demonstrate that the implicit logic of Halakhah embraces both classical Greek logic and the logic of complementarity.[16] Thus, two divergent opinions by talmudic sages—say, Bet Hillel permits, Bet Shammai forbids—may both be halakhically true as complementary theses (thus the Talmud's statement that "both these and these are the words of the living God"), but each view must stand up under the laws of classical logic.

Of course, this concept of complementarity can be exploited to justify all ideas, no matter how wrong-headed and illegitimate. There is no excuse, other than mental laziness, for so distorting the theory of complementarity that it leads to the relativistic thesis that all propositions are equally true or that all ideas have equal claim upon the truth. But genuine mistakes can be made in applying the theory,even by the most sophisticated. Indeed, Niels Bohr himself erroneously argued that the processes of life are complementary to physics and chemistry and represent a different state of matter from the inorganic or lifeless state. The discovery of DNA disproved his theory[17] and also showed how careful one must be in distinguishing between complementarity and simple contradiction and inconsistency, and, as well, in staking a premature claim for complementarity. But this need for caution does not vitiate the vast and powerful claims that the theory of complementarity has upon our attention.

With regard to our theme of Torah Umadda, three consequences emerge. The first relates to the nature of the Torah Umadda itself. Complementarity offers rousing support to the comprehensiveness of the whole approach. Torah, faith, religious learning on one side, and Madda, science, worldly knowledge on the other, together offer us a more overarching and truer vision than either set alone. Each set gives one view of the Creator as well as His creation, and the other a different perspective that may not at all agree with the first. Yet, "they are given from One Shepherd," as Ecclesiastes (12:11) taught.[18] Each alone is true, but only partially true; both together present the possibility of a larger truth, more in keeping with the nature of the Subject of our concern.

The second lesson for us from complementarity applies to the relation of "Torah only" and Torah Umadda (equivalent to Rav Kook's "inward" and "outward" motions), as well as that of the restrictive and expansive versions of the *shelemut* ideal. Both are true, and therefore both are necessary: "Both these and these are the words of the living God." Indeed the coexistence of both, simultaneously and cooperatively, assures us of greater entrée to the totality of Torah life. (It is for this reason that one should not impute dissonance to Yeshiva University and its affiliated institutions when they simultaneously nourish advanced *kollelim*—institutions exclusively devoted to higher talmudic learning—and the whole array of Torah Umadda that exposes the undergraduate both to Torah and to the arts and sciences on a level of excellence. The two together form a whole that is greater than the sum of its parts.)

Is it illegitimate to apply the theory of complementarity to a normative as well as a descriptive situation? In other words, is complementarity a way of accommodating different perceptions of reality only, or does it also affirm competing courses of action, such as the Torah Umadda and the "Torah only" approaches?

Our response is that we have not indulged in illicit use of complementarity theory in supporting this kind of pluralism regarding approaches to the Torah community. First, Bohr himself was not beyond such application of complementarity. And second, the normative aspects of our problem are reducible to descriptive questions: What is the view of Torah in our situation? What is the will of the Creator and what does He demand of us in the time and place in which He has placed us? As such, we are dealing with the actional implications of fundamental but differing visions.

We turn now to the third consequence of complementarity for our theme, and this relates to the varying interpretations or kinds of Torah Umadda. Our conclusion must be that while we may feel strong preference for one over the other models, each retains a core of validity and does not necessarily invalidate competing models. There is no model of Torah Umadda that is exclusively valid for all people at all times. There is a plurality of versions or paradigms to choose from. Hence, Torah Umadda can embrace the natural scientist, the businessman, and the professional *talmid hakham*—who, although he experiences no inner encounter between Torah and Madda, understands and sympathizes with the problems with which others must perforce wrestle—and, as well, the academic Judaic scholar who finds that encounter most sharply and sometimes painfully evident in his own discipline as he experiences the most direct interaction between the two. Each has his own "way," as Rabbi Akiva Eger taught, and in the fullness of time each of them will be vindicated in one aspect or another, for we are arrayed in a circle about the Truth.

The divine Choreographer has not yet chosen to reveal His

plan, but it is for us an act of faith—no less outrageous than the
acceptance of the theory of complementarity—that there *is* a
plan; that what appears to be cacophonous is really part of a
larger harmony; that what seems divergent is merely the
apparent contradiction of the top and the bottom of the circle
going in opposite directions; and that what looks like chaos is
part of a larger pattern of exquisite order.

Let the dance go on!

תם ונשלם שבח לאל בורא עולם

Notes

1. *Kiddushin* 82a.

2. *Eruvin* 13b.

3. See *Hiddushei Maran RYZ ha-Levi* (Jerusalem, 1962) to *Hayyei Sarah,*
pp. 11–13.

4. *Taanit* 31a.

5. R. Yehudah Leib Eger, *Torat Emet* (Lublin: 1889–1902), vol. 2,
101a. R. Yehudah Leib broke with the family's mitnagdic tradition and
became a hasid of R. Menaham Mendel of Kotzk and later joined the Rebbe
of Izhbitz. He ultimately became the Rebbe of Lublin.

6. A similar pluralistic approach was recommended by Rav Kook; see
Zvi Yaron, *Mishnato shel ha-Rav Kook* (Jerusalem: World Zionist Organization, 1974), p. 187, notes 9 and 10; also see Chapter 6 in this book.

7. For elaboration on this theme, see my "Seventy Faces," in *Moment
Magazine,* June 1986, vol. 11, no. 6, pp. 23–28. See also my "Pluralism and
Unity in the Orthodox Jewish Community," *Jewish Life,* Fall 1979, pp.
41–47.

8. This point is treated in much greater detail in Norman Lamm and
Aaron Kirschenbaum, "Freedom and Constraint in the Jewish Judicial
Process," in *Cardozo Law Review* 1 (1980), pp. 99–133, especially pp.
100–105.

9. See, too, the list of eight or nine items in Shimon Schwab's *These
and These* (New York: Feldheim, 1966), pp. 26f., in opposition to the
opinion of the majority of the heads of Lithuanian yeshivot.

10. In an Op Ed article in The New York Times, June 10, 1989.

11. Victor S. Weisskopf, *The Privilege of Being a Physicist* (New York: W. H. Freeman, 1989), pp. 42–43 and *passim*.

12. See my *Torah Lishmah* (New York: Yeshiva University Press, 1989), pp. 73–78.

13. Ibid., pp. 83f. and p. 99, note 140. For the use of this dichotomy in formulating halakhically the meditation necessary for the reading of the Shema, see my *Halakhot ve'Halikhot* (Jerusalem: Yeshiva University Press, 1990), Chapter 2.

14. According to Maimonides, *Hil. Issurei Biah* 13:9.

15. *Resisei Lailah* 17.

16. See Daniel Weil, "Complementarity in Rabbinic Logic" (Heb.), in *Higayon* (Jerusalem: Alum, 1989), ed. Moshe Koppel and Ely Merzbach, no. 1, pp. 101 ff.

17. Weisskopf, pp. 44f.

18. The whole verse reads, "The words of the wise are as goads, and as nails well planted are the words of masters of assemblies, which are given from One Shepherd" (Ecclesiastes 12:11). The Talmud's comment (*Hagigah* 3b) is quite significant and relevant to our point. It reads:

The disciples of the wise sit in manifold assemblies and occupy themselves with the Torah, some pronouncing unclean and others pronouncing clean, some prohibiting and others permitting, some disqualifying and others declaring valid. Should a man say: How in these circumstances (of contradictory views of the scholars) shall I learn Torah? Therefore Scripture says, "All of them are given from One Shepherd"—One God gave them, one prophet uttered them from the mouth of the Lord of all creation.

INDEX